# First World War
## and Army of Occupation
# War Diary
## France, Belgium and Germany

1 DIVISION
Divisional Troops
Royal Army Medical Corps
141 Field Ambulance
1 July 1916 - 21 September 1919

WO95/1259/2

The Naval & Military Press Ltd
www.nmarchive.com
**Published in association with The National Archives**

Published by

## The Naval & Military Press Ltd

Unit 10 Ridgewood Industrial Park,

Uckfield, East Sussex,

TN22 5QE England

Tel: +44 (0) 1825 749494

www.naval-military-press.com

www.nmarchive.com

*This diary has been reprinted in facsimile from the original. Any imperfections are inevitably reproduced and the quality may fall short of modern type and cartographic standards.*

**© Crown Copyright**
**Images reproduced by permission of The National Archives, London, England, 2015.**

# Contents

| Document type | Place/Title | Date From | Date To |
|---|---|---|---|
| Heading | WO95/1259/2 141 Field Ambulance July 16-Sept 19 | | |
| Heading | 1st Division Medical 141st Field Ambulance 1916 July-1919 Jun | | |
| Heading | July 141th Field Ambulance. | | |
| Heading | 141st Field Ambulance From 1st July 1916 To 31st July 1916 (Volume 1) | | |
| War Diary | Bracquemont (Noeux-Les-Mines) | 01/07/1916 | 04/07/1916 |
| War Diary | Divion | 05/07/1916 | 06/07/1916 |
| War Diary | Chocques | 07/07/1916 | 07/07/1916 |
| War Diary | Havernas | 08/07/1916 | 08/07/1916 |
| War Diary | Behencourt | 09/07/1916 | 09/07/1916 |
| War Diary | Henencourt | 11/07/1916 | 31/07/1916 |
| Heading | Vol II War Diary, No. 141. Field Ambulance, For The Month Of August, 1916. | | |
| War Diary | Henecourt Wood | 01/08/1916 | 31/08/1916 |
| Heading | War Diary of 141st Field Ambulance From 1st August 1916 To 31st August 1916. (Volume 2) | | |
| War Diary | 1st Div Vol 4 War Diary Officer Commanding No. 141 Field Ambulance For Month Of Septembe, 1916. | | |
| War Diary | Henencourt | 01/09/1916 | 30/09/1916 |
| Heading | War Diary of 141 Field Ambulance. From 1.9.16 To 30.9.16 (Volume 3) | | |
| Heading | Vol 5 140/1788 War Diary 141 Field Ambulance. From 1st October 16 To 31st October 16 (Volume) | | |
| War Diary | Henecourt | 01/10/1916 | 03/10/1916 |
| War Diary | Ercourt | 04/10/1916 | 31/10/1916 |
| Heading | Vol 6 140/1849 War Diary No. 141 Field Ambulance November 1916 | | |
| War Diary | Bazieux | 01/11/1916 | 05/11/1916 |
| War Diary | Millencourt | 05/11/1916 | 16/11/1916 |
| War Diary | Millencourt Bazentin-Le-Petiy | 17/11/1916 | 21/11/1916 |
| War Diary | Bazentin-Le-Petit | 21/11/1916 | 30/11/1916 |
| Heading | War Diary of 141th Field Ambulance From 1st November 1916 To 30th November 1916 (Volume No 4) | | |
| Heading | Vol 7 140/1900No 141 Field Ambulance December 1916 | | |
| War Diary | Basautu-Le-Petil | 01/12/1916 | 02/12/1916 |
| War Diary | Bottom Wood | 03/12/1916 | 31/12/1916 |
| Heading | War Diary of 141 Field Ambulance. From 1st December 16 To 31st December 16 (Volume No 6) | | |
| Heading | 140/19471 Vol 8 War Diary of 141th Field Ambulance From 1st January 1917 To 31st January 1917 (Volume No 7) | | |
| War Diary | Lavieville | 01/01/1917 | 31/01/1917 |
| Heading | 140/1994 Vol 9 War Diary of From 1st February 1917 To 28th February 1917 (Volume No 8) | | |
| War Diary | Lavieville | 01/02/1917 | 02/02/1917 |
| War Diary | Mericourt-Sur-Somme | 03/02/1917 | 04/02/1917 |
| War Diary | Fontaine-Les-Cappy | 05/02/1917 | 28/02/1917 |

| | | | |
|---|---|---|---|
| Heading | Vol 10 140/2042 War Diary of 141st Field Ambulance. From 1st March 1917 To 31st March 1917. (Volume No: 9) | | |
| War Diary | Fontaine Les. Cappy | 01/03/1917 | 31/03/1917 |
| Heading | Vol 11 140/2086 War Diary of 141st. Field Ambulance For The Month Of April 1917. (Volume No: 10) | | |
| Miscellaneous | Summary Of Medical War Diaries Of 142nd F.A. 3rd Div. 6th Corps. 3rd Army. 18th Corps From May 19th. | | |
| Miscellaneous | 142nd F.A. 3rd Div. 6th Corps. 3rd Army. | | |
| War Diary | Villers Bretonneux | 01/04/1917 | 23/04/1917 |
| War Diary | Camp 131 | 24/04/1917 | 30/04/1917 |
| Heading | Vol 12 140/2161 War Diary 141st Field Ambulance. From 1st May 1917 To 31st May 1917 (Volume No: 11) | | |
| War Diary | Camp 131 Morcourt | 01/05/1917 | 01/05/1917 |
| War Diary | Morcourt | 02/05/1917 | 19/05/1917 |
| War Diary | Warfusee-Abancourt | 20/05/1917 | 27/05/1917 |
| War Diary | R. 34 C.4.0 (Map Refce Sheet 27 2nd Ed"n) | 28/05/1917 | 31/05/1917 |
| Miscellaneous | Summary Of Medical War Diaries Of 142nd F.A. 3rd Div. 6th Corps. 3rd Army. 18th Corps From May 19th. | | |
| Miscellaneous | 142nd F.A. 3rd Div. 6th Corps. 3rd Army. | | |
| Heading | 141st Field Ambulance. From 1st June 1917 To 30th June 1917 (Volume No: 12) | | |
| Miscellaneous | Summary Of Medical War Diaries | | |
| Miscellaneous | 141st F.A. 1st Divn. 14th Corps. 5th Army. | | |
| War Diary | R.34 C. 4.0 (Sheet 27) | 01/06/1917 | 11/06/1917 |
| War Diary | Wallon Cappel | 12/06/1917 | 21/06/1917 |
| War Diary | C.28 D. 6.2. (Sheet 27). | 22/06/1917 | 22/06/1917 |
| War Diary | Uxem | 23/06/1917 | 25/06/1917 |
| War Diary | D.2.d.4.4 (Sheet 19) | 26/06/1917 | 30/06/1917 |
| Heading | Vol 14 140/2298 War Diary of 141st Field Ambulance. From 1st July 1917 To 31st July 1917 (Volume No: 13) | | |
| War Diary | D.2.D.4.4. Sheet 19 | 01/07/1917 | 26/07/1917 |
| War Diary | Le Clipon Camp. | 27/07/1917 | 31/07/1917 |
| Heading | Vol 15 140/3601 War Diary of 141st Field Ambulance. From 1st August 1917 To 31st August 1917 (Volume No: 14) | | |
| War Diary | Le Clipon Camp. | 01/08/1917 | 31/08/1917 |
| Heading | Vol 16 140/3601 War Diary 141 Field Ambulance. From 1st September 1917 To 30th September 1917 (Volume No 15) | | |
| War Diary | LeClipon Camp. | 01/09/1917 | 30/09/1917 |
| Heading | Vol 17 140/2499 War Diary of 141st Field Ambulance. From 1st October 1917 To 31st October 1917. (Volume No: 16) | | |
| War Diary | Le Clipon Camp. | 01/10/1917 | 21/10/1917 |
| War Diary | Rubrouck | 21/10/1917 | 22/10/1917 |
| War Diary | Hubrouck | 23/10/1917 | 25/10/1917 |
| War Diary | E. 19. a. 0.9. (Sheet 27) | 26/10/1917 | 31/10/1917 |
| Heading | Vol 18 140/2578 Nov. 1917 War Diary 141 Field Ambulance War Diary For Month Of November 1917 | | |
| War Diary | E.19 a. 0.9 Sheet 27 | 01/11/1917 | 06/11/1917 |
| War Diary | Schools Camp | 07/11/1917 | 07/11/1917 |
| War Diary | Irish Farm | 07/11/1917 | 13/11/1917 |
| War Diary | Duhallow | 14/11/1917 | 16/11/1917 |
| War Diary | Duhallow (1.1.b.3.8.sheet 28) | 17/11/1917 | 23/11/1917 |

| | | | |
|---|---|---|---|
| War Diary | Schools Camp | 24/11/1917 | 26/11/1917 |
| War Diary | Phillippo Farm (D 8 C. 7. 7.) Sheet 27 | 27/11/1917 | 30/11/1917 |
| Miscellaneous | | | |
| Miscellaneous | Vol 19 140/2618 War Diary of 141st Field Ambulance. From 1st December 1917 To 31st December 1917 (Volume No: 18) | | |
| War Diary | Phillippo Farm (D8.c.7.7.) Sheet 27 | 01/12/1917 | 03/12/1917 |
| War Diary | Portland Camp X 28, a 1.8 Sheet 19 | 04/12/1917 | 05/12/1917 |
| War Diary | Zuidhuis S 28.b. 5.5. Sheet 20 | 06/12/1917 | 06/12/1917 |
| War Diary | Zuidhuis S 28.b. 5.5. | 07/12/1917 | 10/12/1917 |
| War Diary | Zuidhuis Farm (S 28.b. 5.5.) Sheet 20 | 11/12/1917 | 31/12/1917 |
| Heading | Vol 20 140/2696 War Diary of 141st Field Ambulance. From 1st January 1918 To 31st January 1918. (Volume No. 19) | | |
| War Diary | S.28.b.5.5. Sheet 20. | 01/01/1918 | 31/01/1918 |
| Heading | Vol 21 140/2784 War Diary of 141st Field Ambulance. From 1st February 1918 To 28th February 1918 (Volume No. 20.) | | |
| War Diary | S.28 b. 5.5. Sheet 20. | 01/02/1918 | 08/02/1918 |
| War Diary | Duhallow C. 25 D. 1.1 (Sheet 28) | 09/02/1917 | 27/02/1917 |
| Heading | Vol 22 140/2849 War Diary of No 141 Field Ambulance. From 1st. March 1918 To 31st. March 1918. (Volume No. 21) | | |
| War Diary | Duhallow C. 25d.1.1. (Sheet 28) | 28/02/1918 | 28/02/1918 |
| War Diary | C.25.d.1.1 (Sheet 28) | 01/03/1918 | 28/03/1918 |
| War Diary | Gwalia Farm A 22.d.8.9 sheet 28 | 29/03/1918 | 31/03/1918 |
| Heading | Vol 23 140/2900 War Diary of No 141 Field Ambulance. From 1st April 1918 To 30th April 1918 (Volume No 22) | | |
| War Diary | Gwalia Farm A 22.d. 8.9. Sheet 28. | 01/04/1918 | 08/04/1918 |
| War Diary | F 7 a. 5.2. (Sheet 36b) | 09/04/1918 | 11/04/1918 |
| War Diary | D 30. D. 1.1. Sheet 36 B. N.E. | 12/04/1918 | 15/04/1918 |
| War Diary | E 15. a. 1.3. (Sheet 36 B.) Fouquiere | 16/04/1918 | 21/04/1918 |
| War Diary | D 30. d. 1.1. (Sheet 36B) | 22/04/1918 | 24/04/1918 |
| War Diary | K 20.a. 5.5. (Sheet 36B) Ruitz | 25/04/1918 | 30/04/1918 |
| Heading | Vol 24 140/2983 War Diary of No. 141 Field Ambulance. From 1st May 1918 To 31st May 1918 (Volume No 23) | | |
| War Diary | K 20.a.5.5. (Sheet 36B) | 01/05/1918 | 31/05/1918 |
| Heading | Vol 25 140/3076 War Diary of No. 141 Field Ambulance From. 1st June 1918 To 30th June 1918 (Volume No 24) | | |
| War Diary | K 20.a. 5.5. Sheet 44B | 01/06/1918 | 30/06/1918 |
| Heading | Vol 26 140/3131 War Diary of No. 141 Field Ambulance From-1st July, 1918 To-31st July, 1918. (Volume No. 25) | | |
| War Diary | K. 20. a.5.5. Sheet 44b. | 01/07/1918 | 31/07/1918 |
| Heading | Vol 27 140/3259 War Diary of No. 141 Field Ambulance. From 1st August 1918 To 31st August 1918. (Volume No. 26) | | |
| War Diary | K.20.a.5.5. Sheet 44b | 01/08/1918 | 21/08/1918 |
| War Diary | H. 13 C. Sheet 44b | 21/08/1918 | 31/08/1918 |
| Heading | Vol 28 140/3259 War Diary of No. 141 Field Ambulance. From 1st September 1918 To 30th September 1918. (Volume No. 27) | | |
| War Diary | | 01/09/1918 | 01/09/1918 |

| | | | |
|---|---|---|---|
| War Diary | Arras | 02/09/1918 | 08/09/1918 |
| War Diary | Avesnes-le-Comte | 09/09/1918 | 10/09/1918 |
| War Diary | Villers Bretonneux | 11/09/1918 | 12/09/1918 |
| War Diary | O. 33. a. 8.2. Sheet 62 C | 13/09/1918 | 14/09/1918 |
| Heading | Vol 29 140/3327 War Diary of No. 141 Field Ambulance. From 1st October 1918 To 31st October 1918 (Volume No. 28) | | |
| War Diary | Estrees En Chaussee | 15/09/1918 | 24/09/1918 |
| War Diary | Poeuilly | 25/09/1918 | 30/09/1918 |
| Miscellaneous | 141st Field Ambulance | | |
| War Diary | Poeuilly | 01/10/1918 | 02/10/1918 |
| War Diary | Vadencourt | 03/10/1918 | 10/10/1918 |
| War Diary | Magny La Fosse | 11/10/1918 | 18/10/1918 |
| War Diary | Bohain | 19/10/1918 | 20/10/1918 |
| War Diary | Bohain | 21/10/1918 | 31/10/1918 |
| Heading | Vol 30 140/3401 War Diary of 14 1st. Field Ambulance From 1st November 1918 To 30th November 1918 (Volume No. 29) | | |
| War Diary | Bohain | 01/11/1918 | 05/11/1918 |
| War Diary | Q. 35 D. | 06/11/1918 | 11/11/1918 |
| War Diary | Sheet 57b | 12/11/1918 | 13/11/1918 |
| War Diary | B Azuel R.8.b. Sheet 57b | 14/11/1918 | 15/11/1918 |
| War Diary | Marbaix I 16.d. 8.8. Sheet 57a | 16/11/1918 | 16/11/1918 |
| War Diary | Sars Poteries F 19.d.8.2. Sheet 57a. | 17/11/1918 | 18/11/1918 |
| War Diary | Beaumont C4. 80. 80. N Nmur 1: 100000 | 19/11/1918 | 19/11/1918 |
| War Diary | Walcourt F 4. Namur 1:100000 | 20/11/1918 | 23/11/1918 |
| War Diary | Florennes 3 H 25. 04. | 24/11/1918 | 30/11/1918 |
| Heading | Vol 31 140/3481 War Diary of 141st Field Ambulance From 1st December 1918 To 31st December 1918 (Volume No. 30) | | |
| War Diary | | 01/12/1918 | 01/12/1918 |
| War Diary | Corennes | 02/12/1918 | 02/12/1918 |
| War Diary | Weillen | 03/12/1918 | 03/12/1918 |
| War Diary | Boiseilles | 04/12/1918 | 09/12/1918 |
| War Diary | Chevetogne Abbey | 10/12/1918 | 10/12/1918 |
| War Diary | Baillonville | 11/12/1918 | 11/12/1918 |
| War Diary | Deulin | 12/12/1918 | 14/12/1918 |
| War Diary | Sadzot | 15/12/1918 | 15/12/1918 |
| War Diary | Vaux Chavanne | 16/12/1918 | 16/12/1918 |
| War Diary | Bihain | 17/12/1918 | 17/12/1918 |
| War Diary | Honvelez | 18/12/1918 | 18/12/1918 |
| War Diary | Maldingen | 19/12/1918 | 19/12/1918 |
| War Diary | Schonberg | 20/12/1918 | 21/12/1918 |
| War Diary | Baasem | 22/12/1918 | 22/12/1918 |
| War Diary | Schmidtheim | 23/12/1918 | 23/12/1918 |
| War Diary | Eicherscheid | 24/12/1918 | 24/12/1918 |
| War Diary | Odendorf | 25/12/1918 | 31/12/1918 |
| Heading | 1Div Troops 141 Fld Amb 1919 Jan To 1919 June | | |
| Heading | 1st Div Box 926 Vol 32 140/3490 War Diary of 14 1st Field Ambulance. From 1st January 1919 To 31st January 1919. (Volume No. 31) | | |
| War Diary | Odendorf | 01/01/1919 | 02/01/1919 |
| War Diary | Rheinbach | 03/01/1919 | 31/01/1919 |
| Heading | Vol 33 140/3524 War Diary For The Period 1st. To 28th. February 1919 Volume No. 32 | | |
| War Diary | Rheinbach Germany 9 B. | 01/02/1919 | 09/02/1919 |

| | | | |
|---|---|---|---|
| War Diary | Rheinbach | 10/02/1919 | 18/02/1919 |
| War Diary | Rheinbach Germany | 19/02/1919 | 28/02/1919 |
| Heading | Vol 34 140/3551 War Diary 1st. March 1919 To 31st. March 1919 Volume No. 35 | | |
| War Diary | Rheinbach Germany | 01/03/1919 | 31/03/1919 |
| Heading | 14 1st. Field Ambulance. War Diary for the period 1st. April 1919 To 30th April 1919 Volume No. 34 | | |
| War Diary | Rheinbach Germany | 01/04/1919 | 30/04/1919 |
| Heading | May 1919 War Diary No 141 Field Ambulance | | |
| War Diary | Rheinbach Germany | 01/05/1919 | 31/05/1919 |
| Heading | June 1919 No. 14 1st Field Ambulance. For The Period 1st To 30th June 1919 Volume No. 36 | | |
| War Diary | Rheinbach Germany | 01/06/1919 | 19/06/1919 |
| War Diary | Lengsdorf Germany | 20/06/1919 | 30/06/1919 |
| Heading | War Diary 141st Field Ambulance July 1919 | | |
| War Diary | Rheinbach Germany | 01/07/1919 | 31/07/1919 |
| Heading | No. 141. Y.A | | |
| War Diary | Rheinbach Germany | 01/08/1919 | 28/08/1919 |
| War Diary | Kinmel Park Camp. | 29/08/1919 | 31/08/1919 |
| Heading | Sept. 1919 No. 141 Field Ambulance. | | |
| Miscellaneous | History. 23. | | |
| War Diary | Kinmel Park | 01/09/1919 | 21/09/1919 |

WO95/1259 (2)
141 Field Ambulance
July '16 – Sept '19

1ST DIVISION
MEDICAL

141ST FIELD AMBULANCE
~~JAN - DEC 1918~~

1916 JLY — 1919 JUN

141st Field Ambulance

141st F.A.

Confidential

War Diary
of
141st Field Ambulance.

from 1st ~~June~~ July 1916   to   31st July 1916

(Volume 1.)

# WAR DIARY
## or
## INTELLIGENCE SUMMARY.

*(Erase heading not required.)*

Army Form C. 2118.

| Place | Date | Hour | Summary of Events and Information | Remarks and references to Appendices |
|---|---|---|---|---|
| BOAC QUEMONT | 1.7.16 | | Casualties admitted 12 sick 65 wounded: 2 Officers 1 O.R. died in Headquarters. | |
| (NOEUX-LES-MINES) | 2.7.16 | | Casualties admitted 9 sick 11 wounded. | |
| | 3.7.16 | | Casualties admitted 9 sick 11 wounded. Captain C.C. FORSYTH transferred from 98 Seaforths to R.A.M.C. and posted to this unit. Assumed charge of section at BULLY GRENAY and advanced aid post at CALONNE handed over to 135th Fd. Amb. Coys Aid. | |
| | 4.7.16 | | Headquarters, after equipment and vehicles remaining handed over to 135th F.D. Amb. Marched to DIVISION and took over school buildings and remaining fittings from 135th F.D. Weather extremely wet. Area selected and 10 sick admitted. Admitted 1 sick. | |
| DIVISION | 5.7.16 | | Captain D. MacIntyre R.A.M.C. posted to duty. Admitted 18 sick. | |
| | 6.7.16 | | Ambulance marched at 8.30 P.M. to CHOCQUES | |
| CHOCQUES | 7.7.16 | | R.A.M.C. personnel entrain at CHOCQUES at 1 A.M. Horse transport breakfast at 8.30 P.M. to HAVERNAS at 7 A.M. arrived by road to HAVERNAS at 7 A.M. R.A.M.C. personnel detrained at DOULLENS at 6.30 A.M. and marched to HAVERNAS arriving at 1 P.M. followed by horse transport arriving at 4 P.M. Very heavy rain all night. | |
| HAVERNAS | 8.7.16 | 5 P.M. | Sick at offices admitted. — 23 sick. Unit marched to BEHENCOURT and took over large farm house and outhouses. | |
| BEHENCOURT | 9.7.16 | 4 P.M. | Admitted 3 sick. A section marched to BOIS-DE-HENENCOURT and took over divisional rest station from 38th F.A. | |

Army Form C. 2118.

# WAR DIARY
## or
## INTELLIGENCE SUMMARY.
(Erase heading not required.)

Instructions regarding War Diaries and Intelligence Summaries are contained in F.S. Regs., Part II. and the Staff Manual respectively. Title pages will be prepared in manuscript.

| Place | Date | Hour | Summary of Events and Information | Remarks and references to Appendices |
|---|---|---|---|---|
| HENENCOURT | 11.7.16 | | 1. 12th Div. Casualties taken over Sick 143 Wounded 215. Divisional Rest Station extremely wet and muddy. | |
| | 12.7.16 | | B. & C. Sections marched in to D.R.S. at 11 A.M. A system of drainage commenced and a cook house and bathing room started. Casualties admitted 15 sick. | |
| | 13.7.16 | | Admitted direct 24 sick 2 wounded and as transfers 10 sick 11 wounded. | |
| | 14.7.16 | | Admitted direct 5 sick 1 wounded and as transfers 11 sick 9 wounded. Drainage finished. Cook house finished. Weather fine and conditions improving. Canteen and coffee bar to be erected and commenced. Casualties admitted 2 sick and as transfers 61. | |
| | 15.7.16 | | A. Section leaves with Captains Donaldson, I.E. BRUNEAU and C.C. FORSYT proceed to No.2. F.A. to be attached for duty at advanced dressing station. Also 5 ambulance cars. Casualties admitted 8 sick 1 wounded and as transfers 51 | |
| | 16.7.16 | | A. Section leaves with cars rejoined us. | |
| | 17.7.16 | | Admitted direct 13 sick 1 wounded and as transfers 9 sick 9 wounded. B. Section leaves with Captains J.D. MACCORMACK and I.C.D. KNOX and 5 ambulance cars proceeded to join No.2. F.A. for temporary duty at advanced dressing station. Casualties admitted 35 sick 1 wounded and as transfers 7 sick and wounded. Canteen was finished. | |
| | 18.7.16 | | 58182 Pte FIELD W. and 55989 Pte MURPHY, T. of this unit slightly wounded while attached to No. 2 F.A. and admitted here as transfers from No. 1. F.A. New fit latrines dug. | |

Army Form C. 2118.

# WAR DIARY
or
## INTELLIGENCE SUMMARY.
(Erase heading not required.)

Instructions regarding War Diaries and Intelligence Summaries are contained in F. S. Regs. Part II. and the Staff Manual respectively. Title pages will be prepared in manuscript.

| Place | Date | Hour | Summary of Events and Information | Remarks and references to Appendices |
|---|---|---|---|---|
| | 19.7.16 | | Casualties admitted 31 sick and as transfers 16 sick & 2 wounded. Officers were equipment much untrued by excellent attention from Red Cross. | |
| HENENCOURT | 20.7.16 | | Casualties admitted 31 sick and as transfers 18. | |
| | 21.7.16 | | A. Section leaves with Captain I. E. BUNGAY attached to No. 2. F.A. Captain C.C. FORSYTH R.A.M.E. left this unit for permanent duty with Sgt Bgle R.F.A. Casualties admitted dvied 39 sick 1 wounded as transfers 40 sick 3 wounded. | |
| | 22.7.16 | | New kit retain undertaking and sucde. Have been filled in and arrangements made for incineration. Admitted dvied 41 sick and as transfers 47 wounded. | |
| | 23.7.16 | | Admitted dvied 28 sick 2 wounded. Transferred to D.R.S. 35. 62235 Pte GREATBANKS, W. R.A.M.C. G.S.W. face & both legs, 56496 Pte WRIGHT J. G.S.W. face right arm, left knee — 59115 Pte WHELAN T. abrasion right thigh (mild). 6977 Pte MILNER S. G.S.W. chin & this man unit wounded while with No 2. F.A. Pte WHELAN admitted to D.R.S., the rest were evacuated. | |
| | 24.7.16 | | Admitted 8 sick & as transfers 27. | |
| | 25.7.16 | | Admitted 31 sick & as transfers 16. A. & B. sections rejoined from No. 2. F.A. | |
| | 26.7.16 | | Daris in connected roll. Admitted 22 sick and as transfers 30. | |
| | 27.7.16 | | Admitted 20 sick and as transfers 9. | |

Army Form C. 2118.

# WAR DIARY
## or
## INTELLIGENCE SUMMARY.
*(Erase heading not required.)*

Instructions regarding War Diaries and Intelligence Summaries are contained in F. S. Regs., Part II. and the Staff Manual respectively. Title pages will be prepared in manuscript.

| Place | Date | Hour | Summary of Events and Information | Remarks and references to Appendices |
|---|---|---|---|---|
| HENENCOURT | 28.7.16 | | Lieut. C.R. BECKITT R.A.M.C. (T.C.) joined the unit. | |
| | | | Admitted 22 sick 4 wounded and as transfers 3. | |
| | 29.7.16 | | Admitted djvel - 41 sick and as transfers 5 | |
| | | | Convert hut for patients and personnel – disinfected band erected. | |
| | 30.7.16 | | Admitted dited 43 sick and as transfers 8 | |
| | 31.7.16 | | Admitted dited 14 sick and as transfers 3. | |

Charles Headwich Col.
R.A.M.C.
O.C. 141st Field Ambulance.

# WAR DIARY,

## No. 141. FIEED AMBULANCE,

### FOT THE MONTH OF

### AUGUST, 1916.

Army Form C.2118.

# WAR DIARY
## or
## INTELLIGENCE SUMMARY.

(Erase heading not required.)

Instructions regarding War Diaries and Intelligence Summaries are contained in F. S. Regs., Part II. and the Staff Manual respectively. Title pages will be prepared in manuscript.

| Place | Date | Hour | Summary of Events and Information | Remarks and references to Appendices |
|---|---|---|---|---|
| HENENCOURT WOOD | Aug.10 | | | |
| | 1. | | Admissions = 16. Field ambulance fairly full. Weather very hot. | |
| | 2. | | Admissions 24. Transfers 1. Drew heavy draught to replace casualty. | |
| | 3. | | Admissions 21. Transfers 0. | |
| | 4. | | Admissions 14. Foot-Divisional shots. | |
| | 5. | | Admissions 19. | |
| | 6. | | Admissions 10. | |
| | 7. | | Admissions 22 (1 wounded) | |
| | 8. | | Admissions 13. | |
| | 9. | | Admissions 16. | |
| | 10. | | Admissions 27. Transfers 2. | |
| | 11. | | Admissions 11. Transfers 2. | |
| | 12. | | Admissions 31. Lieut. C.R.RECKITT R.A.M.C. (ienf) proceeded to No.2 Field Ambulance | |
| | 13. | | Admissions 10. for temporary duty. | |
| | 14. | | Admissions 39. Transfers 1. | |
| | 15. | | Admissions 58. Transfers 2. | |
| | 16. | | Admissions 51. Transfers 3. | |
| | 17. | | Admissions 50. Transfers 15. C. Bearer Sub-Subdivision with Captains T.D. MACCORMICK | |

# WAR DIARY
## or
## INTELLIGENCE SUMMARY.
*(Erase heading not required.)*

Army Form C.2118.

| Place | Date | Hour | Summary of Events and Information | Remarks and references to Appendices. |
|---|---|---|---|---|
| HENENCOURT WOOD | August 1916 | | and D. McINTYRE proceeded to No1 F.A. for Sanitary duty. Also mining party of 3 men and 1 N.C.O. to dig dug out for advanced dressing station. Captain A.C.W. KNOX R.A.M.C. (T.C.) detailed to permanently in medical charge of 2nd Royal Sussex Regt. vice Captain A.G. BAKER R.A.M.C. wounded. | |
| | 18th | | Admissions 37. Transfers 7. 7090 Pte KELLY J. R.A.M.C. accidentally wounded (G.S.W. hand and face - slight). | |
| | 19 | | Admissions 56. 58878 Pte BROWN A. 56225 Pte CROSSLEY S. of this unit-killed in action. | |
| | 20. | | Admissions 79. Transfers 30. 61048 Pte LLOYD A.L. of this unit held in action. 69331 Pte SUTTON E.C. of this unit were also wounded (gas shell). Captain D. McINTYRE rejoined by Captain I.E. BRUNEAU and rejoined me. | |
| | 21 | | Admissions 42. Transfers 38. A. Bearer subdivision sent to relieve C. Bearer subdivision. Officers not relieved | |
| | 22. | | Admissions 58. Transfers 34. Captain J.F. WOLFE LITTLE (T.C.) joined as reinforcement. Medical board, self, & Captains L.T. POOLE and C.L. CHALK found Pte 14120 Pte WYNNE 1st L.N.L. unfit for service on account as insane. | |

Army Form C. 2118.

# WAR DIARY
## or
## INTELLIGENCE SUMMARY.
*(Erase heading not required.)*

Instructions regarding War Diaries and Intelligence Summaries are contained in F. S. Regs., Part II. and the Staff Manual respectively. Title pages will be prepared in manuscript.

| Place | Date | Hour | Summary of Events and Information | Remarks and references to Appendices |
|---|---|---|---|---|
| HENENCOURT WOOD | August 1918 23 | | Albuertus 53  Transfers 9 | HENENCT |
| | 24 | | Albuertus 27  Transfers 3. | |
| | | | 56701 Pte PRICE, J. of this unit proceeded to Rouen for Course to have as munition worker | |
| | 25. | | Albuertus 23  Transfers 3. | |
| | | | 104349 Pte CHEESMAN, J. 105399 Pte COOPER, E. 105399 Pte CUMPSTEY, E. join this unit as reinforcements. | |
| | 26. | | Albuertus 30  Transfers 4 | |
| | | | Rev. H.D. BOWEN C.F. temporarily attached to this unit. | |
| | 27. | | Albuertus 23  Transfers 3. | |
| | 28. | | Albuertus 61  Transfers 14. | |
| | 29. | | Albuertus 32  Transfers 23. | |
| | 30. | | Albuertus 30  Transfers 21.  Bearer sub-division with No.1 F.A. relieved. Muir's party exchanged with No.1 F.A. rejoined me in conjunction of duty. | |
| | 31. | | Albuertus 16  Transfers 12. | |
| | | | 1902 L/Cpl BARRON F.P. 6971 Pte ALLEN C. 81718 Pte CROSS D. 05064 Pte THOMAS C.A. 75540 Pte GILDEA J. 78426 Pte BENNET W.E. 56000 Pte BEIER H. 73479 Pte PICKUP J. join this unit as reinforcements | |

[signature]
R.A.M.C.
O.C. 141st Field Ambulance.

# CONFIDENTIAL

## War Diary
### of
### 141st Field Ambulance.

From 1st August 1916 To 31st August 1916.

(Volume 2.)

SECRET

WAR DIARY

Officer Commanding, No. 141 Field Ambulance

for month of

SEPTEMBER, 1916.

Army Form C. 2118.

# WAR DIARY
## or
## INTELLIGENCE SUMMARY.
(Erase heading not required.)

Instructions regarding War Diaries and Intelligence
Summaries are contained in F. S. Regs. Part II.
and the Staff Manual respectively. Title pages
will be prepared in manuscript.

| Place | Date | Hour | Summary of Events and Information | Remarks and references to Appendices |
|---|---|---|---|---|
| HENENCOURT | 1/9/16 | | Casualties admitted 25. Casualties transferred to Divisional Rest Station. 9. A.D.M.S. inspects proposed "Temporary unfits". | L.Y.R. |
| | 2/9/16 | | Casualties admitted. 48. Casualties transferred to D.R.S. 10. | L.Y.R. |
| | | | Lieut. C.R. Rockitt, R.A.M.C. (Temp.) rejoins unit from No 2. F.A. and subsequently posted to 26th Bde. R.F.A. for permanent medical charge. | |
| | 3/9/16 | | Casualties admitted 66. Casualties transferred to D.R.S. 13. | L.Y.R. |
| | | | No 58870 Pte. Moon G., R.A.M.C. transferred to 75th SIS.B.'s for war duties. | |
| | | | No. 72357. Pte. Dawes A. and No 57978. Pte. Longmore J. transferred to 2nd Welsh for war duties. | |
| | 4/9/16. | | Casualties admitted 31. Casualties transferred to D.R.S. 55. | L.Y.R. |
| | 5/9/16 | | do. do. 34. do. 22. | L.Y.R. |
| | 6/9/16. | | Casualties do. 46. do. 8. | |
| | | | Sent relief Bearer Party consisting of 2. N.C.O.'s & 16 men to No.I. Field Ambulance. Capt. G.G. Marshall, R.A.M.C. (SR) reports his arrival from 10th Gloucesters. and is temporarily taken on the strength of this unit. | L.Y.R. |

Army Form C. 2118.

# WAR DIARY
## or
## INTELLIGENCE SUMMARY.

(Erase heading not required.)

| Place | Date | Hour | Summary of Events and Information | Remarks and references to Appendices |
|---|---|---|---|---|
| HENENCOURT. | 6.9.16 | | No 58733. Pte Purnell, J.C. R.A.M.C. evacuated sick to L. of C. A.D.M.C. 1st Division inspects proposed "Temporary unfits". | P.28. |
| | 7.9.16 | | Casualties admitted, 72. Transferred to Divisional Rest Station, 12. | P.28. |
| | 8.9.16 | | do. do. 62. do. 11. | P.28. |
| | | | No. 78 & 62. Pte. Bennett, W.B., R.A.M.C. classified by A.D.M.S. 1st Div. as Temporary unfit transferred to 1st Div. Coy for duty. No. 74 64 Pte Brown, G., R.A.M.C. admitted with G. S.W. Rt. Shoulder. No. 58709 Pte Allington W.C. R.A.M.C. admitted with G. S.W. Left Shoulder, both these men were wounded while with No. 1 Field Ambulance. | L.Y.F. |
| | 9.9.16 | | Casualties admitted 38. Casualties transferred to D.R.S. 76. a Bearer, party consisting of 2 N.C.Os. and 24 men proceeded at 3 P.M. to No. 1 Field Ambulance for duty. 2 N.C.Os and 17 men returned to this unit at 6 P.M. from No. 1 Fd. Amb. | L.P. |
| | 10.9.16 | | Casualties admitted 64. Transferred to D.R.S. & P.S. Capts. MacCormack, MacIntyre, and Bruneau, and Bearers return from No. 1 Field Ambulance. | P.28. |

Army Form C. 2118.

# WAR DIARY
## or
## INTELLIGENCE SUMMARY.
*(Erase heading not required.)*

Instructions regarding War Diaries and Intelligence Summaries are contained in F.S. Regs., Part II. and the Staff Manual respectively. Title pages will be prepared in manuscript.

| Place | Date | Hour | Summary of Events and Information | Remarks and references to Appendices |
|---|---|---|---|---|
| HENENCOURT. | 11.9.16 | | Casualties admitted 57. Casualties transferred to D.R.S. 42. | R.V.F. |
| | 12.9.16 | | do. 17. do. do. 4. | |
| | | | No 57882. Actg. Corporal Lightwood. B. R. auce. + No I 058951. Dr. Stead. H, A.S.C. M.T, admitted to hospital and evacuated to L. of C. | |
| | | | Capt. H.T. Lippiatt, R.A.M.C. (Temp) ceases to and taken on the strength of this unit. | R.V.F. |
| | 13.9.16 | | Casualties admitted 21. Casualties transferred to D.R.S. 8. | |
| | | | Capt. G.G. Marshall R. Amc. (SR.) proceeds from this unit to report to D.A.D.M.S. | |
| | | | Ambulance trains ABBEVILLE for duty, and is struck off the strength of this unit. | R.V.F. |
| | 14.9.16 | | Casualties admitted 20. Casualties transferred to B.R.S. 16. | R.V.F. |
| | 15.9.16 | | Casualties admitted 11. do. do. 1. | |
| | | | Capt. D. MacIntyre, R. Amc. (SR.) proceeds to 1st D.A.C. to assume temporary medical charge. | R.V.F. |
| | 16.9.16 | | Casualties admitted 62. Casualties transferred to D.R.S. 41. | |
| | | | Under instructions from D.D.M.S. III Corps. this unit is opened up as a Dressing Station. The wounded man died in Dressing Station. | R.V.F. |
| | 17.9.16. | | Casualties admitted 84. Casualties transferred to D.R.S. 11. | |
| | | | Medical Board assembles. President Lt. Col. Headlam D.A.D. R.Amc. members. Capt. Clark R.Amc. and Capt. Lippiatt, and reported on mental condition of No R.18364. Rfmn. L. Goossens, 2nd K.R.R.C. | R.V.F. |

Army Form C. 2118.

# WAR DIARY
## or
## INTELLIGENCE SUMMARY.
(Erase heading not required.)

Instructions regarding War Diaries and Intelligence Summaries are contained in F. S. Regs., Part II. and the Staff Manual respectively. Title pages will be prepared in manuscript.

| Place | Date | Hour | Summary of Events and Information | Remarks and references to Appendices |
|---|---|---|---|---|
| HENENCOURT | 18.9.16 | | Casualties admitted 29. Casualties transferred to D.R.S. 5 | R.Y.P. |
| | 19.9.16 | | Casualties admitted 4.9. do. do. 32. | R.Y.P. |
| | 20.9.16 | | A.D.M.S. 1st Division inspected horses before "Temporary flight." Casualties admitted 66. Casualties transferred 2. Capts. S.S. Bruneau & H.T. Lippiatt, R.A.M.C. and 25 O.Ranks. proceed to No.1. Fd. Amb. for duty. | R.Y.P. |
| | 21.9.16 | | Casualties admitted 31. Casualties transferred 9. One horse ambulance with four horses and one motor ambulance proceed to No I Field Ambulance for temporary duty. | R.Y.P. |
| | 22.9.16 | | Casualties admitted 21. Casualties transferred to D.R.S. 17. | R.Y.P. |
| | 23.9.16 | | do. 71. do. 37. | R.Y.P. |
| | 24.9.16 | | do. 42. do. 14. | R.Y.P. R.Y.P. |
| | 25.9.16 | | No 14.07. Pte Regan J, R.A.M.C. transferred to 25th Bde. for trade duties. Casualties admitted 44. Casualties transferred to D.R.S. 19. 46 O.Ranks proceed to No.1. Fd. Ambulance for temporary duty. | R.Y.P. |
| | 26.9.16 | | Casualties admitted 54. Casualties transferred to D.R.S. 21. | R.Y.P. |

**WAR DIARY**
*or*
**INTELLIGENCE SUMMARY.**
(Erase heading not required.)

Army Form C. 2118.

| Place | Date | Hour | Summary of Events and Information | Remarks and references to Appendices |
|---|---|---|---|---|
| HENENCOURT. | 26.9.16 | | Casualties admitted 54. Casualties transferred to D.R.S. 21. | R.Y.P. |
| | 27.9.16 | | Casualties do. 46. do. to. do. 28. | R.Y.P. |
| | 28.9.16 | | do. do. 42. do. do. do. 31. | R.Y.P. |
| | | | Capt. W. E. James R. A. M. C. (Temp.) temporarily attached to this unit. | |
| | 29.9.16. | | Casualties admitted 69. Casualties transferred to D.R.S. 18. | R.Y.P. |
| | | | No 6979. 96. Allen C. R.A.M.C. admitted to hospital and evacuates to O. of C. Shock Relt (Corris) | |
| | | | No T. 3886 Pt. Shaw E. A.S.C. H.T. T.F. posted to this unit for duty. | |
| | | | Capts. Bruneau & Lippeatt R.A.M.C. and bearer party return to this unit from No. 1 F.A. | |
| | 30.9.16. | | Casualties admitted 90. Casualties transferred to D.R.S. 9. | R.Y.P. |
| | | | Capt. W. E. James R.A.M.C. attached to this unit admitted to hospital sick, & evacuates to O. of C. | |

[signature] Lieut. Col.
R.A.M.C.
O.C. 141st Field Ambulance

Confidential.

War Diary

of

141 Field Ambulance.

From. 1.9.16
To. 30.9.16
(Volume 3)

Vol 5

MO/785

1st Div

141 Field Ambulance

COMMITTEE FOR THE
MEDICAL HISTORY OF THE WAR
Date -2 DEC. 1916

Confidential

War Diary
of
141 Field Ambulance.

From 1st October 16 to 31st October 16
(Volume No. 4)

Army Form C. 2118.

# WAR DIARY
## or
## INTELLIGENCE SUMMARY.

(Erase heading not required.)

141 Field Ambulance.

| Place | Date | Hour | Summary of Events and Information | Remarks and references to Appendices |
|---|---|---|---|---|
| HENENCOURT | 1/10/16 | | Casualties admitted 91. Casualties transferred to D.R.S. 33. Under instructions received from A.D.M.S. 1st Division, the 1st Divisional rest Station is closed. Advanced party from 47th Field Ambulance arrive at 6 p.m. and take over the 1st Divisional Rest Station, together with all remaining patients. | gomad |
| | 2/10/16 | | Horse Transport left HENENCOURT at 6.30 A.M. and moved with the 2nd Brigade group to new area. Route QUERRIEUL - AMIENS. N of SOMME-LA CHAUSSEE. Lieut A.T. THURSTON. RAMC (temp.) posted to and taken on the strength of this Unit. | gomad |
| | 3/10/16 | 6 A.M. | Field Ambulance, less Horsed Mechanical Transport, leave HENENCOURT, & proceed by motor bus to new area. arriving 11 P.M. 6.30 A.M. Motor Cyclists and Motor Ambulances left for new area, arriving at 11.30 A.M. Horse Transport arrived at 6 P.M. | gomad |
| ERCOURT. | 4/10/16 | | Open out Hospital, collecting and treating sick from the 2nd and 3rd Brigade Areas. Casualties admitted 7.c. No 58186 Pte G. HAMPSON. R.A.M.C. transferred to Fourth Army Water Column for duty. | gomad |
| | 5/10/16 | | Casualties admitted. 6. Capt. J.F. Wolfe R.A.M.C. (temp) proceeded to report to the D.D.M.S. ROUEN for duty. | gomad |
| | 6/10/16 | | Casualties admitted 17 | gomad |

Army Form C. 2118.

# WAR DIARY
## or
## INTELLIGENCE SUMMARY.
(Erase heading not required.)

| Place | Date | Hour | Summary of Events and Information | Remarks and references to Appendices |
|---|---|---|---|---|
| ERCOURT | 7/10/16 | | Casualties admitted 9 | g3mack |
| | 8/10/16 | | Casualties admitted 19 | g3mack |
| | 9/10/16 | | Casualties admitted 21 | g3mack |
| | 10/10/16 | | Casualties admitted 20. 3 Motor Ambulance cars proceed to report to No 2. Fd. Ambulance at HENENCOURT WOOD for duty. 1 NCO + 6 men proceed to FRESSENVILLE to take over + run baths in the Chateau there. | g3mack |
| | 11/10/16 | | Casualties admitted 11. Casualties transferred 1. | g3mack |
| | 12/10/16 | | Casualties admitted 18 | g3mack |
| | 13/10/16 | | Casualties admitted 14. Transferred 1. No. 6802 Cpl. A.C. BALL. R.A.M.C. evacuated sick to L of C. | g3mack |
| | 14/10/16 | | Casualties admitted 20. Transferred 1 | g3mack |
| | 15/10/16 | | Casualties admitted 14. The 3 Motor Ambulance cars returned to unit from No 2. Fd. Amb. No. 58194 Pte A.W. GORHAM. R.A.M.C. evacuated sick to L of C. | g3mack |

Army Form C.2118.

# WAR DIARY
## or
## INTELLIGENCE SUMMARY.

*(Erase heading not required.)*

Instructions regarding War Diaries and Intelligence Summaries are contained in F.S. Regs., Part II. and the Staff Manual respectively. Title pages will be prepared in manuscript.

| Place | Date | Hour | Summary of Events and Information | Remarks and references to Appendices |
|---|---|---|---|---|
| ERCOURT | 16/10/16 | | Casualties admitted 13. Lt. A.T. THURSTON. R.A.M.C. (temp) proceeded from this unit to take over temporary medical charge of the 10th Glosters, & 1st Royal Highlanders. | appd |
| | 17/10/16 | | Casualties admitted 13. Transferred 1 Capt H.T. LIPPIAT. R.A.M.C. (temp) proceeded from this unit to take over temporary medical charge of the 4th Army School - Guards Division. | appd |
| | 18/10/16 | | Casualties admitted 16. No. 57800 Pte CARRUTHERS. R. R.A.M.C. posted to this unit from no. 3 Machine gun corps. | appd |
| | 19/10/16 | | Casualties admitted 22. Transferred 1 No. M.36401 Sgt. POWELL.A.C. A.S.C. "M.T" No. M/2 081607 Pte SLATER.W. A.S.C. "M.T" No. 57709 Pte. ELLIS.C.C. R.A.M.C. No. 61708. Pte. GRAHAM.S. R.A.M.C. } evacuated sick to L. of C. | appd |
| | 20/10/16 | | Casualties admitted - 16 | appd |

Army Form C. 2118.

# WAR DIARY
## or
## INTELLIGENCE SUMMARY.
(Erase heading not required.)

Instructions regarding War Diaries and Intelligence Summaries are contained in F.S. Regs., Part II. and the Staff Manual respectively. Title pages will be prepared in manuscript.

| Place | Date | Hour | Summary of Events and Information | Remarks and references to Appendices |
|---|---|---|---|---|
| ERCOURT | 21/10/16 | | Casualties admitted 9 | |
| | | | No. 57344 Pte. BUTLER.I.R. RAMC. evacuated sick to L. of C. Field Ambulance Convoy. | journal |
| | 22/10/16 | | Casualties admitted 15. | |
| | | | Capt. H.T. LIPPIATT, RAMC (Temp) rejoined this unit from 4th Army School, Guards Division | journal |
| | 23/10/16 | | Casualties admitted 9. Transfers. 5. | journal |
| | 24/10/16 | | Casualties admitted 17. | journal |
| | 25/10/16 | | Casualties admitted 14. | |
| | | | No. 57344. Pte. I.R. BUTLER. RAMC. rejoined the unit from No 2 Canadian general hospital | journal |
| | 26/10/16 | | Casualties admitted 17. | |
| | | | No. 6190. Pte. O'DONOVAN.C. RAMC. transferred to No. 3. Machine Gun Company for water duties. | |
| | | | No. 62232 Pte. GLEESON.J. RAMC. joined this unit from No 3. Machine Gun Company. | journal |
| | 27/10/16 | | Casualties admitted 14 | |
| | | | Divisional Route March. | journal |

# WAR DIARY or INTELLIGENCE SUMMARY

Army Form C. 2118.

| Place | Date | Hour | Summary of Events and Information | Remarks and references to Appendices |
|---|---|---|---|---|
| ERCOURT | 28/10/16 | | Casualties Admitted 14. Transferred 1. | journal |
| | 29/10/16 | | Horse Transport leave ERCOURT at 1.30 P.M. for III rd Corps reserve area. Casualties admitted 25. | journal |
| | 30/10/16 | | Casualties admitted 14. Transferred 6. No. 57344. Pte. J.R. BUTLER, RAMC ” 55677 ” C.H. RYMILL ” ” 57970 ” R. ELLIOTT ” ” 105398 ” E. COOPER ” } evacuated sick to L of C. | journal |
| | 31/10/16 | | Casualties admitted 32. Field ambulance less Horse+mechanical transport, leaves ERCOURT at 5.45 A.M. & march to FEUQUIRES, proceeded from there at 10 A.M. to new area in motor buses arriving at BAZIEUX @ 7 P.M. Motor Ambulances proceeded by road from ERCOURT to BAZIEUX. Take over hospital building situate at BAZIEUX from 1st South Midland Fd. Amb. | journal |

[signature] R.A.M.C.
O.C. 141st Field Ambulance.

# WAR DIARY

# No 141

# FIELD

# AMBULANCE

## NOVEMBER 1916

# WAR DIARY
## or
## INTELLIGENCE SUMMARY.

*(Erase heading not required.)*

Army Form C. 2118.

| Place | Date | Hour | Summary of Events and Information | Remarks and references to Appendices |
|---|---|---|---|---|
| BAZIEUX | 1.11.16 | | Enlisted reconnaissance Fair weather. Pop 80-150. Latitude d.R. Now for officers. Billets for personnel fairly good. Accommodation for horse standing good. Admitted 6 sick. | |
| | 2.11.16 | | Admissions 8 sick. One case German measles from 1st Signal Coy. | |
| | 3.11.16 | | Admissions 15 sick. One case German measles from 3rd Machine Gun Coy. | |
| | 4.11.16 | | Admissions 6 sick. No. 5600 Pte BEYERS A. 141 F.A. Transferred to 5th L.M.L. Pg. for water duties. 1 horse drought's training horse drawn to inflate casualties; quality moderate. One case German measles from 1st D.E. Signals. | |
| | 5.11.16 | | Admissions 10 sick. Hospital billets and buildings at BAZIEUX handed over to 45 Field Ambulance, and 141 F.A. marches to MILLENCOURT at 1.30 P.M. Take over hospital accommodation and billets at MILLENCOURT from 45th Field Ambulance, together with latrine renaming. Orders to billet and treat sick from units of 1st Division at ALBERT and MILLENCOURT. No.55415 Pte MILLARD J. 58706 Pte GILLINGHAM F. A.S.C. (H.T.) 17397 of QMS. BARRETT B.J. (10th H.L.I. att) and 7/14905 a/staff S/Major WIMBLETON F. A.S.C. (H.T.) & W/2 081092 Pt VINER S. A.S.C. (M.T.) att. that unit admitted and transferred to 45 F.A. | |
| MILLENCOURT | 6.11.16 | | Admissions 7 from 1st Brigade 45th P.A. U. 0920 PtE YEO, G. transferred to 26 Fd Cay R.E. for water duties: 57841 Sgt E.T.H. DAVIS RMTE & 55115 Cpl MANCER C. admitted & transferred to 40 N. Zealand Ind Hsr. 3rd M.G. Coy B.T.M. Bg. 3rd Bgde sent dispatch in separate cases for German measles. Admissions 22 - one case German measles from M.G. Coy. | |
| | 7.11.16 | | Admissions 16 - German measles 3rd B. M. Coy. 3 cases. | |
| | 8.11.16 | | 57767 Pte FARNWORTH T.E. of this unit evacuated sick to L.A.C. | |

# WAR DIARY
## or
## INTELLIGENCE SUMMARY.

*(Erase heading not required).*

Army Form C. 2118.

| Place | Date | Hour | Summary of Events and Information | Remarks and references to Appendices |
|---|---|---|---|---|
| MILLENCOURT | 9-11-16 | | Allonsons 15. | |
| | | | Colonel H.T. LIPPIATT R.A.M.C. (T.C.) proceeded to 50 Gen. Hosp. Dte. for permanent medical charge. | |
| | 10-11-16 | | German measles. 3rd M.G. Coy. = 1. 2nd Welch = 1. | |
| | | | Allonsons 19. German measles 2nd Welch = 1. | |
| | | | Colonel D. McINTYRE R.A.M.C. (Terr.) rejoined this unit from 5th D.A.C. | |
| | | | Lieut. E.O. MARKS R.A.M.C. (Terr.) posted to unit. | |
| | 11-11-16 | | Allonsons 16. German measles 2nd Welch = 2. 4th Signals R.E = 1. 3rd M.G. Coy = 1. | |
| | 12-11-16 | | Allonsons 17. | |
| | 13-11-16 | | Allonsons 15. | |
| | | | 57261 Pte YOUNG L. transferred from this unit to 5th B.H. for water duties. | |
| | 14-11-16 | | Allonsons 14. German measles (5th R.H.) = 1. | |
| | | | 138 Pte MURRAY F.S. R.A.M.C. joined the unit from 15th R.H. | |
| | 15-11-16 | | Allonsons 10. German measles (1st R.H.) = 1. | |
| | | | Visited BAZENTIN-le-PETIT and interviewed O.C. 2/2 Northumbrian F.A. with a view to taking over from him. | |
| | | | Allonsons 11. | |
| | 16-11-16 | | Captain P. SMITH M.C. R.A.M.C. (Terr.) and 14 O.R. posted to this unit. | |
| | | | Advanced party under Captain MacINTYRE proceeded at 2 a.m. in motor lorries to BAZENTIN-le-PETIT to take over from 2/2 Northumbrian F.A. | |
| | | | 26320 Pte GATEHOUSE T. admitted from this unit & transferred to 38 D.R.S. T/1 5799 Dr WOODFORD G A.S.C. (M.T.) of this unit admitted and transferred to C.R.S. 57920 Pte ELLIOTT R & 57344 Pte BUTLER T.R. rejoined from No 3. Gen Hosp. | |
| | | | German measles 2 of 1st M.G. Coy = 2. 4th R.H. = 1. | |
| | | | Lt & Qr M W.G. Fiske (Terr) transferred to 2/5 London F.A. | |

# WAR DIARY or INTELLIGENCE SUMMARY

Army Form C. 2118.

| Place | Date | Hour | Summary of Events and Information | Remarks and references to Appendices |
|---|---|---|---|---|
| MILLENCOURT | 17.11.16 | 10 a.m. | Handed over hospital buildings, billets etc to No 2 F.A. March with unit to BAZENTIN-le-PETIT and take over from 2.2 Northumbrian F.A. to form Advanced dressing station for the division. Casualties to be cleared from R.A.P.s at EAUCOURT L'ABBAYE by trolley line with hand lineal trolley through SEVEN ELMS A.D. Post. Also that WILL'S hut to BAZENTIN le GRAND. Casualties to be evacuated to M.D.S. at BOTTOM WOOD (Sitting wounded and sick) on to C.C.S. at EQ.E.t.u.? (Stretcher wounded & my abdomen, Skull- wound & etc.) Captain MacCORMACK R.E. Serve put in charge of SEVEN ELMS and Captain DONALD R.E. (attached) with Captain BRUNEAU put in charge of MILLER'S Post. Relieved by 2 Officers and 1 section of No. 1 F.A. Admissions 12. Commune wounded. | |
| BAZENTIN-le-PETIT. | 18.11.16 | | 1st F.A. 21, 3rd M.G. Boy = 2, 1st. M.G. Boy = 3. Accommodation: also small dugouts very poor. Underpants dugouts large good dug-out with sound steel plates in them and bunks. Collecting party (very fair) and in huts at BAZENTIN de GRAND. Ground is being levelled for erection of marquees and Curries huts at LANGLAND'S CROSS at BAZENTIN-le-GRAND. Admissions 50, to wounded 31, 8820 PT. BREEZE A.F. severely wounded and evacuated. Relieved by 2 other bearer subdivisions of No 2 F.A. and 1 Officer and 1 bearer subdiv at F.A. | |
| | 19.11.16 | | Admissions wounded 26, sick 49, Transferred sick to C.C.S. 6933 Pte SUTTON E.C. of the unit (3 sub. 52) Admissions wounded 13, sub. 52, 2nd Australian Division. | |
| | 20.11.16 | | Admissions wounded 17 sub 41. 24479 Pte HOLCOMBE, F. R.A.M.C. at FACTORY CORNER and GOOSE ALLEY Q-station in influence to batn? was evacuation of R.A.P. 9 | |
| | 21.11.16 | | Admissions wounded 17 sub 41. 24479 Pte HOLCOMBE, F. R.A.M.C. was wounded to No. 1 A.D.S. from this unit | |

Army Form C. 2118.

# WAR DIARY
## or
## INTELLIGENCE SUMMARY.

*(Erase heading not required.)*

Instructions regarding War Diaries and Intelligence Summaries are contained in F. S. Regs., Part II. and the Staff Manual respectively. Title pages will be prepared in manuscript.

| Place | Date | Hour | Summary of Events and Information | Remarks and references to Appendices |
|---|---|---|---|---|
| BAZENTIN -LE-PETIT | 21.11.16 | | Evacuation of FACTORY CORNER and GOOSE ALLEY aid posts taken over from 2nd Australian Div. Captain L.T. POOLE given charge of the line with Captain I.E. BRUNEAU. Captain BRUNEAU relieved at MILLERS POST by Lieut MARSH. | |
| | 22.11.16 | | It has been arranged to evacuate Cough Drop hospital previously used for this sector and establish a new post "EDWARDS POST" at a spot about 300 yards N.E. of it. Line of evacuation to be Factory Corner to Edwards Post to Seven Elms and thus on left sector and Goose Alley Post to Edwards Post to Seven Elms. Until trolley line is laid cases to be hand carried as far as Seven Elms. Admissions wounded 26 sick 21. Captain P. SMITH R.C. R.A.M.E. (Temp.) detailed for permanent charge of 1st Glosters. Captain H.T. LIDDIATT RAME (Temp.) joined this unit from 1st Glosters. Visited all advanced dressing posts. | |
| | 23.11.16 | | Admissions wounded 31 sick 49. 88030 Pte BURLEY D. 69351 Pte SUTTON E.C. 75479 Pte PICKUP J. 7/4 094270 Dr SAUNDERS A.S.C.(H.T.) of this unit transferred to No 2. M.D.S. A new post for the KILLERS POST selected about 40 yards from BAZENTIN-LE-GRAND at a spot where the ground is drier and drains less. Mining of dugouts commenced. | |
| | 24.11.16 | | Admissions wounded 18 sick 42. German mines + cases from 103rd Glosters. A new dugout commenced at Seven Elms. | |
| | 25.11.16 | | Admissions wounded 11 sick 34. A new collecting station at LANGLAND CIRCUS was established in marquees and tents. Walking sick will in future be treated here and evacuated direct by train. Dugouts and tents both previously used. | |
| | 26.11.16 | | Admissions wounded 14 sick 62. A considerable number of trench feet. 59882 Pte MARGINSON F. of this unit slight wound, remains at duty. 7/4 02290 Dr DAVIES W. A.S.C. (H.T.) of this unit transferred to No 2 M.D.S. 88032 Pte BURLEY W.D. rejoined from No. 2. M.D.S. | |

2353 Wt. W2541/1454 700,000 5/15 D.D.&L. A.D.S.S./Form/C. 2118.

Army Form C. 2118.

# WAR DIARY
## or
## INTELLIGENCE SUMMARY.
*(Erase heading not required.)*

Instructions regarding War Diaries and Intelligence Summaries are contained in F. S. Regs., Part II. and the Staff Manual respectively. Title pages will be prepared in manuscript.

| Place | Date | Hour | Summary of Events and Information | Remarks and references to Appendices |
|---|---|---|---|---|
| BAZENTIN -LE- PETIT | 27.11.16 | | Admissions wounded 21 sick 95. Our own German wounds from 10th Glosters. A very large number of cases of trench feet. Weather conditions appalling. Heavy rain and very cold. | |
| | 28.11.16 | | Casualties wounded 38 sick 105. A great number of trench feet. The new HILLERS Post is now in occupation and the former one has been abandoned. It is nearly complete but requires more sandbagging owing to the German mines 1 from 10th Glosters. | |
| | 29.11.16 30.11.16 | | Admissions wounded 26 sick 118. Admissions wounded 13 sick 73. Weather better and fewer trench feet. Captain H.T. LIPPIATT proceeded to 1st Glosters for temporary duty. | |

Mulbern Heath Lt. Col.
O.C. 141st Field Ambulance.

War Diary
of
141ˢᵗ Field Ambulance
from 1ˢᵗ November 1916.
to 30ᵗʰ November 1916.

(Volume no. 4.)

CONFIDENTIAL

WAR DIARY

No 141 Field Ambulance

DECEMBER 1916

# WAR DIARY
## or
## INTELLIGENCE SUMMARY

Army Form C. 2118.

| Place | Date | Hour | Summary of Events and Information | Remarks and references to Appendices |
|---|---|---|---|---|
| Bazentin le Petit | 1.12.16 | | Casualties admitted: Sick = 93, wounded = 16 | |
| | 2.12.16 | | Casualties admitted: Sick = 75, wounded = 21. Allowed Dressing Station and part of No.3 to No.1 Field Ambulance. Two complete sections of 141 F.A. attached to No.1 Field Ambulance. Remainder of 141 F.A. moved to Bottom Wood in readiness to take over No.2 Main Dressing Station from 1/3 North Midland F.A. | |
| Bottom Wood | 3.12.16 | | Unit witnessed in the morning by No.2 M.D.S. | |
| | 4.12.16 | | Took over from 1/3 North Midland F.A. No.2 M.D.S. 20 O.R. attached to 141 F.A. from 1/3 N.F.A. | |
| | 5.12.16 | | Casualties admitted: wounded 20; sick 48; transferred sick 35. | |
| | 6.12.16 | | Casualties admitted: wounded 18; sick 112; transfers 49. | |
| | 7.12.16 | | Casualties admitted: wounded 6; sick 80. 21 O.R. from 141 F.A. proceed to join No.1 F.A. 21 O.R. from 1/3 N.F.A. joined 141 F.A. for duty. | |
| | 8.12.16 | | Casualties admitted: sick 105; wounded 14. Captain J.D. McCormack of 141 F.A. slightly wounded and evacuated to C.C.S. | |
| | 9.12.16 | | Casualties admitted: sick 76; wounded 18. | |
| | 10.12.16 | | Casualties admitted. Sick 114 wounded 8 | |

Army Form C. 2118.

# WAR DIARY
## or
## INTELLIGENCE SUMMARY.

(Erase heading not required.)

| Place | Date | Hour | Summary of Events and Information | Remarks and references to Appendices |
|---|---|---|---|---|
| Bottom on Wood. | Dec. 1916 | | | |
| | 11. | | Casualties admitted sick 17 wounded 8. No 23064 Pte Thomas C.A. of this unit transferred to 2 R.H.F. for waste pieces. | |
| | 12. | | Casualties admitted: Sick 92 wounded 14. Driver - riding out 2 H.G. horses to reflect casualties No.7103 Pte ALTREE A. of this unit (att) No.1 F.H. severely wounded. No. 105399 Pte CHIPSTEN L. slightly wounded. No. 57944 St Sgt HARLEY W. admitted Sick & transferred to III Corps rest station. | |
| | 13. | | Capt E.E. BRUNEAU of this unit (att No.1 F.A.) wounded to 45 C.C.S. Casualties admitted: Sick 93 wounded 6. | |
| | 14. | | Casualties admitted Sick 131 wounded 3. | |
| | 15. | | Casualties admitted: Sick 136 wounded 11. No. 12698 Pte SMITH, W.T. of this unit from No. 17 General Hospital for duty. | |
| | 16. | | Casualties admitted sick 91 wounded 9. | |
| | 17. | | Casualties admitted Sick 75 wounded 6. | |
| | 18. | | Casualties admitted Sick 87 wounded 4. Party of 1/3 N.F.A. wound 1/3 N.F.A. (O.L.) this unit leaves to admit cases under instruction of A.D.M.S. | |

# WAR DIARY
## or
## INTELLIGENCE SUMMARY.

Army Form C. 2118.

| Place | Date | Hour | Summary of Events and Information | Remarks and references to Appendices |
|---|---|---|---|---|
| Botom Wood | Dec 1916 | | and ceases to act as No 2 M.D.S. becoming again a F.A. for reception of local sick. | |
| | 19 | | 62384 Pte GATELEY C.E. left to report for duty at No 11 General Hosp. Casualties admitted sick 100 wounded 7. O.C. H.S. assumed 2nd in command of 141 F.A. under instructions of Captain L.F. POOLE RAMC. | |

Hubert _____ Lt Col
FEATRE

Army Form C. 2118.

# WAR DIARY
## or
## INTELLIGENCE SUMMARY.
(Erase heading not required.)

Instructions regarding War Diaries and Intelligence Summaries are contained in F. S. Regs., Part II and the Staff Manual respectively. Title pages will be prepared in manuscript.

| Place | Date | Hour | Summary of Events and Information | Remarks and references to Appendices |
|---|---|---|---|---|
| BOITON WOOD | 20 | | Enemy shell heavy throughout Wood and 2 | L.A.P. |
| | 21 | | " | L.A.P. |
| | 22 | | " | L.A.P. |
| | | | Wounded 3   B.O.R. 18 | |
| | 23 | | Our 1RD Horse & 1 officer to relieve wounded | L.A.P. |
| | 24 | | Enemy shell heavy throughout Wood | L.A.P. |
| | 25 | | | L.A.P. |
| | 26 | | | L.A.P. |
| | 27 | | | L.A.P. |
| | 28 | | 10 Oth Tanks for Unit from B.O.R. Village | L.A.P. |
| | 29 | | No. 58138 Cdr W.H.D. MORRIS F.C., R.A.M.C. transferred to 33rd Field Amb. for further duty. | L.A.P. |
| | 30 | | Casualties heavy through Enemy shell. Sick 25 | L.A.P. |
| | | | Advance party consisting of 1 Officer, 4 Batmen proceeded to LOUVENCOURT to take over Billets from Staffs. | |

Army Form C. 2118.

# WAR DIARY
## or
## INTELLIGENCE SUMMARY.
(Erase heading not required.)

Instructions regarding War Diaries and Intelligence Summaries are contained in F. S. Regs., Part II. and the Staff Manual respectively. Title pages will be prepared in manuscript.

| Place | Date | Hour | Summary of Events and Information | Remarks and references to Appendices |
|---|---|---|---|---|
| BOTTOM WOOD | DECEMBER 1916 30 | | From 1/31 Northumbrian Field Ambulance. Party attached to No. 1 Field Ambulance rejoin Unit. | N.B. |
| | 31 | | Casualties passing through Unit. Sick 24. | N.B. |
| | | 8.30 am | Advance Transport moves to LOUVIEVILLE via FRICOURT, ALBERT & main AMIENS Road. | |
| | | 9.30 pm | Remainder of Unit marches to LOUVIEVILLE Hospital Buildings, Billets & Horse Lines taken over to 1/3rd Northumbrian Field Ambulance. Capt. J. MacRAE R.A.M.C. (Temp) posted to & taken on the strength of the Unit. | L.I.BOYD Capt R.A.M.C. |

Confidential

War Diary
of
141 Field Ambulance.

From 1st December 16    To 31st December 16

(Volume No. 6)

Confidential

War Diary

of

141st Field Ambulance

From 1st January 1917   To 31st January 1917

(Volume No 7)

1st Division

COMMITTEE FOR THE MEDICAL HISTORY OF THE WAR
Date 13 MAR. 1917

# WAR DIARY
## or
## INTELLIGENCE SUMMARY.
(Erase heading not required.)

Army Form C. 2118.

| Place | Date | Hour | Summary of Events and Information | Remarks and references to Appendices |
|---|---|---|---|---|
| Louverne | 1.1.17 | | Casualties admitted to unit Sick 1. | Appendices/Returns |
| | | | Capt A. Irvine Fortescue R.A.M.(C) assumed command of the unit | |
| | 2.1.17 | | No 31327 L/Cpl Laville C.J. R.A.M.C transferred to No 21 M.A.C for duty | A.7. |
| | | | No 15312 L/Cpl Gillespie J R.A.M.C joined this unit from No 21 M.A.C for duty | |
| | 3.1.17 | | Casualties admitted to unit Sick 8. | A.7. |
| | | | Lt. E. D. Marks R.A.M.C. (Temp) of this unit admitted to hospital and transferred to III Corps Rest Sta. | |
| | 4.1.17 | | Casualties admitted to unit Sick 12. | A.7. |
| | | | Casualties admitted to unit Sick 6. | A.7. |
| | | | No 48313 Pte Amos W.J. R.A.M.C No 61945 Pte Archer H.L. R.A.M.C No 20370 Pte Bolton A.W. R.A.M.C | A.7. A.7. A.7. |
| | | | joined this unit from Base Details | |
| | 5.1.17 | | Casualties admitted to unit Sick 4. | |
| | 6.1.17 | | Casualties admitted to unit Sick 8. | |
| | 7.1.17 | | Casualties admitted to unit Sick 27 | |
| | | | No 19612 Sgt J.P. Barron R.A.M.C transferred to No 18 General Hospital for duty | A.7. |
| | 8.1.17 | | Casualties admitted to unit Sick 20. | |
| | | | L/Cpl 60 Marks R.A.M.C (Temp) discharged from III Corps Rest Station and rejoined unit for duty | |
| | | | No 57800 Pte Carruthen R R.A.M.C. No 7090 Pte Baines W. R.A.M.C. No 58025 Cpl Field J R.A.M.C | |
| | | | admitted to Hospital Sick and evacuated to casualty clearing station | |
| | 9.1.17 | | Casualties admitted to unit Sick 39. | A.7. |
| | 10.1.17 | | Casualties admitted to unit Sick 17 | |
| | | | No 5814 Pte Walsh W.F. R.A.M.C No 5882.3 Pte Callaghan J R.A.M.C were admitted to hospital | A.7. |
| | | | and evacuated to casualty clearing station | |

# WAR DIARY
## or
## INTELLIGENCE SUMMARY.
*(Erase heading not required.)*

Army Form C. 2118.

| Place | Date | Hour | Summary of Events and Information | Remarks and references to Appendices |
|---|---|---|---|---|
| Laventie | 10.7.17 | | No 56000 Pte Beyer H R.A.M.C. joined this unit for duty from No 1 St. John Ambulance | A.7. |
| | 11.7.17 | | 5884 w. Sellwood W.J. R.A.M.C. was taken on the man'er establishment | A.7. |
| | | | Casualties admitted to Unit Sick 13 | |
| | | | Lt. Col. Dowling R.A.M.C. (Temp) of this unit, admitted to Hospital Sick and transferred to Officers Hospital Rouen | |
| | | | No 67941 Pte Hitt E. R.A.M.C. transferred to 1st L.A. James for water duties | |
| | | | No 20178 Actg Staff Sgt Major Ruane R.D. A.D.C.H.T. joined this unit from 1 S Divisional Train from No 18 General Hospital for duty | |
| | | | No 15389 Sgt Dunn J. R.A.M.C. joined this unit from No 18 General Hospital for duty | |
| | | | No 106227 Pte Bagley C.A. R.A.M.C. to 56000 Pte Beyer H. R.A.M.C. No 3022762 Pte Humphrey A. A.S.C.H.T. T32160 Dr. Mc Cormack R. A.D.C.H.T. admitted to Hospital Sick and evacuated to No 3 C.C.S. | A.7. |
| | 12.7.17 | | Casualties admitted to Unit Sick 8 | |
| | | | No 6803 Jn Pte Rorman Pte R.A.M.C. No 58196 Pte Heaton C. R.A.M.C. admitted to Hospital Sick and transferred to III Corps Rest Station and evacuated from C.R.S. of C. being struck off our strength | A.7. |
| | | | Casualties admitted to Unit Sick 5 | |
| | 13.7.17 | | No 2 orphy Dr Williams J. A.D.C.H.T. attached to this unit admitted to Hospital Sick and transferred to III Corps Rest Station and evacuated from C.R.S. of C. being struck off our strength | A.7. |
| | | | Casualties admitted to this unit nil | |
| | 14.7.17 | | No 66948 Pte Smith G. R.A.M.C. rejoined this unit from III Corps Rest Station. Lt. R.O. Martin R.A.M.C. (Temp) proceeded to 1st Divisional Officers School for temporary duty | A.7. |

**Army Form C. 2118.**

# WAR DIARY
## or
## INTELLIGENCE SUMMARY.
*(Erase heading not required.)*

Instructions regarding War Diaries and Intelligence Summaries are contained in F. S. Regs., Part II. and the Staff Manual respectively. Title pages will be prepared in manuscript.

| Place | Date | Hour | Summary of Events and Information | Remarks and references to Appendices |
|---|---|---|---|---|
| Laireville | 15.1.17 | | Casualties admitted sick 4 <br> No 56117 a/Cpl Mercer C R.A.M.C admitted to hospital sick and evacuated to L/C <br> No 755 Pte Litton J R.A.M.C admitted to hospital sick and transferred to Div Rest Station <br> Lt F.G. Golding R.A.M.C. (temp) was evacuated from Fifteen hospital early to Casualty Clearing Station and thence to the Base, being struck off our strength <br> No. 21297 Pte Bentock G R.A.M.C. was evacuated from Div Rest Station & L/C being struck off our strength | N.T. |
| | 16.1.17 | | Casualties admitted to unit sick 4 <br> No. 81133 Pte Whelan J R.A.M.C awarded 14 days Field punishment No. 1 and reduced to 15 a.m. P.M. 1st Division <br> No 1500 Pte Burgoyne P R.A.M.C admitted to hospital sick and transferred to Divisional Rest Station. | N.T. |
| | 17.1.17 | | Casualties admitted to unit sick 2 <br> No T 35556 Sr Guest J. A/C HT joined this unit for duty <br> Sr 257 Pte Horsey W R.A.M.C reported unit from III Corps Rest Station | N.T. |
| | 18.1.17 | | Casualties admitted to unit sick 1 <br> 9 other Ranks R.A.M.C joined this unit from Base Details for duty <br> No. 1 2070 Sr Shadow R.A.C HT admitted to hospital sick and evacuated to L/C being struck off our strength | N.T. |

Army Form C. 2118.

# WAR DIARY
## or
## INTELLIGENCE SUMMARY.
(Erase heading not required.)

Instructions regarding War Diaries and Intelligence Summaries are contained in F.S. Regs., Part II. and the Staff Manual respectively. Title pages will be prepared in manuscript.

| Place | Date | Hour | Summary of Events and Information | Remarks and references to Appendices |
|---|---|---|---|---|
| Louvencourt | 19.1.17 | | Casualties admitted to Unit Sick 6 | A.F.B. |
| | | | Rev. J. Edwards C.F. (Temp) reported to this unit and is attached from to-day inclusive | |
| | 20.1.17 | | Rev. A.D. Allen C.F. (Temp) & No. 3562 Pte. Green to Capt. Johnstons R.T.O. proceeded to Havre for duty | |
| | | | Casualties admitted to Unit Sick 1 | |
| | | | A.D.M.S. 1st Division inspected the unit | |
| | | | Capt. J. MacRae R.A.M.C. (Temp) proceeded to 1st Divisional Officers School to relieve L.D. Martin Rake (Temp) of this unit who on relief proceeded to No. 2 F.A. this unit for duty | A.F.B. |
| | | | No. 15389 Sgt. Dunn S. R.A.M.C. admitted to hospital sick and evacuated to C.C.S. being attached offered strengths. | |
| | | | No. 15742 Pte Gillman I. R.A.M.C. regimental unit from Divisional Rest station | |
| | | | No. 1500 Pte Burgoyne B. R.A.M.C. was evacuated from F.A. to casualty clearing station and struck off our strength. | |
| | 21.1.17 | | Casualties admitted to unit sick 7 | |
| | | | Lt. J. Clapperton R.A.M.C. (Temp) joined this unit for duty | A.F.B. |
| | | | Casualties admitted Sick 6 | |
| | 22.1.17 | | Capt. M.J. Lyppiatt R.A.M.C. (Temp) rejoined this unit from 1st Glos Regt. | A.F.B. |
| | | | Casualties admitted to unit Sick 7 | |
| | 23.1.17 | | Capt. M.J. Lyppiatt R.A.M.C. (Temp) proceeded to Officers School for temp duty on relief of Capt. J MacRae R.A.M.C. (Temp) who rejoins this unit for duty | A.F.B. |
| | | | No. 761,305 Pt. Ruane W.C. R.A.M.C. was admitted to hospital and transferred to III Corps Rest Station | |

Army Form C. 2118.

# WAR DIARY
## or
## INTELLIGENCE SUMMARY.
*(Erase heading not required.)*

Instructions regarding War Diaries and Intelligence Summaries are contained in F. S. Regs., Part II. and the Staff Manual respectively. Title pages will be prepared in manuscript.

| Place | Date | Hour | Summary of Events and Information | Remarks and references to Appendices |
|---|---|---|---|---|
| Laventie | 24.1.17 | | Casualties admitted to unit List 6. | A.F.F. |
| | 25.1.17 | | Lt Tarrstone R.M.C. (Temp) joined this unit for duty and was taken on our strength. Casualties admitted to unit List 18. | A.F.F. |
| | 26.1.17 | | Casualties admitted to unit List 37. 3 reinforcements joined this unit from Base Details. No 3 149 665 Pte Simpson E.J. A.C.M. joined this unit from No 1 D.R.S. and was taken on our strength. No 58107 Pte Richardson J Ramc & No 105 357 Pte Renwick J A Ramc were admitted to hospital and transferred to III Corps Rest Station. No 309 305 Sgt Bame J was discharged to duty from III Corps Rest Station. | A.F.F. |
| | 27.1.17 | | Casualties admitted to unit List 30. No 57962 Cpl (A/L/Cpl) Edwards J Ramc awarded the military medal (Authority III Corps No H.R. 1/7/17). Capt J. Mac Rae Ramc Temp proceeded to report to A.M.O. 2 5th Div for temp duty with 1st R.W. Fus. | A.F.F. |
| | 28.1.17 | | Casualties admitted to unit List 40. | A.F.F. |
| | 29.1.17 | | Casualties admitted to unit List 20. No 81133 Pte Whelan J returned to this unit from the A.P.M. | A.F.F. |
| | 30.1.17 | | Casualties admitted List 13. No 9120 Pte Watts R 2nd Welsh Regt was attached to this unit as the chaplains batman. | A.F.F. |

Army Form C. 2118.

# WAR DIARY
## or
## INTELLIGENCE SUMMARY.
(Erase heading not required.)

Instructions regarding War Diaries and Intelligence Summaries are contained in F. S. Regs., Part II. and the Staff Manual respectively. Title pages will be prepared in manuscript.

| Place | Date | Hour | Summary of Events and Information | Remarks and references to Appendices |
|---|---|---|---|---|
| Louvencourt | 31.1.17 | | Casualties admitted to unit with 2.S. | A.F.F. |
| | | | No 15389 L/Cpl Dunn E joined this Unit from No 45 C.C.S being returned on our strength | |
| | | | Capt. H.S. Lyprott RAMC (temp) returned from temporary duty at Officers hospital. | |
| | | | No 68894 Pte Lethonard J & No 56389 Pte Ames W Rode were admitted to hospital and evacuated | |
| | | | to Base being struck off our strength | |

H.Munro Fortescue
B/Col RAMC
F.A.
O.C. No 2/1 141
2-1-17

141 3d Aust
H. 019

Confidential

WAR DIARY

OF

From 1st February 1917 To 28th February 1917

(Volume No: 8)

COMMITTEE FOR THE
MEDICAL HISTORY OF THE WAR
Date 4 APR 1917

# WAR DIARY
## or
## INTELLIGENCE SUMMARY.

Army Form C. 2118.

| Place | Date 1917 | Hour | Summary of Events and Information | Remarks and references to Appendices |
|---|---|---|---|---|
| LAVIEVILLE | Feb. 1 | | Casualties admitted: Sick 32. No. 57964 Pte. Whitehouse E. was admitted to hospital and evacuated to L. of C. "Sick." | A.77 |
| | " 2 | | Casualties admitted: Sick 22. No. 37788 Cpl. Straughan W.(R.A.M.C.) and No. T 252280 Driver Shaw E. A.S.C. H.T. were admitted to hospital and evacuated to L. of C. "Sick." Captain N. T. Lyppiatt (Temp) R.A.M.C. proceeded to take over temporary medical charge of 1st L.N. Lan., vice Captain J. Mackae, who returned to this Unit for duty. | A.77 |
| MERICOURT-SUR-SOMME. | " 3 | | Casualties admitted: Sick 28. Evacuated admitted at 10.45 a.m. in accordance with 2nd. Inf. Bde. Order No. 120. The Unit moved from Lavieville - Ribemont Road with the main Albert-Amiens joining column at junction of the Lavieville - Ribemont Road with the main Albert-Amiens Road at 11.16 a.m. and marching via Ribemont, Morcourt L'Abbé, Sailly le Sec, Sailly Laurette, Cerisy and Morcourt to Mericourt-sur-Somme, arriving about 6 o'clock. One horse ambulance followed immediately in rear of each Battalion. The hospital was opened at the Mairie and the H.T. and M.T. billeted above, the being billeted in 3 Adrian huts and the Officers in huts. | A.77 |
| | | | R.A.M.C. personnel — | |
| | " 4 | | Casualties admitted: Nil. | A.77 |
| | " 5 | | Casualties admitted: Sick 40. In accordance with verbal instructions the Unit moved off at about 10.30 a.m. via Chuignolles to Fontaine-les-Cappy, arriving at about 2 o'clock in the afternoon. Two Adrian huts were taken over from the 24th French Division. Lieut. J. Fanston proceeded to take over temporary medical charge of the 2nd. R. Sussex, and returned the same date. A party of 3 Officers and 28 Men proceeded to the Scerérie de Flaucourt and Talus d'Achille. | A.77 |
| FONTAINE-LES-CAPPY. | " 6 | | No. 15389 Sgt. Dunn G. was admitted to hospital and evacuated to L. of C. "Sick." Casualties admitted: Sick 6. | A.77 |

Army Form C. 2118.

# WAR DIARY
## or
## INTELLIGENCE SUMMARY.
*(Erase heading not required.)*

Instructions regarding War Diaries and Intelligence Summaries are contained in F.S. Regs., Part II. and the Staff Manual respectively. Title pages will be prepared in manuscript.

| Place | Date 1917 | Hour | Summary of Events and Information | Remarks and references to Appendices |
|---|---|---|---|---|
| FONTAINE-LES-CAPPY. | Feb. 6 (Cont'd) | | The A.D.Ss. at Sucrerie de Flaucourt and the Talus d'Achille were taken over. No. 58182 Pte. Field N.E.A.; R.A.M.C., was admitted to hospital and transferred to 3rd C.R.S. | A.P. |
| " | 7 | | Casualties passing through: Sick 3, Wounded 1. No. 58107 Pte. Richardson J. R.A.M.C., was evacuated from 3rd C.R.S. to L. of C., being struck down at shaft 26.1.17. Captain J.H. Ritchie M.C., R.A.M.C. (Temp.) reported & the Unit from No. 1 Field Amb. for temporary duty. | A.P. |
| " | 8 | | Took over A.D.Ss. Assevillers Foot, and Secondo at Bois de Boulogne Quarry. Five Reinforcements joined this Unit from Cyclists Base Depot. Capt. A.T. Lyquiatt (Temp.) R.A.M.C. returned from temporary duty with 1st L.N.Lanc. | A.P. |
| " | 8 | | Casualties passing through: Sick 18, Wounded 6. One motor ambulance car was attached from No. 1 F.A. with a driver and orderly and one from No. 2 F.A. | A.P. |
| " | 8 | | Opened a section of a hut for French Foot Prophylaxis at Fontaine-les-Cappy. | A.P. |
| " | 9 | | Captain J.H. Ritchie M.C., R.A.M.C. (Temp.) returned to his Unit No. 1 F.A. No. 39367 Private Antelme L.A., R.A.M.C. proceeded to report to P.M., Fourth Army, for duty, and was struck off the strength. | A.P. |
| " | 10 | | Casualties passing through: Sick 24, Wounded 2. No. 7906 Pte. J.F. White, R.A.M.C. proceeded to No. 1 Fld. Amb. to attend a course of lectures on Chiropody. | A.P. |
| " | 11 | | Cases passing through: Sick 14, Wounded 1. Took over the two huts about 300 yards to the left of those already occupied, for hospital. Handed over Flaucourt Brasserie and Talus d'Achille to an Ambulance of the 48th Division. | A.P. |
| " | 12 | | Casualties passing through: Sick 8, Wounded 7. Casualties passing through: Sick 16, Wounded 3. | A.P. |

Army Form C. 2118.

# WAR DIARY
## or
## INTELLIGENCE SUMMARY.
(Erase heading not required.)

Instructions regarding War Diaries and Intelligence Summaries are contained in F.S. Regs., Part II. and the Staff Manual respectively. Title pages will be prepared in manuscript.

| Place | Date 1917. | Hour | Summary of Events and Information | Remarks and references to Appendices |
|---|---|---|---|---|
| FONTAINE-LES-CAPPY. | Feb. 13 | | Casualties passing through: Wounded 6, Sick 28. One A.D. Corps died. | A.F.F. |
| | " 14 | | No.58182 Pte Field W.E.A., R.A.M.C., was discharged from 3rd C.C.S. to duty, and rejoined this Unit on the 14th instant. Capt. H.T. Lipiatt, R.A.M.C. (Temp.) proceeded to 39th Bde., R.F.A. for temporary duty. No.57982 Pte G. Allen, R.A.M.C., and No.56093, Pte Swallow C., R.A.M.C. proceeded to report to 4th Field Survey Coy. for a test in photography. Casualties passing through: Sick 30, Wounded 17. Lose 6 to crucifix. Removed hospital to the hut nearest the road. | A.F.F. |
| | " 15 | | Five re-inforcements joined the Unit from the Base. No.77223 Pte Grainder L.A. was sent to No.2 Fld. Amb. sick. Casualties passing through: Sick 30, Wounded #5. Opened a place at A.D.S. Assevillers for Trench Foot Prophylaxis. | A.F.F. |
| | " 16 | | Cases passing through Unit: Sick 22, Wounded 7. No.57382 Pte McHenry C., R.A.M.C. proceeded to No.3 Coy., 1st Div. Train, and was struck off our strength. Lieut. J. Fanshaw proceeded to 1st Northants for duty and was taken on our strength. | A.F.F. |
| | " 17 | | Casualties passing through Unit: Wounded 1, Sick 23. Captain L.G. Bowker Allen, D.S.O., M.C., R.A.M.C.(Reg.) joined this Unit and was taken on our strength. | A.F.F. |
| | " 18 | | Casualties passing through Unit: Sick 28, Wounded 6. Capt. H.T. Lipiatt, R.A.M.C. (Temp.) posted to medical charge of 39th Brigade R.F.A., vice Capt. L.G. Forsyth, R.A.M.C. (Temp.) who is posted to and joined this Unit. No. 76336, Pte. W.J. Storey, R.A.M.C., admitted to Hospital. G.S.W. (Bot Legs). One Medical Officer, one Bearer-Subdivision and one Motor Ambulance from No.1 Field Ambulance joined this Unit for temporary duty. The Motor Ambulance attached | A.F.F. |

Army Form C. 2118.

# WAR DIARY
## or
## INTELLIGENCE SUMMARY.
(Erase heading not required.)

| Place | Date 1917. | Hour | Summary of Events and Information | Remarks and references to Appendices |
|---|---|---|---|---|
| FONTAINE-LES-CAPPY. | Feb.18 (Contd.) | | From No. 2 Field Ambulance rejoined its Unit. No. 88124 Pte. Walker J., R.A.M.C. No. 88135 Pte. Robertson J.P., R.A.M.C. "83161 " Thompson C., R.A.M.C. " 70711 " Pearce J., R.A.M.C. | A/T. |
| | "19. | | Joined this Unit from Base Details for duty. No.58117 L/Cpl. Hobson A., R.A.M.C. admitted to Hospital of No.2 Fld. Amb. "Sick". No. 7427 Pte. Worthy J., R.A.M.C. Casualties passing through Unit: Sick 14, Wounded 8. "48313 " Amos W.G., R.A.M.C. Transferred to 30th H.A.C. for duty. "60350 " Dillard J.G., R.A.M.C. | A/T. A/T. |
| | "20. | | Casualties passing through Unit: Sick 33, Wounded 2. Two cases of German Measles. 1st S.W.Bs. evacuated to No. 38 Casualty Clearing Station. | A/T. |
| | "21. | | Casualties passing through Unit: Sick 30, Wounded 2. Drew one Nissen Hut for use of Foot Washing Establishment at Fontaine-les-Cappy. | A/T. |
| | "22. | | Casualties passing through Unit: Sick 26, Wounded 4. No. 58003 Sgt. Major Kitchen A.E., R.A.M.C. "58182 Pte. Field W.E.A., R.A.M.C. admitted to hospital of No.2 Field "57970 " Elliot R., R.A.M.C. Ambulance. Sick. "90089 " Houstins F.S., R.A.M.C. "56873 " McGregor W., R.A.M.C. | A/T. |
| | "23. | | Casualties passing through Unit: Wounded 4, Sick 37. No. 58003 Sgt.Majr. Kitchen A.E., R.A.M.C. rejoined Unit. | A/T. |
| | "24. | | Casualties passing through Unit: Sick 27, Wounded 11. No. 77223 Pte. Grenader J., R.A.M.C. rejoined unit from No.2 Field Ambulance. "90337 " McGean J., R.A.M.C. admitted to hospital of No.2 Fld Amb. Sick. | A/T. |
| | "25. | | Casualties passing through Unit: Sick 25, Wounded 3. No. 77223 Pte. Grenader J., R.A.M.C. posted to 50th Divisional School for duty. | A/T. |

Army Form C. 2118.

# WAR DIARY
## or
## INTELLIGENCE SUMMARY.
(Erase heading not required.)

| Place | Date 1917. | Hour | Summary of Events and Information | Remarks and references to Appendices |
|---|---|---|---|---|
| FONTAINE-LES-CAPPY. | Feb. 26. | | Casualties passing through Unit: Sick 31, Wounded 13. No. 57970 Pte. Elliott R! R.A.M.C., rejoined Unit from No. 2 Field Ambulance. One wounded man died at Headquarters. One Motor Ambulance proceeded to and reported at 48th Division from Dressing Station, G.15. c. 2.4. for duty. | A17 |
| | " 27. | | Casualties passing through Unit: Sick 37, Wounded 2. | A17 |
| | " 28. | | Casualties passing through Unit: Sick 23, Wounded 6. | A17 |

J. Anne Fortescue

Lt Col R.A.M.C.
O.C. 141st Field Ambulance.

CONFIDENTIAL.

WAR DIARY

OF

NO: 141st Field Ambulance.

From 1st March 1917    To 31st March 1917.

(Volume No:9)

**Army Form C. 2118.**

# WAR DIARY
## or
## INTELLIGENCE SUMMARY.
*(Erase heading not required.)*

Instructions regarding War Diaries and Intelligence Summaries are contained in F. S. Regs., Part II. and the S.F Manual respectively. Title pages will be prepared in manuscript.

| Place | Date | Hour | Summary of Events and Information | Remarks and references to Appendices |
|---|---|---|---|---|
| FONTAINE LES CAPPY | March 1917 1 | | Casualties passing through Unit. Sick: 28. Wounded: 9. No. 58757 Cpl. McTavish J. RAMC. GSW (Face) Slight. " M/2. 103804 Pte. Payne F.H. ASC. MT. GSW (face) Slight. Both remained at duty. | APP |
| | 2 | | Casualties passing through Unit. Sick: 18. Wounded: 6. 1 Off. RAMC with 1 Aust'n Ambulance Car, 1 other RSC MT. & 1 Car on duty RAMC, proceeded to report to OC Advanced Dressing Station. 1st South Midland Field Ambulance, 448", Bavroux, Foucourt. Brassuc for temporary duty. | APP |
| | 3 | | Casualties passing through Unit. Sick: 21. Wounded: 15. COC 1st Division inspected the Unit. No. 3579. S/Sgt. (Act. S/M.) Davies A. RAMC admitted to No. 2 Fd Ambulance. Sick. | APP |

Maurice Fortescue
Lieut RAMC

# WAR DIARY or INTELLIGENCE SUMMARY

Army Form C. 2118.

| Place | Date | Hour | Summary of Events and Information | Remarks and references to Appendices |
|---|---|---|---|---|
| FONTAINE LES CROIX | Nov 1.17 | 4 | Casualties passing through lines 1. Sick - 16. Wounded - 10. No. 57957 Sgt. Mins. C. RAMC posted to 1st Divisional Officers School for temporary duty. No. 55/56 Pte Shattock R.E. RAMC transferred to C/75 Battery RFA for war duties. | A/1 |
| | | 5 | Casualties passing through lines 1. Sick - 30. Wounded - 1. | A/2 |
| | | | Infantry Units attached to this Unit inspected by A.D.M.S. 1st Division. | |
| | | 6 | Casualties passing through lines 1. Sick. 25. Wounded. 23. No. 54309 Pte. A. Walton R.A.M.C. admitted to Hospital & No. 2 F. Amb. Sickness, sick. | A/4 |
| | | 7 | Casualties passing through lines 1. Sick - 23. Wounded - 56. No. 15721 Sgt. Ryan A.F. Odell R.A.M.C. joined this Unit for duty from No. 4 General Hospital from No. 58003 Sgt. Ryan A.E. Kitchen R.A.M.C. exchange with him. | A/4 |

A. Murie. Lt Colonel RAMC

# WAR DIARY
## INTELLIGENCE SUMMARY

Army Form C. 2118.

| Place | Date | Hour | Summary of Events and Information | Remarks and references to Appendices |
|---|---|---|---|---|
| Fontaine les Cappy | March 1917 7 | | No. 35791 Cpl (Act Sgt) Davies R. RAMC struck off duty from Hospital of No. 2 Ambulance & reported at unit. No. 60 Parr returned duty from Base details Bounty. | MF |
| | 8 | | No. 53003 Sgt Myson P. Kitchen RAMC proceeded on duty to report to No. 4 General Hospital for duty. | MF |
| | 9 | | No. 55117 Pau L/C Hodson R.E. RAMC rejoined Unit from III Corps Rest Station. Casualties today: Wounded - 3. Sick - 29. No. 71945 Gunner H.C Williams M.G. RAMC admitted to Hospital of No. 2 I.S. Ambulance sick. 1 N.C.O & 55 1st Gunners of Janry & Feby Reg'l Reliefs attacked to this Unit & duty at Quarantine Camp Fieffes. Becourt to be run by this Unit. | MF |
| | 10 | | Casualties during though out Wounded 5 Sick - 26. | MF |

Maurice Fortescue
Lieut RAMC

Army Form C. 2118.

# WAR DIARY
## or
## INTELLIGENCE SUMMARY.

(Erase heading not required.)

| Place | Date | Hour | Summary of Events and Information | Remarks and references to Appendices |
|---|---|---|---|---|
| Fortune Les Comp | March 1917 | | | |
| | 11 | | Carrying parties through the night. Sick 24. Evacuated. | App |
| | 12 | | Owing to run a Divisional Sports Meeting at the eighth wounded drawing stamen at Becourincourt. Evacuated. Carrying parties through the night. Sick 23. Evacuated 3. No. 55710 Pt. T. WEBB. RAMC forwarded to sick convoy from No. 3 Stationary Hospital. | App |
| | 13 | | Carrying parties through the night. Sick 26. Evacuated 4. | App |
| | 14 | | Capt. T. Tora, RAMC (Temp) posted to this Unit for temporary duty vice Capt. H.A. SHEATH, MC RAMC into be taken to No. 1 FA for duty. Sick 47. Evacuated 13. | App |
| | 15 | | Carrying parties through the night. Sick 33. Evacuated 1. | App |
| | 16 | | " Sick 43. Evacuated 7. | App |
| | 17 | | " Sick 33. Evacuated 10. | App |

No. 56624 Pte A.T. JOHNSTON. RAMC forward from this Unit to report to the NT. Bank of the R.S.C. for duty.

J. Irvine Fortescue RAMC

# WAR DIARY
## or
## INTELLIGENCE SUMMARY.
(Erase heading not required.)

Army Form C. 2118.

| Place | Date | Hour | Summary of Events and Information | Remarks and references to Appendices |
|---|---|---|---|---|
| Fampoux | 1917 March | | | |
| Les- | 18 | | Casualties passing through Amb: Sick 29. Wounded Nil | A17 |
| Cars | 19 | | Advanced dressing station opened in Railway village - | A17 |
| | | | Sick. 23 | |
| | | | Capt: T. Poole R.A.M.C. (R) proceeded to the Office of the D.D.M.S. | |
| | | | III C. Corps for temporary duty | |
| | | | Casualties passing through Amb: Sick 17 | A17 |
| | 20 | | Capt. J.H. Ritchie, M.C. R.A.M.C. joined this Unit for temporary | |
| | | | duty from No. 1 F.Amb Can: War: Advanced dressing station opened in Villers aux bois | A17 |
| | 21 | | Casualties passing through Amb: Wounded 1 | A17 |
| | 22 | | " " Evacuated Railway | A17 |
| | " | | Sick 17 Wounded 1 | A17 |
| | | | No. 47810 Pte M.C. Scofer, R.A.M.C joined the Amb: for duty from | |
| | | | No. 51 Stanac Hospital | |
| | 23 | | Casualties passing through Amb: Sick 8. 10. Wounded 1 | |
| | 24 | | " " Sick 12 | |
| | | | Bearer Sub division of No. 1 & 3 Ambulances attached | |
| | | | rejoin own Amb: | |
| | | | Casualties passing through Amb: Sick 7 | A17 |
| | 25 | | 3 O.R.s R.A.M.C. from No. 1 Amb: Can: Base Depot (1st Canadian |

F. Murray Lt.Col. Officer Comg

# WAR DIARY
## or
## INTELLIGENCE SUMMARY.

*(Erase heading not required.)*

Army Form C. 2118.

| Place | Date | Hour | Summary of Events and Information | Remarks and references to Appendices |
|---|---|---|---|---|
| Fortune les Croix | March 1919 26 | | Cancelled parade through Chal Sick. 9 Orrs Officer Staff Sgt W Morley RAMC remand to L of C Sick | 9/7 |
| | 27 | | Cancelled parade through Chal Sick. 8 Pte down to Divisional Rest Station at Becquincourt No. 58161 Sgt T. Bonnon RAMC proceed from this unit to report to No 31 General Hospital for duty | 9/44 |
| | 28 | | Cancelled parade through Chal Sick. 3 O.Rs attached to the Unit for duty at the Soup Kitchen upon its Divisional Cr | 9/13 |
| | 29 | | Cancelled parade through Chal Sick. 9 | 9/14 |
| | 30 | | " " " Sick. 11 | 9/73 |
| | 31 | | "B" Section of Unit march from Fontaine les Cappy to Vilers Bretonneux to take over III Cor Rest Station (Guards) X III Corps Bearer Section from 2/3rd N.Mid Field Ambulance to Cambresi came Even parade Divisional Chal Sick. 9 | 9/74 |

Maurice Fortescue
Lt Col RAMC
OC 141 Field Ambulance.

SECRET,

WAR DIARY
OF
141st. FIELD AMBULANCE
FOR THE MONTH OF
APRIL 1917.

(VOLUME No:10)

B.E.F.

Summary of Medical War Diaries of 142nd F.A. 3rd Div. 6th Corps.

3rd ARMY.

18th Corps from May 19th.

OPERATIONS ON WESTERN FRONT - April - May 1917.

Officer Commanding - Lt. Col. Habgood A.H.

Summarised under the following headings :-

Phase "B" - Battle of Arras - April - May 1917.

   1st Period - Attack on Vimy Ridge - April.

   2nd Period - Capture of Siegfried Line - May.

---------

B.E.F.

142nd F.A.   3rd Div.   6th Corps.   3rd ARMY.     Western Front.
O.C. = Lt. Col. Habgood A.H.                        April 1917.


PHASE "B" - Battle of Arras - April - May 1917.
   1st Period - Attack on Vimy Ridge -   April.


Headquarters at Hauteville.

| | |
|---|---|
| April 4th. | Moves. To Wanquetin. |
| 9th. | To Arras. |
| 13th. | Moves. Detachment. Bearers rejoined Headquarters from clearing wounded between Arras and Tilloy 9th - 13th. |
| | Casualties R.A.M.C. 0 & 6 wounded remained at duty. |
| 14th. | Moves. To Hospital St. Jean 6th C.M.D.S. |
| | Medical Arrangements. T.S.D. available employed under O.C. 6th C.M.D.S. (87th F.A.) |
| 15th-25th. | Ops. R.A.M.C. No entry. |
| 26th. | Medical Arrangements. O.C. 142nd F.A. assumed charge of C.M.D.S. |
| 27th. | T.D. 2/2nd London Field Ambulance joined for duty, also Capt. Kennedy - Abdom. Surg. Spec. Capt. Scarborough - Anaesthetist. |
| 28th. | Moves. Detachment. Bearers to Feuchy La Chapel A.D.S and Gunpits behind Monchy. |
| 30th. | Ops. R.A.M.C. Constructional work at C.M.D.S. |

B.E.F.

142nd F.A.  3rd Div.  6th Corps.  3rd ARMY.  Western Front.
O.C. = Lt. Col. Habgood A.H.                  April 1917.

PHASE "B" - Battle of Arras - April - May 1917.
    1st Period - Attack on Vimy Ridge - April.

             Headquarters at Hauteville.

| | |
|---|---|
| April 4th. | Moves. To Wanquetin. |
| 9th. | To Arras. |
| 13th. | Moves. Detachment. Bearers rejoined Headquarters from clearing wounded between Arras and Tilloy 9th - 13th. |
| | Casualties R.A.M.C. O & 6 wounded remained at duty. |
| 14th. | Moves. To Hospital St. Jean 6th C.M.D.S. |
| | Medical Arrangements. T.S.D. available employed under O.C. 6th C.M.D.S. (87th F.A.) |
| 15th-25th. | Ops. R.A.M.C. No entry. |
| 26th. | Medical Arrangements. O. C. 142nd F.A. assumed charge of C.M.D.S. |
| 27th. | T.D. 2/2nd London Field Ambulance joined for duty, also Capt. Kennedy - Abdom. Surg. Spec. Capt. Scarborough - Anæsthetist. |
| 28th. | Moves. Detachment. Bearers to Feuchy La Chapel A.D.S and Gunpits behind Monchy. |
| 30th. | Ops. R.A.M.C. Constructional work at C.M.D.S. |

Army Form C. 2118.

# WAR DIARY
## or
## INTELLIGENCE SUMMARY.
*(Erase heading not required.)*

Instructions regarding War Diaries and Intelligence Summaries are contained in F. S. Regs., Part II. and the Staff Manual respectively. Title pages will be prepared in manuscript.

| Place | Date | Hour | Summary of Events and Information | Remarks and references to Appendices |
|---|---|---|---|---|
| Villers Bretonneux. | 1st April 1917. | | "B" Section march from Fontaine-les-Cappy to Villers Bretonneux. Take over old 3rd Corps Rest Station (closed) and 3rd Corps Scabies Section from 2/3 North Midland Field Ambulance. "C" Section at Fontaine-les-Cappy. | Annex Folders  |
| | 2nd | | Casualties admitted to Scabies Section...... 15 <br> " " " Field Ambulance...... Nil. <br> Capt F. D. Annesley, RAMC (S.R.) joined Unit for duty from 25th Brigade RFA. | Annex Folders |
| | 3rd | | Casualties admitted to Scabies Section...... 22 <br> " " " Field Ambulance...... 5. <br> Capt L. T. Poole, RAMC. rejoined Unit from Office of DDMS. 3rd Corps. | 9/17 A/17 |
| | 4th | | Casualties admitted to Scabies Section...... 31 <br> " " " Field Ambulance...... 14 | |
| | 5th | | " " " Scabies Section...... 21 <br> " " " Field Ambulance...... 17 <br> "C" Section march from Fontaine-les-Cappy to Liancourt, establish a post there and collect sick from the 1st Brigade. Hand over Hospital Buildings situate at Fontaine-les-Cappy to an Ambulance of the 32nd Division. <br> Capt L.T.Poole, RAMC. proceeded from HeadQuarters to take charge of "C" Section at Liancourt. | A/17 |
| | 6th | | Casualties admitted to Scabies Section,,,,,. 18 | A/17 |
| | 7th | | " " " " " 9 | A/17 |
| | 8th | | " " " " " 5 <br> " " " Field Ambulance....... 3 | A/17 |

Army Form C. 2118.

# WAR DIARY
## or
## INTELLIGENCE SUMMARY.
(Erase heading not required.)

| Place | Date | Summary of Events and Information | Remarks and references to Appendices |
|---|---|---|---|
| Villers Brettoneux | April 1917. | | |
| | 9th | Casualties admitted to Corps Scabies Section......... 28 | |
| | | " Field Ambulance.................. 14 | |
| | | 1 N.C.O. and 7 men proceed in advance from Villers Bretonneux to Doingt to erect new Corps Scabies Section. | |
| | 10th | Casualties admitted to Corps Scabies Section......... 41 | |
| | | " Field Ambulance.................. 10 | |
| | | 1 Officer, 36 Other Ranks R.A.M.C. 1 Limber Wagon, 1 Water Tank, with necessary A.S.C. personnel proceeded from Villers Bretonneux to Doingt. | |
| | 11th | Casualties admitted to Corps Scabies Section......... 14 | |
| | | " " Field Ambulance.................. 12 | |
| | 12th | " " Corps Scabies Section......... 16 | |
| | | " " Field Ambulance.................. 13 | |
| | 13th | " " Corps Scabies Section......... 15 | |
| | | " " Field Ambulance.................. 9 | |
| | 14th | " " Corps Scabies Section......... 9 | |
| | | " " Field Ambulance.................. 8 | |
| | 15th | " " Corps Scabies Section......... 34 | |
| | | " " Field Ambulance.................. 9 | |
| | | No:39959 Cpl Atkinson G., R.A.M.C. joined this Unit for duty. | |
| | 16th | Casualties admitted to Field Ambulance.............. 9 | |
| | | " Corps Scabies Section.......... 56 | |
| | | Capt L.T.Poole, R.A.M.C. proceeded from Doingt to the Office of A.D.M.S., 1st Division for temporary duty. | |
| | | Capt L.G.Bourdillon., D.S.O., M.C., R.A.M.C. assumes command of "C" Section at Liancourt Liancourt | |
| | | Under instructions received from the D.D.M.S. IIIrd Corps, no further admittances are made to the IIIrd Corps Scabies Section, and arrangements are made to close down this Section. | |

Army Form C. 2118.

# WAR DIARY
## or
## INTELLIGENCE SUMMARY.
*(Erase heading not required.)*

Instructions regarding War Diaries and Intelligence Summaries are contained in F. S. Regs., Part II. and the Staff Manual respectively. Title pages will be prepared in manuscript.

| Place | Date April 1917. | Hour | Summary of Events and Information | Remarks and references to Appendices |
|---|---|---|---|---|
| Villers Bretonneux. | 17th | | Casualties admitted to Field Ambulance........11 | |
| | 18th | | "         "         "       "       "       ........13 | |
| | 19th | | "         "         "       "       "       ........23 | |
| | | | Hand over site for new lllrd Corps Scabies Section at Doingt to 1/2nd S.Midland Field Ambulance. Detachment of this Unit ("B" Section) march from Doingt et/Camp Marly. | |
| | 20th | | "B" Section march from Camp Marly and join the 2nd Brigade at Morcourt. | |
| | | | Casualties admitted to Field Ambulance........22 | |
| | 21st | | "         "         "       "       "       ........12 | |
| | 22nd | | "         "         "       "       "       ........4 | |
| | | | No:39599 Cpl G. Atkinson. R.A.M.C. posted to No:2 Field Ambulance for duty | |
| | 23rd | | Casualties admitted to Unit................1. | |
| | | | Hand over the lllrd Corps Scabies Section (closed) at Villers Bretonneux to a detachment of a 48th Divisional Field Ambulance. | |
| | | | Hand over the lllrd Corps Rest Station (closed) at Villers Bretonneux to a detachment of a 42nd Divisional Field Ambulance. | |
| | | | "A" Section leave Villers Bretonneux at 1-30 p.M. and march to Camp No:131 (Morcourt) and join "B" Section. | |
| | | | Hospital closed. | |
| | | | Casualties passing through "C" Section........6 | |
| | | | "         "         "       "       "       ........7 | |
| Camp 131 | 24th | | One complete section plus one bearer sub division participate in the 2nd Brigade manoeuvres. | |
| | 25th | | Casualties passing through "C" Section........7 | |
| | | | Capt L. T. Poole, R.A.M.C. rejoins Units from the Office of A.D.M.S., 1st Division. | |
| | 26th | | Casualties passing through "C" Section........5 | |
| | | | Capt L.T.Poole., R.A.M.C. proceeds to Liancourt to take over command of "C" Section. | |

Army Form C. 2118.

# WAR DIARY
## or
## INTELLIGENCE SUMMARY.
*(Erase heading not required.)*

Instructions regarding War Diaries and Intelligence Summaries are contained in F. S. Regs., Part II. and the Staff Manual respectively. Title pages will be prepared in manuscript.

| Place | Date April | Hour | Summary of Events and Information | Remarks and references to Appendices |
|---|---|---|---|---|
| Camp 131 | 27th | 17 | Casualties passing through "C" Section........ 7 | |
| | 28th | | "    "    "    "C"    "    ........ 3 No:31679 Pte Harris. R.A.M.C. evacuated to "L of C" sick. | |
| | 29th | | Casualties passing through Unit "C" Section... 9 | |
| | 30th | | "    "    "    "C" Section........ 8 Covering the period 18th to the 30th May a uniform scheme of training as ordered by the A. D. M. S., 1st Division has been carried out. | |

N Finnie Fortescue

Lieut Col R.A.M.C.

Commanding 141st Field Ambulance.

CONFIDENTIAL.

WAR DIARY

of

141st FIELD AMBULANCE.

From 1st May 1917    To 31st May 1917.

(Volumne No:11)

Army Form C. 2118.

# WAR DIARY
## or
## INTELLIGENCE SUMMARY.
(Erase heading not required.)

Instructions regarding War Diaries and Intelligence Summaries are contained in F.S. Regs., Part II. and the Staff Manual respectively. Title pages will be prepared in manuscript.

| Place | Date MAY 1917. | Hour | Summary of Events and Information | Remarks and references to Appendices |
|---|---|---|---|---|
| Camp 131 Morcourt. | 1st | | Casualties passing through Unit........ Sick 4 Lieut T. Clapperton., R.A.M.C. and 20 Other Ranks proceed to Villers Bretonneux for the purpose of dismantling and loading Huts at the old 3rd Corps Rest Station. No:58105 Private L. L. Wilson., R.A.M.C. proceeds to No:3 Canadian Casualty Clearing Station for duty as Dental Mechanic. "A" & "B" Sections march from Camp 131 to Morcourt and take over billets vacated by Units of the 2nd Brigade. | N.T. |
| Morcourt. | 2nd | | Casualties passing through Unit........ Sick 6 No:90158 Pte J. Gunn., R.A.M.C. to the School of 1st Divisional Cookery for a course. Lieut T. Clapperton., R.A.M.C. and 20 Other Ranks rejoin Unit from Villers Bretonneux. | N.T. |
| | 3rd. | | "C" Section march from Biancourt to Brusle, and collect sick from all 3rd Brigade and from the 2nd K. R. R.s, transferring cases to 3rd Corps Rest Station; urgent cases being evacuated to nearest medical Unit. Casualties passing through Unit........ Sick 4 No:22540 Private W. Poole, R.A.M.C. admitted to Hospital "Sick" and evacuated to "L of C" | N.T. |
| | 4th | | Casualties passing through Unit........ Sick 6 Capt Jas MacRae., R.A.M.C. and one R.A.M.C. orderly with a sufficiency of medical inspection material for a medical inspection proceeded to report to Camp Commandant at Querrieu for temporary duty as M. O. i/c Troops, Querrieu area. | N.T. |
| | 5th | | Casualties passing through Unit........ Sick 12 Divisional Field Ambulance Sports held at CERISY (No:1 Field Ambulance) | N.T. |

Army Form C. 2118.

# WAR DIARY
## or
## INTELLIGENCE SUMMARY.

*(Erase heading not required.)*

Instructions regarding War Diaries and Intelligence Summaries are contained in F. S. Regs., Part II. and the Staff Manual respectively. Title pages will be prepared in manuscript.

| Place | Date MAY 1917. | Hour | Summary of Events and Information | Remarks and references to Appendices |
|---|---|---|---|---|
| Morcourt. | 6th | | Casualties passing through Unit...... Sick 4 No:M/2.149665 Pte E. T. Simpson., A.S.C.-"MT" evacuated to "L of C" from 1st Divisional Rest Station. | XI7. |
| | 7th | | Capt L. G. Bourdillon, D.S.O., M.C., R.A.M.C. proceeds to the Office of D.M.S., Fourth Army for instruction in the duties of a D.A.D.M.S., remaining on the strength of this Unit whilst attached there. 1 N.C.O. and 20 Other Ranks proceeds to No:34 Casualty Clearing Station for temporary duty. Casualties passing through Unit...... Sick 4 | XI7. |
| | 8th | | Capt F. D. Annesley, R.A.M.C. proceeds from HeadQuarters to Brusle for duty with "C" Section. Casualties passing through Unit...... Sick 1 | XI7. |
| | 9th | | Casualties passing through Unit...... Sick 2 | XI7. |
| | 10th | | Casualties passing through Unit...... Sick 2 Draw 1 H.D. Horse to replace casualty. | XI7. |
| | 11th | | Casualties passing through Unit...... Sick 2 No:57364 Pte Hemmings W.T., R.A.M.C. proceeds to 2nd Royal Munster Fus. for Water duties. No:90138 Pte Gunn J., R.A.M.C. rejoins Unit from 1st Divisional Bomb School. | XI7. |
| | 12th | | Casualties passing through Unit...... Sick 3 No:2756 Pte Burke A., R.A.M.C. joins this Unit for duty from the 2nd Royal Munster Fus. No:54309 Pte A. Walton., R.A.M.C. rejoined this Unit from No:1 Prisoners of War Coy. Casualties passing through Unit...... Sick 4 | XI7. |
| | 13th | | | XI7. |
| | 14th | | "      "       "       "    ..... Sick 3 | XI7. |
| | 15th | | "C" Section march from Brusle and rejoin Head Quarters at Morcourt. | XI7. |
| | 16th | | No:58046 Pte C. T. Heal., R.A.M.C. proceeded to report to No:216 Machine Gun Coy for Water Duties. | XI7. |

Army Form C. 2118.

# WAR DIARY
## or
## INTELLIGENCE SUMMARY.
(Erase heading not required.)

Instructions regarding War Diaries and Intelligence Summaries are contained in F. S. Regs., Part II. and the Staff Manual respectively. Title pages will be prepared in manuscript.

| Place | Date May 1917 | Summary of Events and Information | Remarks and references to Appendices |
|---|---|---|---|
| Morcourt | 16th | No:7659 Pte Simmons A. (attached as Barber to this Unit) proceeded to rejoining his own Unit :- 1st Gloucestershire Regiment. No:56118 Sgt Blandford R., R.A.M.C. rejoined this Unit for duty from No:1 New Zealand Stationary Hospital. Casualties passing through Unit........ Sick 3 | |
| | 17th | " " " " ........ Sick 2 | |
| | 18th | " " " " ........ Sick 2 Advance party of Unit proceeds from Morcourt to Warfusée-Abancourt to take over billets. | |
| | 19th | Casualties passing through Unit........ Sick 9 Unit marches from Morcourt to Warfusée-Abancourt. Collect and treat sick of all troops, other than 3rd Cavalry Division, in the area. 1 N.C.O. and 20 men rejoined this Unit from No:34 Casualty Clearing Station | |
| Warfusée-Abancourt. | 20th | Casualties passing through Unit........ Sick 3 | |
| | 21st | " " " " ........ Sick 5 Capt Jas MacRae., R.A.M.C. and Medical Orderly rejoined this Unit from the Camp Commandant, QUERRIEU. | |
| | 22nd | Casualties admitted to Unit........... Sick 5. | |
| | 23rd | " " " " ........... Sick 5 | |
| | 24th | " " " " ........... Sick 4 No:105399 Private E. Cumpstey., R.A.M.C. admitted to Hospital "Sick" and evacuated to Lines of Communication. | |
| | 25th | Casualties admitted to Unit........... Sick 7 | |

Army Form C. 2118.

# WAR DIARY
## or
## INTELLIGENCE SUMMARY.
*(Erase heading not required.)*

Instructions regarding War Diaries and Intelligence Summaries are contained in F. S. Regs., Part II. and the Staff Manual respectively. Title pages will be prepared in manuscript.

| Place | Date May 1917. | Hour | Summary of Events and Information | Remarks and references to Appendices |
|---|---|---|---|---|
| Warfusée-Abancourt. | 26th | | Capt C. L. Chalk., R.A.M.C. in charge of Motor Ambulances and Motor Cycles of this Unit leave Unit at 6-15 a.m. and join the Divisional Motor Ambulance Convoy at Fork Road. Map Reference 0.23 a.4.6. (Sheet 62 D) at 6-45 a.m. Convoy moves off at 7 a.m. and proceeds to Berthen area.  Cars and Cycles of this Unit arrive at R. 34 c. 4.0. (Map Reference Sheet 27. Second Edition). Casualties admitted to Unit.............. Sick 13. No:28767 Cpl A. Hutton., R.A.M.C. admitted to Hospital "Sick" and evacuated to L of C. | J.F. |
| do | 27th | | Casualties admitted to Unit.............. Sick 5. Unit leaves Warfuséé Abancourt at 8-45 p.m. and marches to Guillaucourt.  Entrain and move off from Guillaucourt at 10-30 p.m. | J.F. |
| R.34 c.4.0. (Map Refce Sheet 27 2nd Ed'n) | 28th | | Unit arrives at Caestre at 10-45 a.m. and disentrain at that hour.  March to R.34 c.4.0. Arriving at 4-0 p.m. Open up Hospital and collect and treat Sick of the 3rd Brigade. Casualties admitted to Unit.............. Sick 2. 6 Other Ranks join the Unit for duty from Base Details. | J.F. |
| do | 29th | | Casualties admitted to Unit.............. Sick 7. Capt L.G.Bourdillon., D.S.O., M.C., R.A.M.C. taken off the strength of this Unit. | J.F. |
| do | 30th | | Casualties admitted to Unit.............. Sick 4. No:58877 Pte A.E.Whiting., R.A.M.C. and No:59835 Pte W.Wood., R.A.M.C. proceeded from this Unit to report to O.C. 39th Brigade R.F.A. for Water duties. | J.F. |
| do | 31st | | Casualties admitted to Unit.............. Sick 5. | J.F. |

*[signature]*
Lieut Col R.A.M.C.
Commanding 141st Field Ambulance.

B.E.F.

Summary of Medical War Diaries of 142nd F.A. 3rd Div. 6th Corps.

3rd ARMY.

18th Corps from May 19th.

OPERATIONS ON WESTERN FRONT - April - May 1917.

Officer Commanding - Lt. Col. Habgood A.H.

Summarised under the following headings :-

Phase "B" - Battle of Arras - April - May 1917.
   1st Period - Attack on Vimy Ridge - April.
   2nd Period - Capture of Siegfried Line - May.

---------

B.E.F.

142nd F.A.   3rd Div.   6th Corps.   3rd ARMY.     Western Front.
O.C.= Lt.Col. Habgood A.H.                          May 1917.

18th Corps from 19th May.


PHASE "B" - Battle of Arras - April - May 1917.
  2nd Period - Capture of Siegfried Line - May.

May 1st.      Accommodation. Ward with 48 beds for abdominal wounds.
    3rd.      Ops. Enemy. Hospital shelled several times during day.
              Casualties R.A.M.C. O & 3 killed. O & 17 wounded. 87th
              F.A.
              Medical Arrangements. In consequence of shelling wounded
              removed to ground floor. Sisters returned to C.C.S.
              (20), as many wounded as possible evacuated, and wounded
              diverted to No. 1. 6th C.M.D.S.
              Casualties. 20 and 259 through C.M.D.S. during day.
    4th.      Casualties R.A.M.C. O & 4 wounded Bearers.
              Moves. F.A. 87th F.A. left C.M.D.S. Arras.
  14th-15th.  Moves. Detachment. Bearers rejoined Headquarters.
    18th.     Moves. To Liencourt on relief by 2/2nd Ldn. F.A.
    19th.     Transfer. To 18th Corps.

142nd F.A.   3rd Div.   18th Corps.   3rd ARMY.   Western Front.
O.C. = Lt. Col. Habgood A.H.                     May 1917.


PHASE "B". Battle of Arras - April - May 1917.
  2nd Period - Capture of Siegfried Line - May.

May 19th.  Transfer. To 18th Corps.

21st.  Casualties R.A.M.C. Capt. A. Gilmour M.O. 7 K.S.L.I. evacuated to 93rd C.C.S.

31st.  Ops. R.A.M.C. Unit acted as D.R.S. 18th-31st.

Accommodation. Up to 100 with special arrangements for Scabies.

Moves. To Noyellette.

B.E.F.

142nd F.A.   3rd Div.   6th Corps.   3rd ARMY.         Western Front
O.C.= Lt.Col. Habgood A.H.                              May 1917.

18th Corps from 19th May.

PHASE "B" - Battle of Arras - April - May 1917.
   2nd Period - Capture of Siegfried Line - May.

May 1st.   Accommodation. Ward with 48 beds for abdominal wounds.
3rd.   Ops. Enemy. Hospital shelled several times during day.
   Casualties R.A.M.C. O & 3 killed. O & 17 wounded. 87th
   F.A.
   Medical Arrangements. In consequence of shelling wounded
   removed to ground floor. Sisters returned to C.C.S.
   (20), as many wounded as possible evacuated, and wounded
   diverted to No. 1. 6th C.M.D.S.
   Casualties. 20 and 259 throughout M.D.S. during day.
4th.   Casualties R.A.M.C. O & 4 wounded Bearers.
   Moves. F.A. 87th F.A. left C.M.D.S. Arras.
14th-15th. Moves. Detachment. Bearers rejoined Headquarters.
18th.   Moves. To Liencourt on relief by 2/2nd Ldn. F.A.
19th.   Transfer. To 18th Corps.

B.E.F.

142nd F.A.  3rd Div.  18th Corps.  3rd ARMY.  Western Front.
O.C. = Lt. Col. Habgood A.H.                  May 1917.

PHASE "B". Battle of Arras - April - May 1917.
  2nd Period - Capture of Siegfried Line - May.

May 19th.  Transfer. To 18th Corps.
    21st.  Casualties R.A.M.C. Capt. A. Gilmour M.O. 7 K.S.L.I.
evacuated to 93rd C.C.S.
    31st.  Ops. R.A.M.C. Unit acted as D.R.S. 18th-31st.
Accommodation. Up to 100 with special arrangements for
Scabies.
Moves. To Neyellette.

CONFIDENTIAL.

WAR DIARY

of

141st FIELD AMBULANCE.

From 1st JUNE 1917 to 30th JUNE 1917

(Volume No: 12)

COMMITTEE FOR THE
MEDICAL HISTORY OF THE WAR
Date —7 AUG.1917

B.E.F.

SUMMARY OF MEDICAL WAR DIARIES FOR

141st F.A., 1st Divn. 14th Corps, 5th Army. from 10.6.17

8th Corps from 14/6/17.

15th Corps, 4th Army from 20/6/17.

WESTERN FRONT June 1917.

O.C. Lt. Col. A.J. Fortescue.

SUMMARISED UNDER THE FOLLOWING HEADING

Phase "D" Battle of Messines June 1917.

B.E.F. 1.

<u>141st F.A. 1st Divn. 14th Corps. 5th Army.</u>  <u>WESTERN FRONT</u>
<u>O.C. Lt. Col. A.I. Fortescue.</u>  <u>June 1917.</u>
<u>8th Corps from 14/6/17.</u>

<u>Phase "D" Battle of Messines June 1917.</u>

1917.  <u>Headquarters.</u> at Wallon Cappel Sheet 27.

June 10th.  <u>Moves and Transfer.</u> Unit transferred with 1st Divn. to 5th Army and arrived at Wallon Cappel (Sheet 27)

14th  <u>Transfer.</u> Unit transferred to 8th Corps with 1st Divn.

B.E.F.

141st F.A. 1st Divn. 8th Corps, 5th Army.   WESTERN FRONT.
O.C. Lt. Col. A.J. Fortescue.                June 1917.
15th Corps, 4th Army from 20/6/17.


Phase "D" Battle of Messines June 1917.

1917.
June 14th.    <u>Transfer.</u>  Unit transferred to 8th Corps with 1st Divn.
20th.         <u>Moves and Transfer.</u>  Unit transferred with 1st Divn.
              to 15th Corps, 4th Army and moved to C.28.d.6.2. (Sheet
              27).

B.E.F.

SUMMARY OF MEDICAL WAR DIARIES FOR
141st F.A., 1st Divn. 14th Corps, 5th Army. from 10.6.17
8th Corps from 14/6/17.
15th Corps, 4th Army from 20/6/17.

---

WESTERN FRONT June 1917.

---

O.C. Lt. Col. A.J. Fortescue.

SUMMARISED UNDER THE FOLLOWING HEADING

Phase "D" Battle of Messines June 1917.

B.E.F.

141st F.A. 1st Divn. 14th Corps. 5th Army.   WESTERN FRONT

O.C. Lt. Col. A.I. Fortescue.   June 1917.

8th Corps from 14/6/17.

Phase "D" Battle of Messines June 1917.

| | |
|---|---|
| 1917. | Headquarters. at Wallon Cappel Sheet 27. |
| June 10th. | Moves and Transfer. Unit transferred with 1st Divn. to 5th Army and arrived at Wallon Cappel (Sheet 27) |
| 14th | Transfer. Unit transferred to 8th Corps with 1st Divn. |

141st F.A. 1st Divn. 8th Corps, 5th Army.   WESTERN FRONT.
O.C. Lt. Col. A.J. Fortescue.                June 1917.
15th Corps, 4th Army from 20/6/17.


Phase "D" Battle of Messines June 1917.

1917.
June 14th.  Transfer. Unit transferred to 8th Corps with 1st Divn.
20th.       Moves and Transfer. Unit transferred with 1st Divn.
            to 15th Corps, 4th Army and moved to C.28.d.c.2. (Sheet 27).

Army Form C. 2118.

# WAR DIARY
## or
## INTELLIGENCE SUMMARY.

(Erase heading not required.)

Instructions regarding War Diaries and Intelligence Summaries are contained in F. S. Regs., Part II. and the Staff Manual respectively. Title pages will be prepared in manuscript.

| Place | Date June 1917. | Hour | Summary of Events and Information | Remarks and references to Appendices |
|---|---|---|---|---|
| R.34 c.4.0 (Sheet 27) | 1st. | | No:28767 Cpl Hutton A., R.A.M.C. and No:105399 Pte Cumpstey E., R.A.M.C. rejoined nit from C. C. Station. | A/17. |
| -do- | 2nd | | Capt Jas MacRae., R.A.M.C. rejoined Unit from temporary duty with 2nd Royal Munster Fus. Casualties admitted to Unit........ Sick 5. | A/17. |
| | | | Capt F. D. Annesley., R.A.M.C. (S.R) proceeds to 25th Brigade R.F.A. for duty as M.O. 1/c that Unit. | |
| | | | No:54309 Pte Walton A., R.A.M.C. proceeded to 409th Lowland Field Coy R.E. for Water duty, Capt S.D.Fairweather., R.A.M.C. (T.C.) joined this Unit for duty from No:2 Field Ambulance. Casualties admitted to Unit........ Sick 4. | A/17. |
| -do- | 3rd. | | Casualties admitted to Unit........ Sick 3. | A/17. |
| -do- | 4th | | Casualties admitted to Unit........ Sick 4. No:88124 Private Walker J., R.A.M.C. admitted to Hospital of this Unit and evacuated to "L of C" "Sick" | A/17. |
| -do- | 5th | | Casualties admitted to Unit........ Sick 4. | A/17. |
| -do- | 6th | | Casualties admitted to Unit........ Sick 5. No:M/2.082048 Pte Baker H. E., A.S.C. "MT" admitted to Hospital of this Unit and evacuated to "L of C" "Sick" | A/17. |
| | | | No:56232 Pte Poole P.G., R.A.M.C. rejoined this Unit from temporary duty at D.M.S., Fourth Army. | |
| | | | No:5991 Pte Proce B., R.A.M.C. joined this Unit for duty from 2nd Royal Sussex Regt | |
| -do- | 7th | | Casualties admitted to Unit........ Sick 6. Capt Jas MacRae., R.A.M.C. and Capt S.D.Fairweather., R.A.M.C. proceeded to report to D.D.M.S. Xth Corps for temporary duty. | A/17. |
| -do- | 8th | | Casualties admitted to Unit........ Sick 16. 20 Other Ranks from this Unit proceeded to report to No:12 C. C. Station for temporary duty. No:57251 Sgt Minns C., R.A.M.C. rejoined this Unit for duty from 1st Divisional Officers School. | A/17. |

Army Form C. 2118.

# WAR DIARY
## or
## INTELLIGENCE SUMMARY.
(Erase heading not required.)

Instructions regarding War Diaries and Intelligence Summaries are contained in F. S. Regs., Part II. and the Staff Manual respectively. Title pages will be prepared in manuscript.

| Place | Date 1917. June | Hour | Summary of Events and Information | Remarks and references to Appendices |
|---|---|---|---|---|
| R.34 c.4.0 (Sheet 27) | 9th | | Casualties admitted to Unit........ Sick 15. Capt Jas MacRae., R.A.M.C. and Capt S.D.Fairweather., R.A.M.C. rejoined this Unit from D.D.M.S., Xth Corps. | A.17. |
| do | 10th | | Casualties admitted do Unit........ Sick 8. No:28767 Cpl A. Hutton., R.A.M.C. admitted to Hospital of this Unit "Sick" and evacuated to "L of C" 20 Other Ranks of this Unit rejoin Head Quarters from No:12 C. C. Station. | A.17. |
| do | 11th | | Unit leaves R. 34 c. 4. O. Sheet 27 (2nd Edition) at 7-30 a.m. and marches with the 3rd Infantry Brigade Group to the WALLON CAPPEL area via FLETRE - CAESTRE - LA BREARDE. Unit arrives at WALLON-CAPPEL at 1-30 p.m. Open out sufficient accommodation to deal with sick of the 3rd Brigade; retaining all cases that are likely to be well in three days. Capt L. T. Poole., R.A.M.C. proceeded to the Office of A.D.M.S., 1st Division for temporary duty. No:58824 Corporal Knapton A., R.A.M.C., joined this Unit for duty. | A.17. |
| Wallon Cappel | 12th | | Casualties admitted to Unit........ Sick 2. No:T/2.60203 Driver Stockdale J., A.S.C. "HT" attached, admitted to Hospital "Sick" and evacuated to "L of C". | A.17. |
| do | 13th | | Casualties admitted to Unit........ Sick 7. Capt S.D.Fairweather., R.A.M.C. proceeded to 1st S. W. Bs for temporary medical charge of that Unit. | A.17. |
| do | 14th | | Casualties admitted to Unit........ Sick 4. | A.17. |
| do | 15th | | Casualties admitted to Unit........ Sick 7. | A.17. |
| do | 16th | | Casualties admitted to Unit........ Sick 12. | A.17. |

Army Form C. 2118.

# WAR DIARY
## or
## INTELLIGENCE SUMMARY.
(Erase heading not required.)

Instructions regarding War Diaries and Intelligence Summaries are contained in F.S. Regs., Part II. and the Staff Manual respectively. Title pages will be prepared in manuscript.

| Place | Date Hour June 1917. | Summary of Events and Information | Remarks and references to Appendices |
|---|---|---|---|
| Wallon Cappel. | 17th | Casualties admitted to Unit....... Sick 8. No:DM2/18538 Private New G., A.S.C. "MT" joined this Unit for duty from No:1 Divisional Supply Column. Capt Jas MacRae., R.A.M.C. proceeded to 25th Brigade R.F.A. for temporary medical charge of that Unit. | A/17. |
|  | 18th | Casualties admitted to Unit....... Sick 17. | A/17. |
|  | 19th | Casualties admitted to Unit....... Sick 30 No:12698 Private W. J. Smith., R.A.M.C. admitted to Hospital "Sick" and evacuated to "L of C". | A/17. |
|  | 20th | Casualties admitted to Unit....... Sick 22 No:T/1. 4270 Sgt E.J.Watts., A.S.C. "HT" admitted to Hospital "Sick" and evacuated to "L of C". | A/17. |
| Wallon Cappel | 21st | Unit leaves C. 28 d. 6. 2 (Sheet 27) at 4 a.m. and marches to Les Trois Rois (Map Refce O. 28 d. 2.9. Sheet 27) and marches from that point with the 3rd Brigade Group to the Wormhoudt Area. via Zuytpeene- Wemaers Cappel- Cross roads I. 29 b. - C. 23 c. 4. 6. (Sheet 27). Unit arrives at billets allotted in C. 28 d. 6. 2. (Sheet 27) at 8-30 a.m. Collect and treat sick of the 3rd Brigade Units. Casualties admitted to Unit...... Sick 3. | A/17. |
| C.28 d. 6.2. (Sheet 27). | 22nd | Unit leaves C. 28 d. 6. 2 (Sheet 27) at 3 a.m. and marches to Church WYLDER and marches from that point with the 3rd Brigade Group to the Leffrinckhoucke area via Tax - Galghouck. Unit arrives at billets allotted in Uxem at 8-40 a.m. Collect and treat sick of the 3rd Brigade Units. Casualties admitted to Unit...... Sick 5. | A/17. |

Army Form C. 2118.

# WAR DIARY
## or
## INTELLIGENCE SUMMARY.
(Erase heading not required.)

Instructions regarding War Diaries and Intelligence Summaries are contained in F. S. Regs., Part II. and the Staff Manual respectively. Title pages will be prepared in manuscript.

| Place | Date June 1917. | Hour | Summary of Events and Information | Remarks and references to Appendices |
|---|---|---|---|---|
| UXEM. | 23rd | | Casualties admitted to Unit........ Sick 13. Capt. S. D. Fairweather, R.A.M.C. rejoins Unit from 1st S.W.Bs. Lieut & Qr Mr G. Sellex., R.A.M.C. joins Unit for temporary duty from No:2 Field Ambulance. | A17 |
| | 24th | | Casualties admitted to Unit........ Sick 11. | A17. |
| | 25th | | Casualties admitted to Unit........ Sick 4. Under instructions received from the A.D.M.S. 1st Division. Unit leaves UXEM at 9 a.m. and proceeds to establish a Corps Rest Station and Convalescent Camp (accomodation 2,000) at D.2.d.4.4. (Sheet 19). No:T.35555 Driver G. Guest., A.S.C. "HT" attached. admitted to Hospital "Sick" and transferred to Corps Main Dressing Station. | A17. |
| D.2.d.4.4. (Sheet 19) | 26th | | Capt L.T. Poole., R.A.M.C., and 20 Other Ranks of this Unit proceeded to report to No:2 Field Ambulance. at the Advanced Dressing Station. LAITERIE ROYALE (Map Reference R. 23 d. 9.0. Sheet 11) for the purpose of erecting bomb proof shelters for the accomodation of wounded East of the YSER Canal. Casualties admitted to Unit....... Sick 4. Capt S. D. Fairweather, R.A.M.C. proceeded to report to O.Commanding 25th Brigade R.F.A. R.F.A. for temporary medical duty vice Capt J. MacRae., R.A.M.C. granted leave to the U.K. No:T/1. 4270 Sgt E.J.Watts., A.S.C."HT" rejoins Unit from No:15 Casualty Clearing Station. No:7467 Pte G.Brown., R.A.M.C. is struck off the strength of this Unit from 5th May 1917 having been declared an absentee from that date by a Court of Enquiry assembled on 26th June 1917 in accordance with para. 673 King's Regulations. | A17. |
| | 27th | | No:M.36401 Sgt A.C.Powell., A.S.C. "MT" proceeded to No:1 Divisional Supply Col. for duty. No:M.S. 816 Sgt C.Cameron., A.S.C. "MT" joined this Unit for duty from No:1 Div.Supply Col. Casualties admitted to Unit....... Sick 2. No:T.35555 Driver G. Guest., A.S.C. "HT"attached; evacuated to "L of C" from XVth Corps Main Dressing Station and is accordingly taken off our strength. | A17. |

Army Form C. 2118.

# WAR DIARY
## or
## INTELLIGENCE SUMMARY.
*(Erase heading not required.)*

| Place | Date June 1917. | Hour | Summary of Events and Information | Remarks and references to Appendices |
|---|---|---|---|---|
| D.2.d.4.4. (Sheet 19) | 28th | | Casualties admitted to Unit...... Sick 3. No:7467 Private G. Brown., R.A.M.C. joined this Unit from the United Kingdom off leave and is accordingly taken on our strength. | 977. |
| | 29th | | Casualties admitted to Unit...... N I L. | 977. |
| | 30th | | Casualties admitted to Unit...... Sick 2. No:T/1.4270 Sergeant E.J.Watts., A.S.C. "HT" attached. admitted to Hospital "sick" and transferred to XVth Corps Main Dressing Station. | 977. |

F. Irvine Fortescue

Lieut Col R.A.M.C.
Commanding 141st Field Ambulance.

CONFIDENTIAL.

WAR DIARY

of

141st FIELD AMBULANCE.

From 1st JULY 1917 to 31st JULY 1917.

(Volume No: 13).

Army Form C. 2118.

# WAR DIARY
## or
## INTELLIGENCE SUMMARY.

(Erase heading not required.)

Instructions regarding War Diaries and Intelligence Summaries are contained in F. S. Regs., Part II. and the Staff Manual respectively. Title pages will be prepared in manuscript.

| Place | Date JULY 1917. | Hour | Summary of Events and Information | Remarks and references to Appendices |
|---|---|---|---|---|
| D.2.d.4.4. Sheet 19. | 1st | | Casualties admitted to Unit...... Sick Nil No:35791 Sgt A.Davies., R.A.M.C. proceeded from this Unit to report to No:2 Field Ambulance for temporary duty with the party of Miners from this Unit. | J/1/7. J/2/. |
| | 2nd | | Casualties admitted to Unit...... Sick 1. | J/3. |
| | 3rd | | Casualties admitted to Unit...... Sick 3. | J/4. |
| | 4th | | Casualties admitted to Unit...... Sick 4. Capt S.D.Fairweather., R.A.M.C. rejoined Unit from temporary duty with 25th Brigade R.F.A. No:57944 Staff Sergeant W.Marley., R.A.M.C. joined this Unit for duty from the Cyclists Base Depot. No:T/2. 11098 Driver C.Lovelock., A.S.C. "HT" attached, admitted to Hospital "Sick" and transferred to XVth Corps Main Dressing Station. | J/4. |
| | 5th | | Casualties admitted to Unit...... Sick 1. | J/7. |
| | 6th | | Casualties admitted to Unit...... Sick 3. Capt L.T.Poole., R.A.M.C. and party of 21 Other Ranks R.A.M.C. (Miners) rejoined this Unit from No:2 Field Ambulance. Revd J. Edwards., C.F. (United Board) proceeded from this Unit to report to 3rd Infantry Brigade Head Qrs for duty. | J/7. J/7. |
| | 7th | | Casualties admitted to Unit...... Sick 2 | J/7. |
| | 8th | | Casualties admitted to unit...... Sick Nil No:T/1.4270 Sgt E.J.Watts., A.S.C. "HT" attached. rejoined Unit from XVth Corps M.D.Station | J/7. |
| | 9th | | Casualties admitted to unit...... Sick 1. | J/7. |
| | 10th | | Casualties admitted to Unit...... Sick 1. | J/7. |

Army Form C. 2118.

# WAR DIARY
## or
## INTELLIGENCE SUMMARY.
*(Erase heading not required.)*

Instructions regarding War Diaries and Intelligence Summaries are contained in F.S. Regs., Part II. and the Staff Manual respectively. Title pages will be prepared in manuscript.

| Place | Date | Hour | Summary of Events and Information | Remarks and references to Appendices |
|---|---|---|---|---|
| D.2.d.4.4. (Sheet 19). | JULY 1917. | | | |
| | 11th | | Casualties admitted to Unit...... 5.(Sick) Casualties admitted on transfer to Corps Rest Station..... 148.(Sick) ...... 40 (Wounded) | 31/7 |
| | 12th | | Casualties admitted to Unit....... Sick 2. Casualties admitted on transfer to Corps Rest Station.... Sick 78. Wounded 17. Capt S.D.Fairweather & Capt Jas MacRae., R.A.M.C. proceeded from Unit to report at XVth Corps Main Dressing Station for temporary duty. No:T/2 10942 Cpl S. Salter., A.S.C. "HT" attached admitted to Hospital "Sick" and evacuated to "L of C". | 31/7 |
| | 13th | | Casualties admitted to Unit........ Sick 3 Casualties admitted on transfers to Corps Rest Station..... Sick.... 50 Wounded..... 3 Capt S.D.Fairweather. & Capt Jas MacRae., R.A.M.C. rejoined unit from XVth Corps Main Dressing Station | 31/7 |
| | 14th | | Casualties admitted to Unit....... Sick...... 2 Casualties admitted on transfers to Corps Rest Station..... Sick.... 125 Wounded.... 3 | 31/7 |
| | 15th | | Casualties admitted to Unit....... Sick..... Nil Casualties admitted on transfer to Corps Rest Station..... Sick 62 Wounded. 8 Lieut & Qr Mr G. Sellex., R.A.M.C. proceeds from Unit to report to No:1 Field Ambulance for temporary duty. Capt C. C. Forsyth., R.A.M.C. and No:56118 Sgt R.Blandford., R.A.M.C. proceed to report to No:2 Field Ambulance for temporary duty. | 31/7 |

Army Form C. 2118.

# WAR DIARY
## or
## INTELLIGENCE SUMMARY.
*(Erase heading not required.)*

Instructions regarding War Diaries and Intelligence Summaries are contained in F. S. Regs., Part II. and the Staff Manual respectively. Title pages will be prepared in manuscript.

| Place | Date July 1917. | Hour | Summary of Events and Information | Remarks and references to Appendices |
|---|---|---|---|---|
| D.2.d.4.4. Sheet 19. | 16th | | Casualties admitted to Unit...... Sick 1. Casualties admitted to Corps Rest Station on transfer..... Sick 84 Wounded.. 25 | A/2 |
| | 17th | | Captain Jas Byrne., R.A.M.C. (T.C) joined this Unit for duty. Casualties admitted to Unit...... Sick 2 Casualties admitted to Corps Rest Station on transfer..... Sick 74 Wounded.. 11 | A/2 |
| | 18th | | Casualties admitted to Unit...... Sick 10 Casualties admitted to Corps Rest Station on transfer..... Sick 51 Wounded.. 1 No:22541 Private G. P. Pickles., R.A.M.C. admitted to Hospital "Sick" and evacuated to "L of C". The Revd J.A.G.Morton., C.F. accompanied by his servant No:202541 Pte C.M.Kaye., 1/4 East Lancs Field Ambulance joined this Unit for duty at the Corps Rest Station. | A/7 |
| | 19th | | Casualties admitted to Unit...... Sick 1 Casualties admitted to Corps Rest Station on transfer..... Sick 45 Wounded.. 7 17 Other Ranks R.A.M.C. of the 1/2nd West Riding Field Ambulance joined this Unit for temporary duty at the Corps Rest Station. | A/7 |
| | 20th | | Casualties admitted to Unit...... Sick 1 Casualties admitted to Corps Rest Station on transfer..... Sick 42 Wounded.. 28 | A/7 |
| | 21st | | Casualties admitted to Unit...... Sick 1 Casualties admitted on transfer to Corps Rest Station..... Sick 33 Wounded.. 16 No:T/1. 14308 Driver H. Grote., A.S.C. "HT" admitted to Hospital "Sick" and evacuated to "L of C" | A/7 |

Army Form C. 2118.

# WAR DIARY
## or
## INTELLIGENCE SUMMARY.
(Erase heading not required.)

| Place | Date | Hour | Summary of Events and Information | Remarks and references to Appendices |
|---|---|---|---|---|
| D.2.d.4.4. Sheet 19. | JULY 1917. 22nd. | | Casualties admitted to Unit...... Sick 3 Casualties admitted on transfer to Corps Rest Station.... Sick.. 35 Wounded.. 676 Lieut E.O.Marks., R.A.M.C. No:61111 Lance Cpl J.C.Madden., R.A.M.C. and No:77223 Private S.Gransden., R.A.M.C., proceeded from this Unit to report to the Administrative Commandant., Petite Synthe. for temporary medical duty in the Back Area, Fourth Army. | |
| | 23rd | | Casualties admitted to Unit...... Sick 1. Casualties admitted on transfer to Corps Rest Station.... Sick 21 Wounded. 308 | |
| | 24th. | | Casualties admitted to Unit...... Sick Nil. Casualties admitted on transfer to Corps Rest Station.... Sick 31 Wounded. 77 | |
| | 25th | | Casualties admitted to Unit...... Sick Nil. " on transfer to Corps Rest Station NIL. Capt Jas MacRae., R.A.M.C., one Cyclist and 10 Other Ranks (Pioneers) proceeded from Unit to report to the Officer Commanding No:1 Field Ambulance for the purpose of pitching Camp and erecting Nissen Hut for the Unit in Le Clipon Camp. Hand over XVth Corps Rest Station together with all remaining patients at 12 noon to the 2/3rd East Lancashire Field Ambulance. Before handing over, returned to duty or transferred to No:1 Field Ambualnce as many patients of the 1st Division as possible, and arranged with the O.Commanding 2/3rd East Lancashire Field Ambulance that no cases of the 1st Division left remaining are otherwise disposed of than to duty or to No:1 Field Ambulance. | |
| | 26th | | Units leaves D.2.d.4.4. at 8 a.m. and marches to Le Clipon Camp via St Pol and Mardick. Arriving 2-30 p.m. Two water carts and horses taken into Camp, the remainder of the transport bivouac with the 3rd Brigade Transport near Loon Plage. Transport Officer remains outside the Camp in charge. | |

Army Form C. 2118.

# WAR DIARY
## or
## INTELLIGENCE SUMMARY.
(Erase heading not required.)

Instructions regarding War Diaries and Intelligence Summaries are contained in F.S. Regs., Part II. and the Staff Manual respectively. Title pages will be prepared in manuscript.

| Place | Date | Hour | Summary of Events and Information | Remarks and references to Appendices |
|---|---|---|---|---|
| Le Clipon Camp. | JULY 1917. 27th | | Casualties admitted to Unit.... N I L. Medical Officer of this Unit detailed for temporary medical charge of the 1st R.Highlanders. No:55415 Private J. Millard., R.A.M.C. proceeds from this Unit to report to the Officer Commanding., 1st Btn L.N.Lancs for Water duties. No:93373 Private Renel L.V., R.A.M.C. admitted to Hospital of No:1 Field Ambulance "Sick" | 31/7 |
| | 28th | | Casualties admitted to Unit.... N I L. | 31/7 |
| | 29th | | Casualties admitted to Unit.... N I L. Capt J. MacRae., R.A.M.C. and Capt S.D.Fairweather., R.A.M.C. proceeded from Unit to report to D.D.M.S., XVth Corps for temporary medical duty. No:26900 Private J.F. Gatehouse., R.A.M.C. attached to No:1 Field Ambulance for temporary duty as Dental Mechanic. | 31/7 |
| | 30th | | Casualties admitted to Unit.... N I L. The clothing of personnel of Unit and the whole equipment, Medical, Surgical and Ordnance of Unit inspected and checked by Lieut & Qr G. Sellex, R.A.M.C. (No:2 Field Ambulance). Revd J. W. S. Irvine., C.F. joined this Unit for duty. No:88022 Pte L. F. Bennett., R.A.M.C. of this Unit ceased to be attached to the Office of the A.D.M.S., 1st Division on the 29th July 1917 and has now been taken on the authorised establishment of that Office. | 31/7 |
| | 31st | | Casualties admitted to Unit.... N I L. No:9373 Pte L.V.Renel., R.A.M.C. discharged from Hospital of No:1 Field Ambulance and rejoined this Unit. 4 Other Ranks A.S.C. "HT" join this Unit for duty from 1st Divisional Train. No:58795 Pte R.Marshall., R.A.M.C. and No:44736 Pte T.Smithson. R.A.M.C., admitted to Hospital of No:1 Field Ambulance "Sick". | 31/7 |

Maurice Fortelure
Lieut Col R.A.M.C.
Commanding 141st Field Ambulance.

C O N F I D E N T I A L.

WAR    DIARY

of

141st FIELD AMBULANCE.

From    1st August 1917 .          To    31st August 1917.

(Volume. No: 14)

Army Form C. 2118.

# WAR DIARY
## or
## INTELLIGENCE SUMMARY.
(Erase heading not required.)

| Place | Date 1917 | Hour | Summary of Events and Information | Remarks and references to Appendices |
|---|---|---|---|---|
| Le Clipon Camp. | August 1st | | Casualties admitted to Unit..... Nil.<br>No:90087 Private S.H.E.Haggis., R.A.M.C. admitted to Hospital of No:1 Field Ambulance "Sick"<br>Capt S. D. Fairweather., R.A.M.C. and Captain Jas MacRae., R.A.M.C. rejoined Unit from temporary duty with the D.D.M.S., XVth Corps. | A/1. |
| | 2nd | | Casualties admitted to Unit..... Nil.<br>No:74427 Private G. Brown., R.A.M.C. tried by Field General Court Martial at Head Qrs of 1st Royal Righrs on the following charge:- "When on Active Service, absenting himself without leave, in that he in the Field absented himself after leave granted to the United Kingdom from Tatoo Roll Call, 25/4/1917 till 7-45 p.m. on the 28/6/17"..... Found "Guilty" and awarded 56 days F.P. No:1.<br>Lieut Col A.Irvine-Fortescue., R.A.M.C. proceeds to the United Kingdom on leave, and the command of the Field Ambulance during his absence devolves on Captain L.T.Poole., R.A.M.C. | A/1. |
| | 3rd. | | Casualties admitted to Unit..... Nil.<br>No:12048 Private J. W. Thompson., R.A.M.C. admitted to Hospital of No:1 Field Ambce "Sick" | A/1. |
| | 4th | | Casualties admitted to Unit..... Nil.<br>No:2424 Private J. Hayes., R.A.M.C. admitted to Hospital of No:1 Field Ambulance "Sick"<br>No:44736 Private T. M. Smithson., R.A.M.C. discharged to duty from Hospital of No:1 Fd Ambulance and rejoined Unit. | A/1. |
| | 5th | | Casualties admitted to Unit..... Nil. | A/1. |
| | 6th | | Casualties admitted to Unit..... Nil.<br>No:72397 Private J. J. Green., R.A.M.C. was admitted to Hospital of No:1 Field Ambulance "Sick" | A/1. |
| | 7th | | Casualties admitted to Unit..... Nil. | A/1. |
| | 8th | | Casualties admitted to Unit..... Nil.<br>No:72397 Pte J.J.Green., R.A.M.C. discharged to duty from Hospital of No:1 Fd Ambce and rejoined Unit. | A/1. |

Army Form C. 2118.

# WAR DIARY
## or
## INTELLIGENCE SUMMARY.
*(Erase heading not required.)*

Instructions regarding War Diaries and Intelligence Summaries are contained in F. S. Regs., Part II. and the Staff Manual respectively. Title pages will be prepared in manuscript.

| Place | Date August 1917. | Summary of Events and Information | Remarks and references to Appendices |
|---|---|---|---|
| Le Clipon Camp. | 9th | Casualties admitted to Unit:- Nil. No:12048 Private J.W. Thompson., R.A.M.C. discharged to duty from Hospital of No:1 Field Ambulance and rejoined Unit. Captain W.T. Munro., R.A.M.C. (T.C.) posted to this Unit for duty, and remains with the 1st Divisional Train for temporary duty. | N/T. |
| | 10th | Casualties admitted to Unit:- Nil. No:2802 Cpl A.C.Ball., R.A.M.C. was transferred to No:1 Field Ambulance for duty. No:57787 Private J. Allan., R.A.M.C. was admitted to Hospital of No:1 Field Ambulance "Sick" | N/T. |
| | 11th | Casualties admitted to Unit:- Nil. No:75685 Cpl T.D. Gaunt., R.A.M.C. joined this Unit for duty from No:1 Fd Ambce vice Cpl A.C.Ball., R.A.M.C. No:T/4. 036205 Driver J.H.Gaskins., A.S.C. "HT" attached was admitted to Hospital of No:1 Field Ambulance "sick on this day. | N/T. |
| | 12th | Casualties admitted to Unit:- Nil. Captain F.E.L.Phillips., R.A.M.C.(T.C.) joined this Unit for duty. No:13828 Cpl J. Reading., R.A.M.C. joined this Unit for duty | N/T. |
| | 13th | Casualties admitted to Unit:- Nil. 16 Other Ranks R.A.M.C. joined the unit for duty. Capt W.T.Munro., R.A.M.C. was admitted to Hospital of No: 1 Field Ambulance and evacuated to "L of C" Sick. | N/T. |
| | 14th | Casualties admitted to Unit:- Nil. No:T/2.13172 Sgt C.Baldwin., A.S.C. "HT" attached was admitted to Hospital of No:1 Fd Ambce "Sick" Nos 2424 Pte J.Hayes., R.A.M.C. and 57787 Pte J.Allen., R.A.M.C. rejoined Unit from No:1 Field Ambulance having been discharged from Hospital Lt Col A.Irvine-Fortescue., R.A.M.C. rejoins Unit off leave and resumes command. No:40838 Cpl F.W.ralin., R.A.M.C. joined the Unit for duty. | N/T. |

Army Form C. 2118.

# WAR DIARY
## or
## INTELLIGENCE SUMMARY.
(Erase heading not required.)

Instructions regarding War Diaries and Intelligence Summaries are contained in F.S. Regs., Part II. and the Staff Manual respectively. Title pages will be prepared in manuscript.

| Place | Date August 1917 | Hour | Summary of Events and Information | Remarks and references to Appendices |
|---|---|---|---|---|
| Le Clipon Camp. | 15th | | Casualties admitted to Unit..... Nil. Captain S.D.Fairweather., R.A.M.C. (T.C.) proceeded to report to the A.D.M.S. 32nd Division for permanent duty | A/1.7. |
| | 16th | | Casualties admitted to Unit..... Nil. No:44738 Private T. M. Smithson., R.A.M.C. proceeded to report to the 3rd Bgde Hd qrs for temporary duty as Cyclist Runner. No:93329 Pte J. Bowman., R.A.M.C. was admitted to hospital of No:1 Fd Ambce "Sick" Horsed Transport moved from Loon Plage to Mardick. | A/1.7. |
| | 17th | | Casualties admitted to Unit..... Nil. Draw one Heavy Draught Horse to replace casualty. Nos 61111 L.Cpl J.C.Madden and 77223 Pte S.A.Gransden rejoin Unit for duty from Administrative Commandant., Petite Synthe. | A/1.7. |
| | 18th | | Casualties admitted to Unit..... Nil. No:56232 Pte P.G.Poole., R.A.M.C. admitted to Hospital of No:1 Field Ambulance "Sick" Captain L.T.Poole., R.A.M.C. appointed D.A.D.M.S., 1st Division. From this date inclusive 8 T.Unfits posted to this Unit for temporary duty at the Transport Lines. | A/1.7. |
| | 19th | | Casualties admitted to Unit..... Nil. The sentence of Field General Court Martial of 56 days Field Punishment No:1 on No:74467 Private G.Brown., R.A.M.C. has been remitted by 28 days. (Authority Fourth Army letter C.M. 6590 dated 19/8/17") | A/1.7. |
| | 20th | | Casualties admitted to Unit..... Nil. | A/1.7. |
| | 21st | | Casualties admitted to Unit..... Nil. No:58795 Private R.Marshall., R.A.M.C. discharged from Hospital of No:1 Fd Ambce and rejoined Unit. | A/1.7. |

Army Form C. 2118.

# WAR DIARY
## or
## INTELLIGENCE SUMMARY.

*(Erase heading not required.)*

Instructions regarding War Diaries and Intelligence Summaries are contained in F.S. Regs., Part II. and the Staff Manual respectively. Title pages will be prepared in manuscript.

| Place | Date | Hour | Summary of Events and Information | Remarks and references to Appendices |
|---|---|---|---|---|
| Le Clipon Camp. | August 1917. | | | |
| | 21st | | No:50253 Private W.Farmer., 2nd Welsh (Temporary Unfit) attached to this Unit was admitted to Hospital "Sick" and evacuated to "L of C" No:104661 Private W. Hacking., R.A.M.C. admitted to Hospital of No:1 Field Ambulance "Sick" | A.17. |
| | 22nd | | Casualties admitted to Unit..... Nil. No:29342 Private S. Smith., R.A.M.C. was admitted to Hospital of No:1 Field Ambulance "Sick" No:93329 Private J. Bowman., R.A.M.C. was discharged from the Hospital of No:1 Field Ambulance and rejoined this Unit. 8 Other Ranks R.A.M.C. of this Unit proceed to No:1 Field Ambulance for temporary duty. | A.17. |
| | 23rd | | Casualties admitted to Unit..... Nil. No:10304 L. Cpl Macey., (Temporary Unfit) 2nd Welsh Regt. attached to this Unit for duty at the Transport Lines, was returned to his own Battalion for duty. | A.17. |
| | 24th | | Casualties admitted to Unit..... Nil. No:104661 Pte W. Hacking., R.A.M.C. and No:T/4.036205 Driver J. H. Gaskins., A.S.C. "HT" attached, evacuated from No:1 Field Ambulance to "L of C" "Sick". | A.17. |
| | 25th | | Casualties admitted to Unit..... Nil. Unit attends the Divisional Ceremonial Parade for presentation of Medal Ribbons by the Army Commander. The following N.C.Os and man of this Unit were recipients of Medal Ribbons No:57962 Sergeant E.K. Edwards., R.A.M.C............... "Military Medal". No:58752 Corporal J. McTurk., R.A.M.C............... "Bar to the Military Medal". No:M/2.048544. Private R.G. Masters., A.S.C. "HT" attached....... "Croix de Guerre." Number 7799 Private R.Collier., R.A.M.C., rejoins this Unit for duty from the Office of the D. D. M. S., XVth Corps. | A.17. |

Army Form C. 2118.

# WAR DIARY
## or
## INTELLIGENCE SUMMARY.
*(Erase heading not required.)*

Instructions regarding War Diaries and Intelligence Summaries are contained in F.S. Regs., Part II. and the Staff Manual respectively. Title pages will be prepared in manuscript.

| Place | Date August 1917. | Hour | Summary of Events and Information | Remarks and references to Appendices |
|---|---|---|---|---|
| Le Chipon Camp. | 26th | | Casualties admitted to Unit...... NIL. Consequent upon the reduction of Establishment of Riding Horses in Field Ambulances, from 14 to 8, the 8 surplus Riders in this Unit are transferred as follows:-<br>1 to 1st Brigade Hd. Qrs.,    2 to No:1 M.Gun Coy.,<br>1 to 2nd K.R.Rifles.,         1 to No:2 M.Gun Coy.,<br>2 to 2nd R.Munster Fus.,      1 to Belgian Mission. | A/17/ |
| | 27th | | Casualties admitted to unit..... NIL.<br>Number T/2.249551 Driver A. Berry., A.S.C. "HT" joined this Unit for duty from the 1st Divisional Train. | A/17 |
| | 28th | | Casualties admitted to Unit...... NIL.<br>Number 56130 Private " . Cathie., R.A.M.C. admitted to Hospital of No:7 Field Ambulance "Sick" | A/17. |
| | 29th | | Casualties admitted to Unit...... NIL.<br>No:69342 Pte S. Smith., R.A.M.C. was discharged to duty from Hospital of No:1 Field Ambulance, and is attached to that Unit for temporary duty.<br>Captain F.E.L.Phillips., R.A.M.C. proceeds to the 39th Brigade R.F.A. for temporary duty vice Captain J.Tate., R.A.M.C. who joins this Unit for temporary duty. | A/17 |
| | 30th | | Casualties admitted to Unit...... NIL. | A/17 |
| | 31st | | Casualties admitted to Unit...... NIL.<br>During the month a scheme of training as ordered by the A.D.M.S., 1st Division has been carried out, special attention being paid to the following points.<br>1. Physical Training.<br>2. Carrying of Loads.    Men were exercised carrying gradually increased weight.<br>3. Negotiating Obstacles.<br>4. Loading and Off-Loading. Motor Ambulance with special load. | A/17. |

Army Form C. 2118.

# WAR DIARY
## or
## INTELLIGENCE SUMMARY.

(Erase heading not required.)

Instructions regarding War Diaries and Intelligence Summaries are contained in F. S. Regs., Part II. and the Staff Manual respectively. Title pages will be prepared in manuscript.

| Place | Date | Hour | Summary of Events and Information | Remarks and references to Appendices |
|---|---|---|---|---|
| Le Clipon Camp. | August 1917. | | 5. Packing Panniers.<br>6. Swimming, Football and All Games.<br>7. Semaphore Signalling.<br>8. Night operations. | |

*Fiennes Fulleylove*
Lieut Col R.A.M.C.
Commanding 141st Field Ambulance.

Confidential.

War Diary

of

141 Field Ambulance.

From 1st September 1917 To 30th September 1917

(Volume No. 15)

Army Form C. 2118.

# WAR DIARY
## or
## INTELLIGENCE SUMMARY.
*(Erase heading not required.)*

| Place | Date Sept 1917 | Hour | Summary of Events and Information | Remarks and references to Appendices |
|---|---|---|---|---|
| Le Clipon Camp. | 1st | | Casualties admitted to Unit......... NIL. | Nil. |
| | 2nd | | Casualties admitted to Unit......... NIL. | Nil. |
| | 3rd | | Casualties admitted to Unit......... NIL. Number 7467 Private G. Brown., R.A.M.C. rejoined the Unit from A.P.M., 1st Division. | Nil. |
| | 4th | | Casualties admitted to Unit......... NIL. Temporary Unfits attached to this Unit inspected by the A.D.M.S., 1st Division. | Nil. |
| | 5th | | Casualties admitted to Unit......... NIL. Commanding Officer attends Conference of Unit Commanders at Divisional Head Qrs. | Nil. |
| | 6th | | Casualties admitted to Unit......... NIL. No:56730 Pte W. Cathie., R.A.M.C. was discharged from Hospital of No:1 Field Ambulance, and remained with that Unit for temporary duty. | Nil. |
| | 7th | | Casualties admitted to Unit......... NIL. | Nil. |
| | 8th | | Casualties admitted to Unit......... NIL. No:90139 Pte J. Gunn., R.A.M.C. rejoined Unit from No:1 Field Ambulance. | Nil. |
| | 9th | | Casualties admitted to Unit......... NIL. | Nil. |
| | 10th | | Casualties admitted to Unit......... NIL. Commanding Officer attends Conference of Unit Commanders in 3rd Bgde at Bgde Hd Qrs. | Nil. |
| | 11th | | Casualties admitted to Unit......... NIL. Commanding Officer attends Conference of Unit Commanders in 3rd Bgde at Bgde Hd Qrs. | Nil. |

Army Form C. 2118.

# WAR DIARY
## or
## INTELLIGENCE SUMMARY.
*(Erase heading not required.)*

Instructions regarding War Diaries and Intelligence
Summaries are contained in F. S. Regs., Part II.
and the Staff Manual respectively. Title pages
will be prepared in manuscript.

| Place | Date | Hour | Summary of Events and Information | Remarks and references to Appendices |
|---|---|---|---|---|
| Le Clipon Camp. | September 1917. | | | |
| | 12th | | Casualties admitted to Unit....... NIL. Unit participates in the 3rd Brigade Manoeuvres. | N.T. |
| | 13th | | Casualties admitted to Unit....... NIL. Commanding Officer attends Conference of Unit Commanders in 3rd Brigade. No:T/2.13172. Sergeant O.J.Baldwin., A.S.C. "HT" attached, discharged from Hospital of No:1 Field Ambulance and rejoined Unit. | N.T. |
| | 14th | | Casualties admitted to Unit....... NIL. Unit participates in the 3rd Brigade Manoeuvres. Commanding Officer attends the Conference of 3rd Brigade Unit Commanders. No:T/2. 19962 Corporal S. Salter., A.S.C. "HT" attached, rejoined this Unit for duty from the Base Horse Transport Depot. | N.T. |
| | 15th | | Casualties admitted to Unit....... NIL. No:T/1.19866 Farrier Staff Sergeant J.A.Grant., A.S.C. "HT" attached proceeded to No:10 Veterinary Hospital, NEUFCHATEL. to attend the Veterinary Course. | N.T. |
| | 16th | | Casualties admitted to Unit....... NIL. | N.T. |
| | 17th | | Casualties admitted to Unit....... NIL. No:7473 Private C. Rudd., R.A.M.C. Joined this Unit for duty from the Camp Comm. in dent 1st Division. | N.T. |
| | 18th | | Casualties admitted to Unit....... NIL. No:68032 Private L.F.Bennett., R.A.M.C. taken off the strength of this Unit, having been taken on the strength of 1st Division Head Qrs. Unit participates in the 3rd Brigade Manoeuvres. Commanding Officer attends the Conference of 3rd Brigade Unit Commanders. | N.T. |
| | 19th | | Casualties admitted to Unit....... NIL. | N.T. |
| | 20th | | Casualties admitted to Unit....... NIL. | N.T. |

Army Form C. 2118.

# WAR DIARY
## or
## INTELLIGENCE SUMMARY.
*(Erase heading not required.)*

Instructions regarding War Diaries and Intelligence Summaries are contained in F.S. Regs., Part II. and the Staff Manual respectively. Title pages will be prepared in manuscript.

| Place | Date September 1917. | Hour | Summary of Events and Information | Remarks and references to Appendices |
|---|---|---|---|---|
| Le Clipon Camp. | 20th | | No:55791 Cpl (act Sergeant) Davies A.F., R.A.M.C. reverted to his permanent rank of Corporal. | N.7. |
| | 21st | | Casualties admitted to Unit..... NIL. No:47810 Sergeant H.G.Scorer., R.A.M.C. proceeded to No:1 Field Ambce for temporary duty. Captain W.L. Webster., R.A.M.C. (Res) was posted to and taken on the strength of this Unit on this date. | N.7. |
| | 22nd | | Casualties admitted to Unit..... NIL. No:44736 Private T.M.Smithson., R.A.M.C. proceeded to 3rd Brigade Signals for duty vice No:56499 Private E.A.Hicks., R.A.M.C. who rejoined this Unit for duty. | N.7. |
| | 23rd | | Casualties admitted to Unit..... NIL. | N.7. |
| | 24th | | Casualties admitted to Unit..... NIL. No:52740 Cpl T.F.Webb., R.A.M.C. was tried by Field General Court Martials on the following charge:- "When on active service, using insubordinate language to his superior Officer". Found "Guilty". Sentence "Reduced to the Ranks and 90 days F.P. No:1" Captain J.Tate., R.A.M.C. proceeded to 90th Brigade R.F.A. for duty vice Capt.F.E.L. Phillips., R.A.M.C. who rejoined this Unit for duty. | N.7. |
| | 25th | | Casualties admitted to Unit..... NIL. | N.7. |
| | 26th | | Casualties admitted to Unit..... NIL. Lieut-Col A.Irvine-Fortescue., R.A.M.C. proceeded on 5 days leave in France granted from the 24th instant, and the command of the Ambulance during his absence devolves on Captain C.L. Chalk., R.A.M.C. | N.7. |
| | 27th | | Casualties admitted to Unit..... NIL. | N.7. |

Army Form C. 2118.

# WAR DIARY
## or
## INTELLIGENCE SUMMARY.
(Erase heading not required.)

Instructions regarding War Diaries and Intelligence Summaries are contained in F. S. Regs., Part II. and the Staff Manual respectively. Title pages will be prepared in manuscript.

| Place | Date | Hour | Summary of Events and Information | Remarks and references to Appendices |
|---|---|---|---|---|
| LE CIDON CAMP | September 1917 28th | | Evacuation admitted to Unit...... Nil. Unit participated in 3rd Brigade Manoeuvres. Capt. J. Mac Rae, R.A.M.C. proceeds to the 16th Welsh Regiment for temporary medical charge. No. 70866 Farrier S/Sgt. J.A. CROFT, A.S.C. "M.T." rejoined the Unit from a course at No. 10 Veterinary Hospital. | A/5 |
| | 29th | | Evacuation admitted to Unit...... Nil. Cpl. W.R. WEBSTER, R.A.M.C. reported to this Unit to take over the duties & assume command of the Unit during the absence on leave of Sgt. for A. Laurence Laurence, R.A.M.C. | A/7 |
| | 30th | | Evacuation admitted to Unit...... Nil. No. 7380 Driver D. PAUL, A.S.C. "M.T." transferred to 1st Divisional Train for duty. | A/7 |

A. Munn Fortescue
Lt.C. R.A.M.C.
O.C. 141st Field Ambulance.

**CONFIDENTIAL.**

WAR DIARY

of

141st Field Ambulance.

From  1st October 1917  TO  31st October 1917.

****************

(Volume No: 16)

Army Form C. 2118.

# WAR DIARY
## or
## INTELLIGENCE SUMMARY.

*(Erase heading not required.)*

Instructions regarding War Diaries and Intelligence Summaries are contained in F. S. Regs., Part II. and the Staff Manual respectively. Title pages will be prepared in manuscript.

| Place | Date | Hour | Summary of Events and Information | Remarks and references to Appendices |
|---|---|---|---|---|
| Le Clipon Camp. | October 1917 | | | |
| | 1st | | Casualties admitted to Unit...... NIL. Lieut-Col A.Irvine-Fortescue., R.A.M.C. rejoins the Unit off leave and assumes command. Capt W. L. Webster., R.A.M.C. proceeded to report to the Office of the D.M.S., Forth Army for temporary duty. | A/7 |
| | 2nd. | | Casualties admitted to Unit...... NIL. | A/7 |
| | 3rd | | Casualties admitted to Unit...... NIL. | A/7 |
| | 4th | | Casualties admitted to Unit...... NIL. Captain F. E. L. Phillips., R.A.M.C. proceeded from Unit to assume temporary medical charge of the 50th Brigade R.F.A. Captain P. R. Browning., R.A.M.C. in addition to his duties with 1st Divisional Train takes over medical charge of the 3rd Brigade Transport lines and lives in the Wagon lines of this Unit. No:70711 Private J. Rance., R.A.M.C. proceeded to report to the Office of the A.D.M.S., 1st Division for temporary duty. | A/7 |
| | 5th | | Casualties admitted to Unit...... NIL. No:70711 Pte T.F.Webb., R.A.M.C. has been remitted of the sentence of 90 days F.P. No:1 in the case of No:39740 Pte T.F.Webb., R.A.M.C. (Authority Fourth Army G.W. 2227 dated 5/10/17.) | A/7 |
| | 6th | | Casualties admitted to Unit...... NIL. | A/7 |
| | 7th | | Casualties admitted to Unit...... NIL. Lieut & Qr Mr C. Greenhough., R.A.M.C. joined the Unit for duty. | A/7 |
| | 8th | | Casualties admitted to Unit...... NIL No:79462 Private W.H.Bennett., R.A.M.C. rejoined the Unit from No:1 Field Ambulance for duty. | A/7 |
| | 9th | | Casualties admitted to Unit...... NIL. | A/7 |

Army Form C. 2118.

# WAR DIARY
## or
## INTELLIGENCE SUMMARY.
(Erase heading not required.)

| Place | Date October 1917. | Hour | Summary of Events and Information | Remarks and references to Appendices |
|---|---|---|---|---|
| Le Clipon Camp. | 10th | | Casualties admitted to Unit...... NIL. | NIL |
| | 11th | | Casualties admitted to Unit...... NIL. | NIL |
| | 12th | | Casualties admitted to Unit...... NIL. The A.D.M.S., 1st Division inspects the Ambulance Personnel and Transport in full marching order at 11-0 a.m. on the main LOON PLAGE-DUNKERQUE Road half a mile West of GRANDE SYNTHE. Captain C.L.Chalk., R.A.M.C. of this Unit takes over temporary Medical Charge of the 25th Brigade R.F.A. from 12th October 1917, until Captain P.D.Annesley returns from leave. Captain James Byrne R.A.M.C. of this Unit is posted to and assumes Medical Charge of the 39th Brigade R.F.A., and Captain F.E.L.Phillips., R.A.M.C., rejoins the Transport Lines of this Unit for duty. No:101895 Private P. Fletcher., R.A.M.C. of this Unit admitted to Hospital of No:7 Field Ambulance "Sick" No:54232 Private P. G. Poole., R.A.M.C. discharged from Hospital of No:7 Field Ambulance and rejoined this Unit for duty. | NIL |
| | 13th | | Casualties admitted to Unit..... NIL. | NIL |
| | 14th | | Casualties admitted to Unit..... NIL. No:54113 Sergeant R. Blandford., R.A.M.C. was admitted to Hospital of No:7 Field Ambulance "Sick" No:83161 Private G. Thomson., R.A.M.C. proceeded to the Office of the A.D.M.S., 1st Division for temporary duty. No:T/2.10942 Corporal S. Salter., A.S.C."HT" proceeded to No:10 Veterinary Hospital, Neufchatel, to attend a Veterinary Course. | NIL |
| | 15th | | Casualties admitted to Unit..... NIL. | NIL |
| | 16th | | Casualties admitted to Unit..... NIL. | NIL |
| | 17th | | Casualties admitted to Unit..... NIL. | NIL |

Army Form C. 2118.

# WAR DIARY
## or
## INTELLIGENCE SUMMARY.

(Erase heading not required.)

Instructions regarding War Diaries and Intelligence Summaries are contained in F. S. Regs., Part II. and the Staff Manual respectively. Title pages will be prepared in manuscript.

| Place | Date October 1917. | Hour | Summary of Events and Information | Remarks and references to Appendices |
|---|---|---|---|---|
| Le Clipon Camp. | 18th | | 7 O.Ranks R.A.M.C. att. to No:1 Fd Ambce rejoined this Unit for duty. Casualties admitted to Unit...... NIL. No:5418 Sergeant R. Blandford., R.A.M.C. evacuated to "L of C" from No:1 Field Ambulance "Sick" Captain C. L. Chalk., R.A.M.C. rejoined the Unit for duty from the 25th Brigade R.F.A. Captain C. C. Forsyth, R.A.M.C. proceeded from No:1 Field Ambulance to report to 1st L.N. Lancs. for temporary medical duty. No:70711 Private J. Rence., R.A.M.C. rejoined the Unit for duty from the Office of the A.D.M.S. 1st Division. | X17 |
| do | 19th | | Casualties admitted to Unit...... NIL. No:4604 Private B. Dempster., R.A.M.C. rejoined the Unit from the office of the D.M.S., Fourth Army. No:26900 Private J. F. Gatehouse., R.A.M.C. rejoined the Unit from No:1 Field Ambulance for duty. | X17 |
| do | 20th | | Casualties admitted to Unit...... NIL. Field Ambulance leaves Le Clipon Camp and marches with the 3rd Brigade Group to the ERINGHEM Area. (B 24 c 5.8 SR-4 27) Unit billeted in Farm at Collect and treat sick of the Brigade Group, Divisional Engineers, and arrange for the medical attention of the Brigade Train Company. | X17 |
| RUBROUCK. | 21st | | Casualties admitted to Unit........ Nil. Field Ambulance leaves the ERINGHEM area and marches with the 3rd Brigade Group to the RUBROUCK Area. Unit billeted in RUBROUCK. Open up Hospital for the treating of "Sick". | X17 |
| do | 22nd | | Casualties admitted to Unit...... Sick 5. Open out and run the 3rd Brigade Baths situate at G.12 c. c. 9. (Sheet 27) and at G.18 d.9.3. (Sheet 27) | X17 |

Army Form C. 2118.

# WAR DIARY
## or
## INTELLIGENCE SUMMARY.

*(Erase heading not required.)*

| Place | Date Hour October 1917. | Summary of Events and Information | Remarks and references to Appendices |
|---|---|---|---|
| HUBROUCK | 23rd | Casualties admitted to Unit..... Sick 5. No:38740 Private T. F. Webb., R.A.M.C. rejoined the Unit for duty from the A. P. M., 1st Division. | A/7. |
| do | 24th | Casualties admitted to Unit..... Sick 5. No:24161 Private T. T. Hall., R.A.M.C. proceeded from this Unit to report to the Officer in charge Reinforcements., ROUEN. for release for Munitions. No:56130 Private W. Cathie., R.A.M.C. and No:M/2.222725 Private J. Breen., A.S.C."MT" of this Unit were admitted to Hospital and evacuated to "L of C" sick. | A/7. |
| do | 25th | Casualties passing through Unit.... NIL. Field Ambulance leaves the RUBROUCK area and marches with the 3rd Brigade Group to the HOUTERQUE Area. Units billeted in Barn and Tents at E.19. a. 0. 9. and are administered by the XVIIIth Corps. Collect and treat Sick of the Brigade Group, Divisional Engineers and arrange for the medical Inspection of the Brigade Train Company. Captain Jas MacRae., R.A.M.C. is posted to permanent medical charge of the 1/6th Welsh Regt vice Captain D.S.Cooper., R.A.M.C. who on return from leave will join this Unit for duty. 5 Austin Ambulance Cars proceeded on the 25th to report to the O.C., No:24 M.A.C. for temporary duty at the XVIII Corps Main Dressing Station. | A/7. |
| E.19.a.0.9. (Sheet 27) | 26th | Casualties passing through Unit..... Sick 2. 2 Ford Ambulances proceeded from this Unit to report to the Advanced Dressing Station, 63rd Division for temporary duty. | A/7. |
| | 27th | Casualties passing through Unit.... Sick 3. 1 Ford Ambulance reported to this Unit from No:2 Field Ambulance for temporary duty. | A/7. |
| | 28th | Casualties passing through Unit.... Sick 7 No:5/2.10962 Cpl S. Salter., A.S.C."HT" rejoined the Unit from the Veterinary Course at No:10 Veterinary Hospital. | A/7. |

Army Form C. 2118.

# WAR DIARY
## or
## INTELLIGENCE SUMMARY.

*(Erase heading not required.)*

Instructions regarding War Diaries and Intelligence Summaries are contained in F. S. Regs., Part II. and the Staff Manual respectively. Title pages will be prepared in manuscript.

| Place | Date | Hour | Summary of Events and Information | Remarks and references to Appendices |
|---|---|---|---|---|
| E.19.a.0.9. (Sheet 27) | October 1917. 28th (cont'd) | | The 2 Ford Ambulance Cars rejoined the Unit for duty from the Advanced Dressing Station., 63rd Division. | A.17. |
| | 29th | | Casualties passing through Unit...... Sick 11. Captain C. L. Chalk., R.A.M.C. proceeded to report to the O.Commanding., XVIIIth Corps Main Dressing Station for temporary duty. 5 Other Ranks proceeded from this Unit to report to the A.D.M.S., 58th Division for temporary duty. The Ford Ambulance attached to this Unit was returned to No:2 Field Ambulance for duty on the evening of the 28th. One Ford Ambulance Car of this Unit proceeded from this Unit to report to the Advanced Dressing Station., 63rd Division for temporary duty. | A.17. |
| | 30th | | Casualties passing through Unit..... Sick 21. Lieut D.W.Cameron., U.S.A., M.O M.O.R.C. and Lieut J.G.Kramer., U.S.A., M.O.R.C. were posted to this Unit for duty. The one Ford Ambulance Car rejoined this Unit from Advanced Dressing Station., 63rd Div. for duty. | A.17. |
| | 31st | | Casualties admitted to Unit....... Sick.8 No:31349 Private G. F. Russell., R.A.M.C. was admitted to Hospital of this Unit "Sick" and evacuated to "L of C". | A.17. |

*A. Huve Fortescue*

Lieut.Col. R.A.M.C.
Commanding 141st Field Ambulance.

Army Form C. 2118.

# WAR DIARY
## or
## INTELLIGENCE SUMMARY.
(Erase heading not required.)

141 Field Ambulance.

War Diary for the month of November 1917.

COMMITTEE FOR THE
MEDICAL HISTORY OF THE WAR
Date 17 JAN. 1918

Army Form C. 2118.

# WAR DIARY
## or
## INTELLIGENCE SUMMARY.
*(Erase heading not required.)*

Instructions regarding War Diaries and Intelligence Summaries are contained in F. S. Regs., Part II. and the Staff Manual respectively. Title pages will be prepared in manuscript.

| Place | Date November 1917. | Hour | Summary of Events and Information | Remarks and references to Appendices |
|---|---|---|---|---|
| E.19 a.0.9. Sheet 27 | 1st | | Casualties passing through Unit..... Sick 6 | H |
| | 2nd | | Casualties passing through Unit..... Sick 9 No:79146 Private M. Scully, RAMC. rejoined the Unit for duty from A.P.M., 1st Div. Lieut-Col A.Irvine_Fortescue., RAMC proceeded to take up a new appointment. | H |
| | 3rd | | Casualties passing through Unit..... Sick 8 Captain F. Casement., D.S.O., R.A.M.C. joined the Unit for duty and assumed command. No:79905 Private R. Collier., R.A.M.C. proceeded to report to the Office of the D.D.M.S. IInd Corps for temporary clerical duties. | H |
| | 4th | | Casualties passing through Unit..... Sick 5 No:M/2.153804 Private F. W. Payne., A.S.C."MT" with one Austin Ambulance Car rejoined the Unit from No:31 M.A.C. for duty. | H |
| | 5th | | Casualties passing through Unit..... Sick 8 One Austin Ambulance Car joined the Unit for temporary duty from No:1 Field Ambulance. No: 63493. Private W. Page., R.A.M.C. was admitted to Hospital "Sick" and evacuated to "L of C" | H |
| | 6th | | Casualties passing through Unit..... Sick 3 Unit leaves E. 19. a. 0. 9. (Sheet 27) and marches with 1st Imperial Brigade Group to Schools Camp. | H |
| Schools Camp. | 7th | | Casualties passing through Unit..... Sick Nil Wounded Nil 2 Tent sub-divisions with Transport and Medical and Surgical Equipment proceeded from Schools Camp to report to the O. C., IInd Corps Main Dressing Station for temporary duty. Lieut. D. W. Cameron., U.S.A., M.O.R.C. proceeded from the Unit to report to the O.C., IInd Corps Rest Station for temporary duty. 1 Bearer Division and 1 Tent Sub-Division leave Schools Camp and proceed by train to IRISH FARM. The rem Transport moves by road to GWAILA FARM. | H |

# WAR DIARY
## or
## INTELLIGENCE SUMMARY.
*(Erase heading not required.)*

Army Form C. 2118.

| Place | Date November 1917. | Hour | Summary of Events and Information | Remarks and references to Appendices |
|---|---|---|---|---|
| IRISH FARM. | 7th (cont'd) | | One Bearer Division and one Tent/Division from No.2 Field Ambulance join the Unit for temporary duty. Captain D. MacIntyre, R.A.M.C. in charge of 50 O.Ranks R.A.M.C. proceeded to take over the Relay Posts at Kansas House and at Dump House from the 1st Canadian Field Ambulance, also the R.A.P. at Vronprinz and the R.A.P. at ALBATROSS. Captain C. L. Chalk., R.A.M.C. rejoined the Unit for duty from IInd Corps Main Dressing Station | H |
| | 8th | | Casualties passing through Unit..... Sick 13   Wounded 25 No:74242 Private W. E. Bennett., R.A.M.C. rejoined the Unit for duty from the A.P.M., 1st Div. Captain C. L. Chalk., R.A.M.C. proceeded to report to the Office of the A.D.M.S., 1st Division for temporary duty. | H |
| | 9th | | Casualties passing through Unit..... Sick 5   Wounded. 11 No:T/4.262062 Driver E. Plant., A.S.C."MT" joined the Unit for duty. The u/m N.C.O. and men were admitted to IInd Corps Main Dressing Station "Wounded",- No:74866 Private W. Easterbrook., RAMC.   suffering from G.S.W. Head. No:M/2.022059 Private R.G.Masters., A.S.C."MT" suffering from G.S.W. Leg (Rt) and Face No:M/2.022062 Private Sergeant J. P. Mitchell., A.S.C."MT" of No:2 Field Ambulance att. to this Unit.   suffering from G. S. W. Thight (Lt) 2 Officers, 18 N.C.O's and 195 men drawn from the Infantry Battalions of the 1st Imperial Division were attached to this Unit for temporary duty as Stretcher Bearers. | H |
| | 10th | | Casualties passing through Unit..... Sick 2   Wounded. 19 2 Infantry Officers and 145 Infantry O.Ranks proceeded from Irish Farm to report to the Officer in charge of this Unit's Bearers. Capt A.G.H.Smart., RAMC. and 70 Infantry O.Ranks proceeded at 10 a.m. from Irish Farm for duty with the Bearers of this Unit. Capt F.Jefferson., RAMC and Capt C.R.MacLeod with 8 O.Ranks proceeded at 4-30 a.m. from Irish Farm to the A.D.Station at Somme Redoubt for duty. | H |

Army Form C. 2118.

# WAR DIARY
## or
## INTELLIGENCE SUMMARY.
*(Erase heading not required.)*

Instructions regarding War Diaries and Intelligence Summaries are contained in F. S. Regs., Part II. and the Staff Manual respectively. Title pages will be prepared in manuscript.

| Place | Date | Hour | Summary of Events and Information | Remarks and references to Appendices |
|---|---|---|---|---|
| IRISH FARM. | November 1917. 10th (cont'd) | | No:M/2. Private R. G. Masters., A.S.C. "MT" was discharged to duty from IInd Corps Main Dressing Station. No:74864 Private W. Easterbrook., R.A.M.C. was evacuated to "L of C" from the IInd Corps Main Dressing Station. Two Heavy Draught Horses were sent in to Mobile Section "Sick" and were evacuated from that Section. 150 O.Ranks Infantry acting as Stretcher Bearers were returned from the Advanced Dressing Stn to Head Qrs at Irish Farm for a rest. The following casualties in the person personnel of this Unit occurred on this date:- No:28074 Private R.H.Parry., RAMC.    Killed in action. No:72342 Private G. Proctor., RAMC.    G.S.W. Left Arm. No:90223 Private K. C. Beeton. RAMC.    G.S.W. Rt Hand. Left Heel. Back and Right Thigh. No:56232 Private P. G. Poole., RAMC.   "Missing" Believed Killed. | H. |
| | 11th | | Casualties passing through Unit..... Sick. 12 Wounded. 86 150 O.Ranks Infantry who have been acting as Stretcher Bearers with this Unit were returned to their own Units. 50 O.Ranks R.A.M.C. with Capt D. MacIntyre., R.A.M.C. rejoined Head Qrs of Unit from the A.D.Station for a rest. Captain 40 O.Ranks R.A.M.C. proceeded from Head Qrs from to the Advanced Dressing Station for duty with the Bearers. 100 O.Ranks Infantry reported at the Advanced Dressing Station., SOMME REDOUBT for duty with the Bearers of this Unit. No:90449 Private J. H. Gettings., R.A.M.C. of this Unit was sent to the Corps Sick Collecting Station suffering from I.C.T. Feet. | H. |
| | 12th | | Casualties passing through Unit..... Sick. 12 Wounded. 95 100 O.Ranks Infantry reported at the Advanced Dressing Station for duty with the Bearers of this Unit. F** 60 O.Ranks Infantry who have been acting as Stretcher Bearers were returned to their own Unit for duty. 60 O.Ranks R.A.M.C. proceeded from Head Qrs to relieve a similar party at the Advanced Dressing Station. The latter party on relief returned to Head Qrs for a rest. | H. |

Army Form C. 2118.

# WAR DIARY
## or
## INTELLIGENCE SUMMARY.
*(Erase heading not required.)*

Instructions regarding War Diaries and Intelligence Summaries are contained in F. S. Regs., Part II. and the Staff Manual respectively. Title pages will be prepared in manuscript.

| Place | Date | Hour | Summary of Events and Information | Remarks and references to Appendices |
|---|---|---|---|---|
| IRISH FARM | 12th (Cont'd) | | No:52458 Private H.Peckham., R.A.M.C. was wounded in action (G.S.W. Left Ankle) and was sent to the IInd Corps Sick Collecting Station. Walking Wounded Collecting Post. | H. |
| | 13th | | Casualties passing through Unit..... Wounded 54   Sick 4. No:93343 Private G. W. Fearnley, R.A.M.C. was admitted to Hospital "Sick" and transferred to IInd Corps Sick Collection Station. The Head Qrs of the Unit moved from IRISH Farm to DUHALLOW. (Map Refce 1. 1. b. 3. a., Sheet 28) | H. |
| DUHALLOW. | 14th | | Casualties passing through Unit..... Wounded 48   Sick 3. Captain O. L. Chalk., R.A.M.C. rejoined the Unit for duty from the Office of the A.D.M.S., 1st Division. The Bearers in the Line were relieved during the day. The D.D.M.S., IInd Corps visited the Advanced Dressing Station at SOMME REDOUBT. Capt C. L. Chalk., R.A.M.C. and 12 Other Ranks R.A.M.C. proceeded to the Advanced Dressing Station, SOMME REDOUBT to relieve the R.A.M.C. personnel doing duty there. | H. |
| | 15th | | Casualties passing through the Unit..... Wounded 43   Sick 12. 15 O.Ranks R.A.M.C. of No:2 Field Ambulance joined this Unit for temporary duty. 5 O.Ranks R.A.M.C. rejoined this Unit for duty from the A.D.M.S., 58th Division. 13 O.Ranks R.A.M.C. proceeded from Head Qrs to report to the A.D.Stn as a further immediate reserve of Bearers | H. |
| | 16th | | Casualties passing through the Unit..... 48 Wounded....  7 Sick. No:65923 Private W. Page., R.A.M.C. was discharged to duty from No:63 Casualty Clearing Station and rejoined this Unit. No:58112 Private G. F. Hooper., R.A.M.C. was admitted to Hospital "Sick" and transferred to the Corps Sick Collecting Station. 57 Bearers were despatched from Head Qrs to the A. D. Stn as a relief for a similar number in the line. | H. |

Army Form C. 2118.

# WAR DIARY
## or
## INTELLIGENCE SUMMARY.

(Erase heading not required.)

Instructions regarding War Diaries and Intelligence Summaries are contained in F. S. Regs., Part II and the Staff Manual respectively. Title pages will be prepared in manuscript.

| Place | Date | Hour | Summary of Events and Information | Remarks and references to Appendices |
|---|---|---|---|---|
| DUHALLOW. (1.1.b.3.8. Sheet 28) | NOVEMBER 1917. 17th | | Casualties passing through Unit..... Wounded. 66   Sick. 6<br>62 Infantry Bearers reported at the A.D.Station at SOMME REDOUBT at daybreak. 42 proceeded to WATERLOO to assist in evacuation and the remaining 20 being retained as reserve at the A.D.Station.  These Infantry Bearers were returned to their Units at 6 p.m. Capt F. E. L. Phillips R.A.M.C. relieved Captain MacLeod at Waterloo.  57 Bearers proceeded from Head Qrs at 8-30 a.m. in relief of a similar number at Somme Redoubt and Kansas.<br>No:58183 Private J. W. Allinson., R.A.M.C. was admitted to Hospital and transferred to the Corps Sick Collecting Station "Sick" on this date. | H. |
| | 18th | | Casualties passing through Unit..... Wounded. 25   Sick 3<br>34 Bearers proceeded from Unit at 8-30 a.m. in relief of a similar number at WATERLOO. 50 Infantry bearers reported at this Unit and 25 were sent to the A.D.Station at 6 p.m. to assist the Bearers of this Unit.<br>No:58077 Private G. J. Elliott., R.A.M.C. of this Unit was evacuated from the Advanced Dressing Station to the Corps Main Dressing Station suffering from ? Ruptured Viscera. (This man was blown up by a Shell in the vicinity of WATERLOO) | H. |
| | 19th | | Casualties passing through Unit..... Wounded 13   Sick nil<br>The 25 Infantry Bearers remaining at Head Qrs were despatched to the A.D.Station at Somme Redoubt for duty with the Bearers.<br>Capt J. W. C. Stubbs., M.C.,  R.A.M.C. and 33 Other Ranks (1 Bearer Sub-Division) reported at this Unit for temporary duty from No:1 Field Ambulance on the evening of the 18th inst. This party proceeded from this Unit's Head Qrs to KANSAS, to relieve the party of Bearers at that post, at 10 a.m.                                   (one Bearer Sub-Division)<br>Capt G. E. Elkington., R.A.M.C. and 33 Other Ranks joined this Unit for temporary duty from No:1 Field Ambulance at 9 a.m.<br>34 Other Ranks proceeded from Head Qrs at 7-30 a.m. to relieve a similar party at SOMME REDOUBT.<br>The following casualties in personnel occurred on this date.  All were evacuated to "L of C" | H. |

Army Form C. 2118.

# WAR DIARY
## or
## INTELLIGENCE SUMMARY.
(Erase heading not required.)

Instructions regarding War Diaries and Intelligence Summaries are contained in F.S. Regs., Part II. and the Staff Manual respectively. Title pages will be prepared in manuscript.

| Place | Date | Hour | Summary of Events and Information | Remarks and references to Appendices |
|---|---|---|---|---|
| DUHALLOW. I.1.b.3.8. (Sheet 28) | November 1917. | | | |
| | 19th (cont'd) | | 78477 Pte G.H.Gill., R.A.M.C., No:2 Fd Ambce.. G.S.W. Foot rt, Leg lt, and Thigh rt. | ※ |
| | | | 57780 Sgt T. Woods., R.A.M.C., No:142 Fd Ambce.. G.S.W. Shoulder lt. | |
| | | | 84183 Pte E.A.Jackson., R.A.M.C. No:2 Fd Ambce.. G.S.W. Hand lt. | |
| | | | 41498 Pte A.Windle., R.A.M.C. No:2 Field Ambce.. G.S.W. Thigh lt. | |
| | | | 56484 L.Cpl J. Hancock., R.A.M.C. No:141 Field Ambce. Shell Gas Poisoning. | |
| | | | 57787 Pte J. Allan., R.A.M.C. No:141 Field Ambce. Shell Gas Poisoning. | |
| | | | 79466 Pte D. Day., R.A.M.C. No:141 Field Ambce. Shell Gas Poisoning. | |
| | 20th | | Casualties passing through Unit...... Wounded. 16 Sick. 1 Captain G. C. Forsyth., R.A.M.C. relieved Capt F. E.L. Phillips., R.A.M.C. at WATERLOO. | ※ |
| | 21st | | Casualties passing through Unit...... Wounded. 18 Sick nil Capt ELKINGTON., R.A.M.C. and 33 Other Ranks proceeded from Head Qrs at 8 a.m. to report for duty at KANSAS to relieve Capt STUBBS., R.A.M.C. and the 33 Other Ranks. This party on being relieved returned to Head Qrs of this Unit at DUHALLOW and proceeded later in the day to report to their own Unit. viz:- No:1 Fd Ambce. 34 Other Ranks proceeded from Head Qrs at 8 a.m. to report to the A.D.S., SOMME REDOUBT to relieve a similar number of Bearers doing duty there. The latter on being relieved returned to Head Qrs. | ※ |
| | 22nd | | Casualties passing through Unit...... Wounded. 4 Sick. 2 A party of 34 Other Ranks proceeded from Head Qrs at 7-30 a.m. to relieve a similar number of Bearers doing duty at WATERLOO. This latter party on being relieved returned to Hd Qrs. Capt. F. E. L. Phillips., Captain R.MacLeod., with 130 Other Ranks of Nos 2 and 141 Field Ambulance proceeded from DUHALLOW by march route to GWALIA FARM. | ※ |

Army Form C. 2118.

# WAR DIARY
## or
## INTELLIGENCE SUMMARY.
(Erase heading not required.)

Instructions regarding War Diaries and Intelligence Summaries are contained in F. S. Regs., Part II. and the Staff Manual respectively. Title pages will be prepared in manuscript.

| Place | Date | Hour | Summary of Events and Information | Remarks and references to Appendices |
|---|---|---|---|---|
| Duhallow. (I 1b. 3.8.) Sheet 28 | November 1917. 23rd. | | Casualties passing through Unit Wounded..5. Sick...Nil. B.D.M.S. II Corps visited SOMME REDOUBT A.D.S. 3 Officers and 120 O.R. of 92nd.Field Ambulance proceeded to take over the Bearer Posts and A.D.S. from 141 Field Ambulance. and No1 F.Amb. Capts.CHALK,FORSYTH and ELKINGTON and the Bearers of 141 Field Ambce. in the Line returned on relief to DUHALLOW. H.Q., 141 Field Ambulance moved to SCHOOLS CAMP (L 3.d.) The u/m men joined the Unit from No2 Field Amb. and were taken on the strength from 23rd. 90332 Pte.Munroe, H. 1910 Pte.McCabe, H. | H. |
| SCHOOLS CAMP. | 24th. | | Casualties passing through Unit- Wounded...Nil. Sick...Nil. Capt.McLeod and 107 O.R. of No.2 Field Amb. rejoined their Unit at TUNNELLING CAMP. Capts.CHALK and FORSYTH and the Bearer personnel from the Line/141 Field Amb. reported to H'qrs. from DUHALLOW. Capt. ELKINGTON and 33 O.R. No1 Field Amb. reported to their Unit's H'qrs. at ROAD CAMP. 58110 Pte.Hayward, A. R.A.M.C. was admitted to hospital and transferred to Corps M.D.S. suffering from Laryngitis ? Gas. 78422 Pte.W.E.Bennett, R.A.M.C. proceeded to R.A.M.C. BASE DEPOT for duty. 44736 Pte.T.M.Smithson, R.A.M.C. rejoined the unit from 3rd.Brigade Signals. 18828 Cpl.J.A.Reading, R.A.M.C.promoted to the rank of Act.Sergt. from 18.10.17. | H. |
| SCHOOLS CAMP | 25th. | | Casualties passing through unit Wounded..Nil. Sick...Nil. The u/m N.C.O's and Men of this unit are awarded the Military Medal :- 64087 Cpl (act S/Sgt) Swindall, A. R.A.M.C. 35791 Cpl. Davies, A. R.A.M.C. 56484 act L/Cpl.Hancock, J. R.A.M.C. 58054 Pte. Davies, E.M. | H. |

Army Form C. 2118.

# WAR DIARY
## or
## INTELLIGENCE SUMMARY.
(Erase heading not required.)

Instructions regarding War Diaries and Intelligence Summaries are contained in F.S. Regs., Part II. and the Staff Manual respectively. Title pages will be prepared in manuscript.

| Place | Date | Hour | Summary of Events and Information | Remarks and references to Appendices |
|---|---|---|---|---|
| SCHOOLS CAMP | November 1917 26 | | Lieut. D.W. CAMERON, M.O.R.C., U.S.A. departed for duty with No.1 Field Ambulance and was struck off the strength of this Unit. Casualties passing through Unit Wounded......Nil.... Sick.....Nil....... | |
| PHILLIPPO FARM (D 8 c.7.7.) Sheet 27 | 27 | quarter 9 o'clock | No.141 Field Ambulance proceeded by march route from SCHOOLS CAMP to PHILLIPPO FARM (D 8 c.7.7.) Sheet 27. Lieut. J.G. KRAMER, M.O.R.C., U.S.A. and 8 O.R. proceeded to X 30 c. Central Sheet 19 (Medical Aid Post) for temporary duty. Casualties passing through Unit Wounded......Nil.... Sick...18. | |
| | 28 | | Casualties passing through Unit Wounded......Nil.... Sick.....5. | |
| | 29 | | Casualties passing through Unit Wounded......Nil.... Sick....16. Lieut. W. TAYLOR, R.A.M.C. joined the Unit for duty. The undermentioned men proceeded to report to the Camp Commandant, XIX Corps Reinforcement Camp for temporary duty :— <br> 101675 Pte. P. FLETCHER, R.A.M.C. <br> 68562 Pte. A.H. GOULD, R.A.M.C. <br> 84441 Pte. A.G. FARNWORTH, R.A.M.C. <br> 77233 Pte. S.A. GRANSDEN, R.A.M.C. | |
| | 30 | | Casualties passing through Unit Wounded......Nil.... Sick....11. Lieut. W. TAYLOR, R.A.M.C. proceeded to take over temporary medical charge of 2nd. Bn. Royal Munster Fusiliers. | |

Harcourt Lt. Col. R.A.M.C.
O.C. 141st Field Ambulance.

Army Form C. 2118.

WAR DIARY
or
INTELLIGENCE SUMMARY.

(Erase heading not required.)

Instructions regarding War Diaries and Intelligence Summaries are contained in F. S. Regs., Part II and the Staff Manual respectively. Title pages will be prepared in manuscript.

| Place | Date | Hour | Summary of Events and Information | Remarks and references to Appendices |
|---|---|---|---|---|

A5834. Wt. W4973/M687 730,000 8/16 D. D. & L. Ltd. Forms/C.2118/13.

## CONFIDENTIAL.

## WAR DIARY

of

141st Field Ambulance.

From 1st December 1917 to 31st December 1917.

(Volume No:18)

Army Form C.2118.

**WAR DIARY**
or
**INTELLIGENCE SUMMARY.**
(Erase heading not required.)

Instructions regarding War Diaries and Intelligence Summaries are contained in F.S. Regs., Part II. and the Staff Manual respectively. Title pages will be prepared in manuscript.

| Place | Date | Hour | Summary of Events and Information | Remarks and references to Appendices |
|---|---|---|---|---|
| | December 1917. | | | |
| PHILLIPPO FARM. (D8.c.7.7.) Sheet 27. | 1 | | Casualties passing through Unit. Wounded... Nil. Sick....9 | H. |
| | 2 | | Casualties passing through Unit. Wounded... Nil. Sick....18. | H. |
| | 3. | | Unit moves by march route to PORTLAND CAMP (X 28. a.1.8. Sheet 19) The undermentioned men are awarded the Military Medal:- No.4604 Pte.B.DEMPSTER, R.A.M.C. and No.90154 Sgt.A.McI.WILSON, R.A.M.C. No.78210 Pte.G.NIXON, R.A.M.C. admitted to hospital and evacuated to No.64.C.C.S. Casualties passing through Unit. Wounded... Nil. Sick....5. | H. |
| PORTLAND CAMP. X.28.a.1.8. Sheet 19. | 4. | | Casualties passing through Unit. Wounded... Nil. Sick....10. Lieut.J.G.KRAMER, M.O.R.C., U.S.A. and 8 Other Ranks rejoined the Unit from the Medical Post at X 30. c. Central (Sheet 19) The undermentioned N.C.O. and man were admitted to hospital and transferred to 1st.Divisional Rest Station :- 44736 No.58161 Cpl.T.SCANLAN, R.A.M.C. and No.2756 Pte.A.BURKE, R.A.M.C. Pte.T.M.SMITHSON, R.A.M.C. proceeded to 3rd.Infantry Brigade Signals for temporary duty. | H. |
| | 5. | | The Ambulance moves by march route to ZUIDHUIS FARM (S 28. b.5.5.) Sheet 20. and forms the 1st. Divisional Main Dressing Station, taking over from the French Ambulance de Triage. Casualties passing through Unit. Wounded... Nil. Sick....Nil. | H. |
| ZUIDHUIS S 28.b.5.5. Sheet 20 | 6. | | Rev.Father Evans, C.F. with his servant, 18301 Pte.P.McCauley, 1st.Bn.Cameron Highdrs. joined the Unit from 1st.Bn.Cameron Highdrs. for temporary duty. 58826 Pte.C.J.PRENTICE, R.A.M.C. was admitted to hospital and transferred to 1st.Div.Rest Stn. Casualties passing through Unit. Wounded...Nil. Sick.... 6. | H. |

Army Form C. 2118.

# WAR DIARY
## or
## INTELLIGENCE SUMMARY.
(*Erase heading not required.*)

Instructions regarding War Diaries and Intelligence Summaries are contained in F. S. Regs., Part II. and the Staff Manual respectively. Title pages will be prepared in manuscript.

| Place | Date | Hour | Summary of Events and Information | Remarks and references to Appendices |
|---|---|---|---|---|
| ZUIDHUIS S 28.b.5.5. | December 1917. 7th. | | Casualties passing through Unit. Wounded....7  Sick....4. The undermentioned men joined the Unit from No.24 M.A.C. for temporary duty; with 2 Motor Ambulance Cars :- <br>     D.M.2/137845 Pte.Saunders, H.W.  A.S.C. MT. <br>     M2/116537 Pte.Taylor, A.  A.S.C. MT. <br> Under authority granted by His Majesty the King, the Field Marshal Commanding-in-Chief has awarded the Military Cross to <br>     T/Captain C.L.Chalk, R.A.M.C.  No.141 Field Ambulance. | |
| | 8th. | | Casualties passing through Unit. Wounded....1  Sick....7 <br> Lieut.J.G.KRAMER, M.O.R.C., U.S.A. with 53445 Pte.A.Housler, R.A.M.C. proceeded to No.2 Field Ambulance for temporary duty. <br> The undermentioned joined the Unit with 2 Motor Ambulance Cars from No.24 M.A.C. for temporary duty. <br>     M2/148313 L/Cpl.LONGHURST. F.  A.S.C. MT. <br>     M2/152711 Pte.MOFFAT.  F.  A.S.C. MT. <br> The undermentioned with Three 3 ton Motor Lorries joined the Unit from No.243 Ammunition Column for temporary duty :- <br>     M2/227583 L/Cpl.ROSS,    W.  A.S.C. MT. <br>     M2/273261  Pte.PARKS,    R.    " <br>     M2/176948  Pte.MORGAN,  W.    " <br>     M2/191961  Pte.DODD,    S.H.  " <br>     M2/191681  Pte.MARTIN,  R.G.  " <br>     M2/200163  Pte.MARRIAGE, T.    " | |
| | 9th. | | Casualties passing through Unit.  Wounded....1  Sick....15 | |
| | 10th. | | Casualties passing through Unit. Wounded....1  Sick....13 <br> 339155 Cpl.H.G.LAWRENCE, R.A.M.C.(T.F.) joined the unit for duty from the Cyclists Base Depot and is taken on the strength accordingly. <br> 101895 Pte.P.FLETCHER, R.A.M.C. rejoined the unit from XIXth Corps Reinforcement Camp. <br> 58080 Pte.J.R.DAVIES, R.A.M.C. proceeded to report to the Camp Commandant, XIXth.Corps Reinf't. Camp for temporary duty. | |

Army Form C. 2118.

# WAR DIARY
## or
## INTELLIGENCE SUMMARY.
*(Erase heading not required.)*

Instructions regarding War Diaries and Intelligence Summaries are contained in F. S. Regs., Part II. and the Staff Manual respectively. Title pages will be prepared in manuscript.

| Place | Date | Hour | Summary of Events and Information | Remarks and references to Appendices |
|---|---|---|---|---|
| ZUIDHUIS FARM. (S28.b.5.5.) Sheet 20 | December 1917. 11th. | | Casualties passing through Unit.  Wounded....Nil.  Sick.....13. 21210 Pte.H.W.HAMILTON, R.A.M.C. was admitted to hospital, sick, and transferred to 1st.Div. Rest Station. 70711 Pte.J.RANCE, R.A.M.C. proceeded to report to the A.D.M.S. 1st.Division, for temporary duty. | GRa |
| | 12th. | | Casualties passing through Unit.  Wounded....2  Sick.....10 Lieut.J.G.KRAMER, M.O.R.C., U.S.A. with 53265 Pte.A.HOUSLER, R.A.M.C. proceeded from No.2 Field Ambulance to 1st.Bn.South Wales Borderers for temporary duty. 44736 Pte.T.M.SMITHSON, R.A.M.C. rejoined the unit from 3rd.Infy.Brigade Signals. Capt.F.E.L.PHILLIPS, R.A.M.C. proceeded to take over the temporary medical charge of the 8th. Bn.Royal Berks. | GRa |
| | 13th. | | Casualties passing through Unit.  Wounded....1  Sick....13 | GRa |
| | 14th. | | Casualties passing through Unit.  Wounded....1  Sick....27 Lieut Col F. Casement., D.S.O., R.A.M.C. proceeded to the United Kingdom on leave and the command of the Unit during his absence devolves on Captain C. L. Chalk., M.C., R.A.M.C. | GRa |
| | 15th | | Casualties passing through Unit.  Wounded....Nil  Sick....13 1 Motor Ambulance Car joined this Unit for temporary duty from the 2/3rd Wessex Field Ambce for temporary duty collecting the Sick of the 57th Division. | GRa |
| | 16th | | Casualties passing through Unit.  Wounded....1  Sick....17 | GRa |
| | 17th | | Casualties passing through Unit.  Wounded....1  Sick....23 No:58826 Pte C. J. Prentice., R.A.M.C., and No:21070 Pte H. W. Hamilton., R.A.M.C. rejoined this Unit on discharge from the 1st Divisional Rest Station. | GRa |
| | 18th | | Casualties passing through Unit.  Wounded....Nil  Sick....12 Lieut W. Taylor., R.A.M.C. proceeded from temporary duty with 2nd R.Munster Fus. to the 1/6th Bttn Welsh Regt to take over temporary medical charge of that Battalion. No:58117 Lce Cpl A.E.Hobson, R.A.M.C. was admitted to Hospital of This Unit "sick" and evacuated to "L of C" | GRa |

Army Form C. 2118.

# WAR DIARY
## or
## INTELLIGENCE SUMMARY.
(Erase heading not required.)

Instructions regarding War Diaries and Intelligence Summaries are contained in F. S. Regs., Part II. and the Staff Manual respectively. Title pages will be prepared in manuscript.

| Place | Date | Hour | Summary of Events and Information | Remarks and references to Appendices |
|---|---|---|---|---|
| | December 1917. | | | |
| ZUIDHUIS FARM S.28 b.5.5. Sheet 20 | 19th | | Casualties passing through Unit....... Sick 21. Wounded 3. Lieut J. J. Kramer, M.O.R.C. U.S.A. proceeded from temporary medical duty with 1st S.W.B.s to assume temporary medical charge of the 1st R. Highrs. No:59191 Cpl T. Scanlan., R.A.M.C. rejoined the Unit on discharge from the 1st Divisional Rest Station. No:38041 Private J. Silverstein., 1st S. W. Bs. attached to this Unit, ceased to be attached to this Unit from the 27/11/17 having been declared an absentee from that date by a Court of Inquiry assembled on the 19/12/17 in accordance with para 673 Kings Regulations. Captain L. L. Hadley., R.A.M.C. (T.C.) joined this Unit for duty. | CRe |
| | 20th | | Casualties passing through Unit....... Sick 14. Wounded Nil. Captain L. L. Hadley., R.A.M.C. proceeded from this Unit to assume temporary medical charge of the 10th Glosters. | CRe |
| | 21st | | Casualties passing through Unit....... Sick 20. Wounded 6. | CRe |
| | 22nd | | Casualties passing through Unit....... Sick 20. Wounded 3. | CRe |
| | 23rd | | Casualties passing through Unit....... Sick 14. Wounded Nil. No:44736/proceeded to report to 3rd Infantry Brde Signals for temporary duty. No:2756 Private A. Burke., R.A.M.C. rejoined the Unit on discharge from 1st Divisional Rest Station. | CRe |
| | 24th | | Casualties passing through Unit....... Sick 21. Wounded 2. No:56355 Private T. Hope., R.A.M.C. was admitted to Hospital of this Unit "Sick" and evacuated to "L of C". | CRe |
| | 25th | | Casualties passing through Unit....... Sick 4. Wounded Nil. | CRe |
| | 26th | | Casualties passing through Unit....... Sick 9. Wounded Nil. | CRe |
| | 27th | | Casualties passing through Unit....... Sick 21. Wounded Nil. | CRe |

Army Form C. 2118.

# WAR DIARY
## or
## INTELLIGENCE SUMMARY.

*(Erase heading not required.)*

Instructions regarding War Diaries and Intelligence Summaries are contained in F. S. Regs., Part II. and the Staff Manual respectively. Title pages will be prepared in manuscript.

| Place | Date | Hour | Summary of Events and Information | Remarks and references to Appendices |
|---|---|---|---|---|
| ZUIDHUIS FARM. S.28.b.5.5. Sheet 20. December 1917. | 28th | | Casualties passing through Unit...... Wounded 2. Sick 18. Captain F. E. L. Phillips., R.A.M.C. rejoined the Unit from temporary medical duty with the 8th Royal Berks Regt. | |
| | 29th | | Casualties passing through Unit...... Sick 13.   Wounded 1. | |
| | 30th | | Casualties passing through Unit...... Sick 31   Wounded 2. Lieut Col F. Casement., D.S.O., R.A.M.C. rejoined the Unit from the U.K. off leave and assumed command. No:222203 Private J. Tunstall J., 204th Employment Coy. joined this Unit for temporary duty. | |
| | 31st | | Casualties passing through Unit...... Sick 42.   Wounded 4. No:54118 Sgt R.Blandford., R.A.M.C. and No:66949 Pte T.Smith., R.A.M.C. rejoined this Unit from the Cyclists Base Depot on this date for duty. | |

F.E.L.P.
Captain R.A.M.C.
for O.C. 141st Field Ambulance.

C O N F I D E N T I A L.

War Diary
of
141st Field Ambulance.

From 1st JANUARY 1918 TO 31st JANUARY 1918.

(Volumne No.19)

Army Form C. 2118.

# WAR DIARY
## or
## INTELLIGENCE SUMMARY.
(Erase heading not required.)

Instructions regarding War Diaries and Intelligence Summaries are contained in F.S. Regs., Part II. and the Staff Manual respectively. Title pages will be prepared in manuscript.

| Place | Date | Hour | Summary of Events and Information | Remarks and references to Appendices |
|---|---|---|---|---|
| S.28.b.5.5. Sheet 20. | January 1918. 1st | | Casualties passing through Unit...... 36 Sick. 7 Wounded. Captain L.T.Poole., R.A.M.C. assumed command of the Unit vice Captain (act Lieut Col) F.Casement., D.S.O., R.A.M.C. who proceeded from this Unit to the 63 (R.N.) Division for duty, reporting to the A.D.M.S. of that Division on arrival. No.56118 Sergeant R. Blandford., R.A.M.C. proceeded to report to No.2 Field Ambulance for duty. Lieut J.G. Kramer., M.O.R.C., U.S.A., is posted to the medical charge of the 1st Battn Royal Highrs. | App.1 |
| | 2nd | | Casualties passing through Unit...... 44 Sick. 7 Wounded. No.56118 Sergeant R. Blandford., R.A.M.C. joined this Unit for temporary duty with the 1st Divisional Dental Centre from No.2 Field Ambulance. | App. |
| | 3rd | | Casualties passing through Unit...... 47 Sick. 11 Wounded. | App. |
| | 4th | | Casualties passing through Unit...... 50 Sick. 7 Wounded. | App. |
| | 5th | | Casualties passing through Unit...... 30 Sick. Nil Wounded. Captain L.L.Hadley., M.C., R.A.M.C. rejoined the Unit from temporary medical duty with the 10th Bttn Glosters. No.10107 Private P.Hunt., 1st Bttn D.C.L.I. is attached to this Unit from this date. Lieut W. Taylor., R.A.M.C. proceeded to the 63rd (R.N.) Division for duty. | App. |
| | 6th | | Casualties passing through Unit...... 26 Sick. Nil Wounded. No.57957 Sgt C. Minns., R.A.M.C. was admitted to Hospital of this Unit "Sick" and evacuated to "L of C". Captain F.E.L.Phillips., R.A.M.C. proceeded from this Unit to assume temporary medical charge of the 1st Bttn Cameron Highrs. | App. |
| | 7th | | Casualties passing through Unit...... 53 Sick. Nil Wounded. No.56118 Sergt R.Blandford., R.A.M.C. is posted to this Unit from No.2 Field Ambulance for duty. No.72898 Pte R. Collier., R.A.M.C. rejoined this Unit from temporary duty with the D.D.M.S. 71nd Corps. | App. |

Army Form C. 2118.

# WAR DIARY
## or
## INTELLIGENCE SUMMARY.
(*Erase heading not required.*)

Instructions regarding War Diaries and Intelligence Summaries are contained in F. S. Regs., Part II. and the Staff Manual respectively. Title pages will be prepared in manuscript.

| Place | Date | Hour | Summary of Events and Information | Remarks and references to Appendices |
|---|---|---|---|---|
| S.28.b.5.5. Sheet 20 | January 1918 7th | | The Motor Ambulance Car and Orderly attached to this Unit collecting Sick of the 57th Div. proceeded to report to O/3rd Wessex Field Ambulance for duty. | CLG |
| | 8th | | Casualties passing through Unit...... 47 Sick. 6 Wounded. | CLG |
| | 9th | | Casualties passing through Unit...... 43 Sick 2 Wounded. | CLG |
| | 10th | | Casualties passing through Unit...... 36 Sick 5 Wounded. | CLG |
| | 11th | | Casualties passing through Unit...... 43 Sick 10 Wounded. | |
| | 12th | | Casualties passing through Unit...... 54 Sick Nil Wounded. | CLG |
| | 13th | | Casualties passing through Unit...... 49 Sick Nil Wounded. Lieut & Qr Mr C. Greenhough., R.A.M.C. and 5 N.C.Os. R.A.M.C. of this Unit proceeded to attend a Course at the XIXth Corps Gas School., assembling on the 13/1/18 and dispersing on the 20/1/1918. | CLG |
| | 14th | | Casualties passing through Unit...... 43 Sick 1 Wounded. | CLG |
| | 15th | | Casualties passing through Unit...... 38 Sick 2 Wounded. | CLG |
| | 16th | | Casualties passing through Unit...... 33 Sick. 3 Wounded. Captain L.L.Hadley., M.C., R.A.M.C. posted, and proceeded, to assume permanent medical charge of the 1st S. W. Bs vice Captain J.T.Kirkland., M.C., R.A.M.C. who joined this Unit on relief. | CLG |
| | 17th | | Casualties passing through Unit...... 54 Sick. 1 Wounded. | CLG |
| | 18th | | Casualties passing through Unit...... 48 Sick. 1 Wounded. Lieut P. J. Flood., R.A.M.C. joined this Unit for duty from the 63rd (R.N.) Division. | CLG |
| | 19th | | Casualties passing through Unit...... 58 Sick 2 Wounded. | CLG |

Army Form C. 2118.

# WAR DIARY
## or
## INTELLIGENCE SUMMARY.
*(Erase heading not required.)*

Instructions regarding War Diaries and Intelligence Summaries are contained in F. S. Regs., Part II. and the Staff Manual respectively. Title pages will be prepared in manuscript.

| Place | Date | Hour | Summary of Events and Information | Remarks and references to Appendices |
|---|---|---|---|---|
| S.28.b. 5.5. Sheet 20 | January 1918. 20th | | Casualties passing through Unit:...... 42 Sick. 1 Wounded. Lieut F. J. Flood., R.A.M.C. is posted, and proceeded, to assume permanent medical charge of the 2nd Battn Royal Munster Fus. | CRC |
| | 21st | | Casualties passing through Unit:...... 42 Sick. Nil Wounded. No:70711 Private J. Rance., R.A.M.C. was awarded 7 days F. P. No:1 for overstaying his pass to the U. K. by one day. | CRC |
| | 22nd | | Casualties passing through Unit:...... 40 Sick. 2 Wounded. | CRC |
| | 23rd | | Casualties passing through Unit:...... 32 Sick Nil Wounded. Captain F. E. L. Phillips., R.A.M.C. rejoined the Unit from temporary medical duty with the 1st Cameron Highrs. | CRC |
| | 24th | | Casualties passing through Unit:...... 35 Sick. 1 Wounded. Captain C. L. Chalk., M.C.R.A.M.C. assumes command on the Unit during the absence on leave of Lieut-Col E. T. Poole., M.C., R.A.M.C. | CRC |
| | 25th | | Casualties passing through Unit:...... 37 Sick. Nil Wounded. | CRC |
| | 26th | | Casualties passing through Unit:...... 32 Sick. Nil Wounded. | CRC |
| | 27th | | Casualties passing through Unit:...... 20 Sick. Nil Wounded. No:7668 Private E. S. Dyer, R.A.M.C. was transferred to the U. K. on this date for transfer to the Home Establishment on expiration of leave on the 27/1/1918. | CRC |
| | 28th | | Casualties passing through Unit:...... 38 Sick. 1 Wounded. | CRC |
| | 29th | | Casualties passing through Unit:...... 44 Sick. Nil Wounded. M2/022014 Private F.B.Candy., A.S.C. "MT" proceeded from this Unit to attend the Selection Committee of the R.N.Air Dept. LONDON. 52262 Lance Cpl N.Franks, RAMC proceeded from this Unit to report to the Office of the A.D.M.S., 1st Division for temporary duty in charge of Medical Inspection Room there. | CRC |

Army Form C. 2118.

# WAR DIARY
## or
## INTELLIGENCE SUMMARY.
*(Erase heading not required.)*

| Place | Date | Hour | Summary of Events and Information | Remarks and references to Appendices |
|---|---|---|---|---|
| S.28 b.5.5. Sheet 20. | Jan'y 1919 30th | | Casualties passing through Unit....... 39 Sick. Nil Wounded. No.DM2/231280 Private J. W. WILKINSON., A.S.C."MT". joined this Unit for duty from No.1 Division Supply Column. | 320 |
| | 31st | | Casualties passing through Unit....... 19 Sick. Nil Wounded. No.7467 Private G. Brown., RAMC. & No.40599 Pte J.P. Howland., RAMC. were each awarded 28 days F.P. No.1. for overstaying their pass to the U.K. by one day. | 220 |

A. Reill
Captain R.A.M.C.
a/O.C., 141st Field Ambulance.

CONFIDENTIAL.

War Diary
of
141st Field Ambulance.

From 1st February 1918 To 28th February 1918.

(Volume No.20.)

Army Form C. 2118.

# WAR DIARY
## or
## INTELLIGENCE SUMMARY.
(Erase heading not required.)

Instructions regarding War Diaries and Intelligence Summaries are contained in F.S.Regs., Part II and the Staff Manual respectively. Title pages will be prepared in manuscript.

| Place | Date February 1919. | Hour | Summary of Events and Information | Remarks and references to Appendices |
|---|---|---|---|---|
| S.28 b.5.5. Sheet 20. | 1st | | Casualties admitted to Unit. Sick 36. Wounded Nil. No.83141 Private C. Thomson., RAMC. rejoined the Unit for duty from the Office of the A.D.M.S., 1st Division. No.58167 Private A. W. Adams., R.A.M.C. was taken on the strength of the 1st Div. Head Qrs from this date vice No.4604 Private B. Dempster., "M.M.", RAMC. posted to this Unit for duty. | Sd. |
| | 2nd | | Casualties passing through Unit. Sick 37. Wounded Nil. No.56535 Private T. Hope., RAMC. and No.82277 Private J. G. Guthrie., RAMC. joined this Unit for duty from the Cyclists Base Depot. | Sd. |
| | 3rd | | Casualties passing through Unit. Sick 37. Wounded Nil. No.1876 Private F. Elliott., RAMC. and No.45075 Private T. E. Phillips., RAMC joined this Unit for duty. | Sd. |
| | 4th | | Casualties passing through Unit. Sick 35. Wounded Nil. No.27562 Private A. Burke., RAMC. was awarded 28 days F.P. No.1 for overstaying his pass to the U.K. by 48 hours. No.T/3. 030844 Driver W. J. Rusk., ASC"HT" was admitted to Hospital of this Unit "Sick" on this date. Open as the 1st Divisional Rest Station at present location from 12 midnight 4/5th instant. | Sd. |
| | 5th | | Casualties passing through Unit. Sick 34. Wounded 1. No.42386 Private W.A.Ricketts., RAMC.) Joined this Unit for duty. 58034 Private C.T.Heel., RAMC. ) No. T2/13899 Driver D.T.Evans., ASC"HT". was awarded 28 days F.P. No.1. for overstaying his pass to the U.K. by 109 hours, 50 minutes. No.78898 Private R. Collier., RAMC. proceeded from this Unit to report to the office of the D.D.M.S., 11nd Corps for temporary clerical duty. | Sd. |
| | 6th | | Casualties passing through Unit. Sick 29. Wounded Nil. No.3696 Pte P. Wild., RAMC. 10055 Pte W. Queripel., RAMC. 55415 Pte J. Millard., RAMC. 9502 " J. W. Dykes., RAMC. 60206 Pte G. Yeo., RAMC. 8100 Pte C. O'Donovan, RAMC. joined this Unit for duty. No.1910 Pte H.McCabe., RAMC. was admitted to Hospital of this Unit "Sick" | Sd. |

Army Form C. 2118.

# WAR DIARY
## or
## INTELLIGENCE SUMMARY.
*(Erase heading not required.)*

Instructions regarding War Diaries and Intelligence Summaries are contained in F.S. Regs., Part II. and the Staff Manual respectively. Title pages will be prepared in manuscript.

| Place | Date | Hour | Summary of Events and Information | Remarks and references to Appendices |
|---|---|---|---|---|
| S.28.b.5.5. (Sheet 20) | February 1918. 7th | | Casualties passing through Unit. Sick 6. Wounded Nil. No.45309 Private A.Walton., RAMC. No. 315051 Private R.Campbell., RAMC. No. 1742 " P.McBride.,RAMC. No. 5456 " A.J.Grogan., RAMC. No.433669 Pte S.Dewhurst., RAMC. joined this Unit for duty. | |
| | 8th | | Casualties passing through Unit. Sick 38. Wounded 1. Captain J.T.Kirkland., M.C., RAMC. in charge of "B" Section left ZUIDHUIS at. 8 a.m. and took over the Advanced Dressing Station at MINTY FARM (C.1c c.1.7., Sheet 28) and all Bearer Posts in advance from the 106th Field Ambulance. Captain F.E.L.Phillips., RAMC. in charge of "C" Section left ZUIDHUIS at 8 a.m. and took over the Advanced Dressing Station at ST. JULIEN (C.18.c.1.8., Sheet 28) and all Bearer Posts in advance from the 106th Field Ambulance. Hand over the Hospital Buildings at ZUIDHUIS together with all remaining patients, viz:- 103 to the 91st Field Ambulance. "A" Section left ZUIDHUIS at noon and took over the Main Dressing Station at DUHALLOW (C.25 d.1.1. Sheets 28) together with all remaining patients. viz:- 37. from the 107th Field Ambulance. 3 Horsed Ambulances., 1 G.S.Wagon and 2 Water Carts are parked at. ISLY FARM. The remainder of the Horsed Transport is parked at GWALIA FARM. Captain D.MacIntyre., RAMC. (of No.2 Field Ambulance) joined this Unit for temporary duty. from 107th Field Ambulance. One Austin Ambulance Car from No.1 Field Ambulance and one Austin Ambulance Car from No.2 Field Ambulance joined this Unit for temporary duty. No.44736 Pte T.M.Smithson., RAMC rejoined the Unit for duty from the 3rd Brigade Signals. | |
| DUHALLOW. C.25 d.1.1. (Sheet 28) | 9th | | Casualties passing through Unit. Sick 42. Wounded 26. Lieut-Col L.T.Poole., M.C., RAMC. resumed command of the Unit. No.10477 Pte A.Cook., RAMC. was awarded 28 days F.P. No.1 for overstaying his Pass to the U.K. by 24 hours, and was handed over to the A.P.M., 1st Div. to undergo this punishment. | |

Army Form C. 2118.

# WAR DIARY
or
## INTELLIGENCE SUMMARY.
(Erase heading not required.)

Instructions regarding War Diaries and Intelligence Summaries are contained in F.S. Regs., Part II. and the Staff Manual respectively. Title pages will be prepared in manuscript.

| Place | Date | Hour | Summary of Events and Information | Remarks and references to Appendices |
|---|---|---|---|---|
| DUHALLOW. C.25 d.7.1. (Sheet 28). | February 1918. 10th | | Casualties passing through Unit. Sick 34. Wounded 2. The 12 O.Ranks from No.1 Field Ambulance attached to this Unit proceeded to rejoin their own Unit for duty. | A. |
| | 11th | | Casualties passing through Unit. Sick 41. Wounded 1. 33 O.Ranks R.A.M.C. from No.1 Field Ambulance joined this Unit for temporary duty. The Transport of the Unit parked at GWALIA FARM moved to ISLY FARM (Map Reference B.29 d.5. Sheet 28). No.T1/5072 Driver C.Munday., ASC"HT" was taken off the strength of this Unit from 27/1/1918 having been declared an absentee by a Court of Enquiry assembled this day in accordance with para. 673 King's Regulations. | A. |
| | 12th | | Casualties passing through Unit. Sick 27. Wounded 2. | A. |
| | 13th | | Casualties passing through Unit. Sick 33. Wounded 2. Lieut C.J.Buckley., M.O.R.C., U.S.A. joined this Unit for duty. | A. |
| | 14th | | Casualties passing through Unit. Sick 42. Wounded 1. Captain D'Arcy Power., M.C., RAMC. (S.R) joined the Unit for duty. No.74217 Private A.Bamfield., RAMC. was admitted to Hospital of this Unit "Sick" and transferred to the IInd Corps Skin Depot. | A. |
| | 15th | | Casualties passing through Unit. Sick 29. Wounded 5. Lieut & Qr Mr C. Greenough., RAMC. proceeded to report to the O.C. 42nd Stationary Hospital for duty. Captain R.MacKinnon., RAMC (S.R) joined the Unit for duty. No.T3/030844 Driver W.J.Rusk., ASC"HT" rejoined this Unit for duty on discharge from Hospital of 91st Field Ambulance. | A. |
| | 16th | | Casualties passing through Unit. Sick 17. Wounded 3. No.52/9427 Driver G.H.R.Day., ASC"HT" attached, was admitted to Hospital "Wounded" (Shell Wounds Head and Arms) and evacuated to "L of C". | A. |

Army Form C. 2118.

# WAR DIARY
## or
## INTELLIGENCE SUMMARY.

*(Erase heading not required.)*

Instructions regarding War Diaries and Intelligence Summaries are contained in F.S. Regs., Part II. and the Staff Manual respectively. Title pages will be prepared in manuscript.

| Place | Date | Hour | Summary of Events and Information | Remarks and references to Appendices |
|---|---|---|---|---|
| DUHALLOW. C.25.d.1.l. (Sheet 28) | February 1919. 16th (cont'd) | | No.315051 Pte R.Campbell., RAMC (T.F.) proceeded for temporary duty with the 409 (L) Field Coy. No.5436 Pte E.J.Grogan., RAMC, proceeded for temporary duty with the 26th Field Coy. No.9502 Pte J.W.Dykes., RAMC "M.M" proceeded for temporary duty with the 23rd Field Coy. | AS. |
| | 17th. | | Casualties passing through Unit. Sick 35. Wounded 13. Capt. R.MacKinnon., RAMC (S.R) was admitted to Hospital of this Unit "Sick" and transferred to "Officers Rest Station" (No.1 Field Ambulance) | AS. |
| | 18th. | | Casualties passing through Unit. Sick 35. Wounded 3. Capt. D.MacIntyre., RAMC attached to this Unit, proceeded to report to No.2 Field Ambulance for duty. No: 40599 Private J.P.Howland., RAMC. rejoined the Unit from the A.D.M., 1st Division. No: 7421 Private A.Bamfield., RAMC. was discharged from the 11nd Corps Skin Depot and rejoined this Unit for duty. Capt. T. Clapperton., RAMC. proceeded to the Office of the A.D.M.S., 1st Division for temporary duty. | AS. |
| | 19th. | | Casualties passing through Unit. Sick 53. Wounded 6. Major A.A.M.Merrick., RAMC (T.F) joined this Unit for duty. Lieut & Qr Mr J.E.Partridge., RAMC. joined this Unit for duty from No.42 Stationary Hospital. | AS. |
| | 20th. | | Casualties passing through Unit. Sick 35. Wounded 5. No.1910 Private H.McCabe., RAMC. was discharged from Hospital of No.8 Field Ambulance and rejoined this Unit for duty. No.58826 Private C.J.Prentice., RAMC. was admitted to Hospital of this Unit "Sick" and transferred to No.2 Field Ambulance. No.T4/108043 Driver H.Munday., ASC "HT" joined this Unit for duty from 1st Divisional Train. No.18828 Cpl (Act Sgt) J.L.Reading., RAMC. was admitted to Hospital of this Unit "Sick" and evacuated to "L of C". | AS. |

Army Form C. 2118.

# WAR DIARY
## or
## INTELLIGENCE SUMMARY.

(Erase heading not required.)

Instructions regarding War Diaries and Intelligence
Summaries are contained in F.S. Regs., Part II.
and the Staff Manual respectively. Title pages
will be prepared in manuscript.

| Place | Date February 1918. | Hour | Summary of Events and Information | Remarks and references to Appendices |
|---|---|---|---|---|
| DUHALLOW. C.25.d.1.1. (Sheet 28) | 21st | | Casualties passing through Unit. Sick 39. Wounded 4. No.463038 Cpl P.J.Teague., RAMC (T.F.) and No.10132 Private A.Bean., RAMC. joined the Unit for duty. | RP. |
| | 22nd | | Casualties passing through Unit. Sick 34. Wounded Nil. No.T3/030844 Driver W.J.Rusk., ASC"HT" was admitted to Hospital "Sick" and evacuated to "L of C" Major A.A.W.Merrick., RAMC (T.F) proceeded to report to the O.C., No.91 Field Ambulance for duty. Lieut C.J.Buckley., M.O.R.C., U.S.A., proceeded from Head Qrs to the Advanced Dressing Station at MINTY FARM for duty. | RP. |
| | 23rd | | Casualties passing through Unit. Sick 67. Wounded 6. No.T2/13899 Driver D.I.Evans., ASC"HT" was admitted to Hospital of this Unit "Sick" and evacuated to "L of C". One Austin Ambulance Car from No.1 Field Ambulance joined this Unit for temporary duty. Captain J.T.Kirkland., RAMC. rejoined Head Qrs from Advanced Dressing Station at MINTY FARM. Captain R.MacKinnon., RAMC (S.R) was evacuated from "Officer Rest Station" (No.7 Field Ambulance) to "L of C". | RP. |
| | 24th | | Casualties passing through Unit. Sick 38. Wounded 5. Captain J.T.Kirkland., M.C., RAMC. proceeded to report to the O.C., IInd Corps Rest Station (No.12 C.C.Station) for temporary duty. | RP. |
| | 25th | | Casualties passing through Unit. Sick 38. Wounded 7. No.38824 Cpl A.Knapton., RAMC. was admitted to Hospital "Sick" and evacuated to "L of C" | RP. |
| | 26th | | Casualties passing through Unit. Sick 35. Wounded 1. | RP. |
| | 27th | | Casualties passing through Unit. Sick 50. Wounded 3. Capt T.Clapperton., proceeded to attend a Course at the Fourth Army R.A.M.C.School. Capt D'Arcy Power., MC., RAMC. proceeded to report to Head Qrs 15th Wing R.F.C. for duty. No.57274 Sgt W.A.Lee., RAMC. proceeded to attend a Course of instruction in Cookery at the Fourth Army School of Cookery. | RP. |

CONFIDENTIAL.

War Diary

of

No 141 Field Ambulance.

From 1st.March 1918 To 31st.March 1918.

(Volume No.21 )

Army Form C. 2118.

# WAR DIARY
## or
## INTELLIGENCE SUMMARY.
(Erase heading not required.)

| Place | Date | Hour | Summary of Events and Information | Remarks and references to Appendices |
|---|---|---|---|---|
| DUHALLOW. C.25.d.1.1. (Sheet 28) | FEBRUARY 1918. 28th | | Casualties passing through Unit.  Sick 47.  Wounded 16. No.7467 Pte G.Brown., RAMC. was admitted to Hospital "Sick" and evacuated to "L.of C" No.T2/11429 Driver A.E.Nixon., ASC "HT" proceeded to attend a Course of Instruction in Farriery assembling at No.22 Veterinary Hospital. | AR |

L.J. Park
Lieut-Col R.A.M.C.
O.C., 141st Field Ambulance.

# WAR DIARY or INTELLIGENCE SUMMARY

Army Form C. 2118.

| Place | Date Hour March 1918 | Summary of Events and Information | Remarks and references to Appendices |
|---|---|---|---|
| C.25.d.7.7. (Sheet 28) | 1st | Casualties passing through Unit..... Sick 40. Wounded 9. No.58870 Pte G.Wood., RAMC, and No.9913 Pte H.W.Round., RAMC joined this Unit for duty: No.104240 Private J. Cheesman., RAMC was admitted to Hospital of this Unit "Sick" and transferred to 11nd Corps Skin Depot. | |
| | 2nd | Casualties passing through Unit..... Sick 35. Wounded 12. No.57941 Pte G.Holts., RAMC. joined this Unit for duty. | |
| | 3rd | Casualties passing through Unit..... Sick 31. Wounded 9. Vacate Transport Lines at ISLY FARM (Map Reference B.29.d.5. Sheet 28) and take over Transport Lines at BRABANT FARM (Map Reference B.29.d., Sheet 28). | |
| | 4th | Casualties passing through Unit..... Sick 38. Wounded 9. | |
| | 5th | Casualties passing through Unit..... Sick 34. Wounded 7. | |
| | 6th | Casualties passing through Unit..... Sick 31. Wounded 3. No.104340 Pte J.Cheesman., RAMC. was discharged from IInd Corps Skin Depot and rejoined this Unit for duty. | |
| | 7th | Casualties passing through Unit..... Sick 40. Wounded 9. No.T1/5072 Driver C.Munday., ASC"H" attached to this Unit was tried by Field General Court Martial for absenting himself after leave granted to the N.K. from Tattoo Roll Call 27/1/1918 till his apprehension by the Civil Police at MOUNTAIN ASH on the 14/2/1918. Plea "GUILTY". Sentence 90 days F.P.No.1. | |
| | 8th | Casualties passing through Unit..... Sick 31. Wounded 3. | |
| | 9th | Casualties passing through Unit..... Sick 41. Wounded 2. 13 Other Ranks RAMC joined this Unit for temporary duty from No.1 Field Ambulance. Captain T. Clapperton RAMC. rejoined the Unit for duty from the Fourth Army RAMC School. Take over from No.107 Field Ambulance the Relay Posts EAGLE TRENCH, TRAFALGAR SQUARE and CEMENT HOUSE, and detail Bearers for R.A.P. IMBROS. Also take over from No.107th Field Ambulance the Foot Washing Shed at RUDOLPH FARM. | |

Army Form C. 2118.

# WAR DIARY
## or
## INTELLIGENCE SUMMARY.
(Erase heading not required.)

Instructions regarding War Diaries and Intelligence Summaries are contained in F. S. Regs., Part II. and the Staff Manual respectively. Title pages will be prepared in manuscript.

| Place | Date March 1918. | Hour | Summary of Events and Information | Remarks and references to Appendices |
|---|---|---|---|---|
| C.25.d.1.1 (Sheet 28) | 9th (Cont'd) | | No.58826 Private C. J. Prentice., RAMC. was discharged from Hospital of No.704 Field Ambulance and rejoined this Unit for duty. | |
| | 10th | | Casualties passing through Unit.... Sick 39. Wounded 30 Captain T. Clapperton., RAMC. proceeded from Head Qrs to the AD+S A.D.Stn at MINTY FARM for duty vice Lieut B.J.Buckley., M.O.R.C., U.S.A. who was admitted to Hospital of this Unit "Sick" and transferred to Officers Rest Station (No.1 Field Ambulance) Lieut H.F.Bailey., M.O.R.C., U.S.A. is posted to this unit for duty. Captain J.T.Kirkland., M.C., RAMC. rejoined the Unit for duty from temporary duty with IInd Corps Rest Station (No.12 C.C.Station) | |
| | 11th | | Casualties passing through Unit.... Sick 44. 22 Wounded. Lieut H.F.Bailey., M.O.R.C., U.S.A. proceeded from Head Qrs to the A.D.Stn at MINTY FARM for duty vice Captain T.Clapperton., RAMC. who proceeded from MINTY FARM to CEMENT HOUSE A.D.Stn for duty. | |
| | 12th | | Casualties passing through Unit.... Sick 41. Wounded 16. Captain L.P.Kilner., RAMC. joined this Unit from No.1 Field Ambulance for temporary duty. No.463009 Lance Sergt P.L.Brown., RAMC (T.F) joined this Unit for duty. The following Officers, N.C.Os and men of this Unit became casuals on this date. Capt.F.E.L.Phillips., RAMC. Admitted to Hospital of Unit suffering from Shell Gas Poisoning "W" and was transferred to No.2 Field Ambulance. No.58024 L.Cpl T.G.Howard., RAMC. Was admitted to Hospital of this Unit suffering from Shell Gas Poisoning "W" No.61111 L.Cpl J.G.Madden., RAMC. )  No.12048 Pte J.W.Thomson., RAMC. ) Were admitted to Hospital of this Unit suffering No.7096 Pte S.F.White., RAMC. ) from Shell Gas Poisoning "W" and transferred to No.58795 Pte R.Marshall., RAMC. ) No.34 Casualty Clearing Station. No.38233 Pte S.T.George., RAMC. ) No.58007 S.Sgt A.J.Tait., "M.M". RAMC. Shell Gas Poisoning "W", remained at duty. Major G.L.Chalk., M.C., RAMC. proceeded to A.D.Stn at St JULIEN for duty vice Capt F.E.L.Phillips., RAMC. admitted to Hospital. | |

Army Form C. 2118.

# WAR DIARY
## or
## INTELLIGENCE SUMMARY.
(Erase heading not required.)

Instructions regarding War Diaries and Intelligence Summaries are contained in F.S. Regs., Part II. and the Staff Manual respectively. Title pages will be prepared in manuscript.

| Place | Date<br>March 1918 | Hour | Summary of Events and Information | Remarks and references to Appendices |
|---|---|---|---|---|
| C.25 d.1.1.<br>(Sheet 28) | 13th | | Casualties passing through Unit.... Sick 35. Wounded 19. | A.R. |
| | 14th | | Casualties passing through Unit.... Sick 29. Wounded 4. No.T/364743 Driver R.F.Kemp., ASC"HT" and No.T/313245 Driver A.L.Kaye., ASC"HT" joined this Unit for duty from the 1st Divisional Train. | A.R. |
| | 15th | | Casualties passing through Unit.... Sick 52. Wounded 7. No.57963 Sergeant E.K.Edwards., RAMC. proceeded to attend a Course of Instruction at the Fourth Army RAMC School.<br>The RAMC Bearers at the R.A.P. IMBROS were withdrawn on this date. | A.R. |
| | 16th | | Casualties passing through Unit.... Sick 39. Wounded 11. No.58112 Private G.F.Hooper., RAMC was admitted to Hospital of this unit "Sick" | A.R. |
| | 17th | | Casualties passing through Unit.... Sick 45. Wounded 8. | A.R. |
| | 18th. | | Casualties passing through Unit.... Sick 49 Wounded 29. | A.R. |
| | 19th | | Casualties passing through Unit.... Sick 61 Wounded 41. Capt.G.J.Farie, R.A.M.C. posted to this Unit for duty from this date. 57274 Sgt.W.A.Lee, R.A.M.C. rejoined the Unit from School of Cookery, PROVEN. | A.R. |
| | 20th | | Casualties passing through Unit.... Sick 57 Wounded 22. Capt.G.J.Farie, R.A.M.C. proceeded to A.D.Stn.,ST.JULIEN, to take over charge of the evacuation of the Right Sub-Sector from Major C.L.Chalk, M.C., R.A.M.C. who returned to H'qrs. | A.R. |
| | 21st. | | Casualties passing through Unit.... Sick 51 Wounded 95. Capt.F.E.L.Phillips, R.A.M.C., rejoined the Unit from the Hospital of No 2 Field Ambulance. 56499 Pte.E.A.Hicks, R.A.M.C., rejoined the Unit from Temporary duty at No.2 Field Ambulance. 56337 Pte.A.Young, R.A.M.C., evacuated to No 36 C.C.S. wounded (G.S.W.(shell) Wrist, left) | A.R. |

Army Form C. 2118.

# WAR DIARY
## or
## INTELLIGENCE SUMMARY.
*(Erase heading not required.)*

Instructions regarding War Diaries and Intelligence Summaries are contained in F.S. Regs., Part II. and the Staff Manual respectively. Title pages will be prepared in manuscript.

| Place | Date March 1918. | Hour | Summary of Events and Information | Remarks and references to Appendices |
|---|---|---|---|---|
| C 25.d.1.1. Sheet 28. | 22nd | | Casualties passing through Unit..... Sick 49 Wounded 29 Capt.T.P.Kilner, R.A.M.C., No 1 Field Amb. attchd. this unit, proceeded to take over the temporary medical charge of 1st.Bn.Royal Highlanders. 58112 Pte.G.F.Hooper, R.A.M.C., discharged to duty from Hospital. | AR |
| | 23rd. | | Casualties passing through Unit..... Sick 46 Wounded 15 Capt.T.P.Kilner, R.A.M.C. No.1 Field Ambulance, rejoined this Unit for temporary duty from temporary duty with 1st.Bn.Royal Highlanders. | AR |
| | 24th | | Casualties passing through Unit..... Sick 35 Wounded 6 T 313645 Dr.A.L.Kaye, ASC HT was admitted to Hospital, sick, and evacuated to No 24 C.C.S. 57664 Pte.M.W.Bell, R.A.M.C. wounded by Bomb Fragments, Right hand and back (slight). Remained at duty. | AR |
| | 25th | | Casualties passing through Unit..... Sick 54 Wounded 24 57962 Sgt.E.K.Edwards, R.A.M.C. rejoined the Unit from a Course of Instruction at Fourth Army R.A.M.C. School. 58046 Pte.C.T.Heal, R.A.M.C. was admitted to Hospital, sick, and evacuated to No 38 C.C.S. | AR |
| | 26th | | Casualties passing through Unit..... Sick 33 Wounded 16 | AR |
| | 27th. | | Casualties passing through Unit..... Sick 39 Wounded 5 57962 Sgt.E.K.Edwards, R.A.M.C. proceeded to 1st.Divisional Baths, REIGERSBURG, for temporary duty. | AR |
| | 28th. | | Casualties passing through Unit..... Sick 11 Wounded 1. No 1 Field Ambulance relieves this Unit in the Line and takes over the 1st.Divisional Main Dressing Station at DUHALLOW ( C 25.d.1.1. Sheet 28) No 141 Field Ambulance proceeds by march route to GWALIA FARM (A22.d.8.9. Sheet 28) and takes over the Hospital there from No 1 Field Ambulance. Number of Patients remaining is 175. Capt.G.J.Farie, R.A.M.C. and 15 Other Ranks proceeded to L'EBBE FARM (F29.d.5.9. Sheet 27) II Corps Skin Depot and took over that Hospital and 57 Patients remaining from No 92 Field Ambulance. | AR |

Army Form C. 2118.

# WAR DIARY
## or
## INTELLIGENCE SUMMARY.
(Erase heading not required.)

Instructions regarding War Diaries and Intelligence Summaries are contained in F. S. Regs., Part II. and the Staff Manual respectively. Title pages will be prepared in manuscript.

| Place | Date | Hour | Summary of Events and Information | Remarks and references to Appendices |
|---|---|---|---|---|
| GWALLIA FARM. A 22.d.8.9. Sheet 28. | March 1918. 29th | | Casualties passing through Unit.... Sick. 18 Wounded 2. 56337 Pte.A.Young, R.A.M.C. was discharged from No 36 C.C.S. on this date and joined the Unit for duty. | A.R. |
| | 30th. | | Casualties passing through Unit.... Sick. 13 Wounded 1. 9913 Pte.H.W.Round, R.A.M.C. was admitted to Hospital of the Unit, sick. | A.R. |
| | 31st | | Casualties passing through Unit.... Sick. 12 Wounded 8 72 N.C.Os and Men, R.A.M.C. rejoined the Unit from temporary duty with No.1 Field Ambulance at DUHALLOW.(C 25.d.1.1. Sheet 28) | A.R. |

L.J.Post.
LT. COL. R.A.M.C.
O.C. 141st FIELD AMBULANCE.

Confidential.

War Diary

of

No 141 Field Ambulance.

From 1st April 1918 to 30th April 1918.

(Volume No 22.)

Army Form C. 2118.

# WAR DIARY
## or
## INTELLIGENCE SUMMARY.
(Erase heading not required.)

Instructions regarding War Diaries and Intelligence Summaries are contained in F.S. Regs., Part II. and the Staff Manual respectively. Title pages will be prepared in manuscript.

| Place | Date April 1918 | Hour | Summary of Events and Information | Remarks and references to Appendices |
|---|---|---|---|---|
| GWALIA FARM. A.22.d.8.9. Sheet 28. | 1st | | Casualties passing through Unit..... Sick 29 Wounded nil. 9913. Pte. A.W. Round, R.A.M.C. was discharged from Hospital to duty. | A.J.P. |
| | 2nd | | Casualties passing through Unit.... Sick 28 Wounded nil. | A.J.P. |
| | 3rd | | Casualties passing through Unit.... Sick 33 Wounded nil. | A.J.P. |
| | 4th | | Casualties passing through Unit.... Sick 24 Wounded 1. 24244 Pte. A. Winstanley, R.A.M.C. admitted sick to Hospital. 40599 Pte. J.P. Howland, R.A.M.C. rejoined the Unit from temporary duty with 1st Bn. M.H. Coy. 316051 Pte. R. Campbell, R.A.M.C. of this unit attached to H.Q. (Lowland) Field Coy. R.E., was admitted to the hospital of No. 1 Field Ambulance, sick. Under authority delegated by the Field Marshal Commanding in Chief, the II Corps Commander has awarded the Military Medal to the undermentioned men, for gallantry and devotion to duty, in action :- <br> M/2/153780 Pte. A. R. Full, A.S.C. M.T. attached No. 141 Field Ambulance. <br> M/2/052643 " A. Anderson, A.S.C. M.T. attached No. 141 Field Ambulance. | A.J.P. |
| | 5th | | Casualties passing through Unit.... Sick 14 Wounded nil. T/50½ Pr. C. Munday, A.S.C. H.T. rejoined the Unit from the A.D.M. 1st Division. Lieut. A.J. Bailey, M.O.R.C. U.S.A. proceeded to take over the temporary medical charge of 1st Bn. Gloucester Regt. | A.J.P. |
| | 6th | | Casualties passing through Unit..... Sick 11 Wounded nil. 24244 Pte. A. Winstanley, R.A.M.C. was discharged to duty from hospital. | A.J.P. |

Army Form C. 2118.

# WAR DIARY
## or
## INTELLIGENCE SUMMARY.
(Erase heading not required.)

Instructions regarding War Diaries and Intelligence Summaries are contained in F. S. Regs., Part II. and the Staff Manual respectively. Title pages will be prepared in manuscript.

| Place | Date | Hour | Summary of Events and Information | Remarks and references to Appendices |
|---|---|---|---|---|
| GWALIA FARM. A 22.d.8.9. Sheet 28. | April 1918 6th (contd.) | | 48898 Pte. R. Collis, R.A.M.C., rejoined the Unit from temporary duty at the office of A.D.M.S. II. Corps. | |
| | | | The undermentioned men rejoined the Unit from temporary duty with Corps Reinforcement Camp:- | |
| | | | 84441 Pte. A. Yarnworth, R.A.M.C. 68562 Pte. A. A. Lowd, R.A.M.C. | |
| | | | The under mentioned men rejoined the Unit from temporary duty with No. 1 Field Ambulance:- | |
| | | | M2/031524 Pte. A. Y. Kew, A.S.C. M.T. M2/031658 Pte. L. Widdows, A.S.C. M.T. | |
| | | | The Hospital at GWALIA FARM is taken over by the 109th Field Ambulance, together with 26 patients remaining. | |
| | | | The Skin Depot at L'EBBE FARM is taken over by the 110th Field Ambulance, together with 54 patients remaining. | |
| | | | 315051 Pte. A. Campbell, R.A.M.C. of this unit, attached to '409 (Lowland) Field Coy. R.E.' a.I.P. is discharged to duty from the Hospital of No. 1 Field Ambulance. | |
| | 7/4/ | | Casualties passing through unit...... Sick. nil.  Wounded. nil. | |
| | | | The Horse Transport of Unit moves by road with Brigade Transport, to new area. | |
| | | | Capt. H. C. Collier, R.A.M.C. joined the unit for temporary duty from 1st Bn. Gloucester Regt. | |
| | | | 57962 Sgt. C. R. Edwards, R.A.M.C. rejoined the unit from temporary duty at 1st Divsnl. Baths. | I.D.P. |
| | 8th | | Casualties passing through unit...... Sick nil. Wounded. nil. Entrained PESELHOEK. | |
| | | | Unit moves by train to CHOCQUES, and then by march route to F.y.d.5.2. (Sheet 36.B) | |
| | | | Horse Transport rejoins the unit at F.y.d.5.2. (Sheet 36.B) | |

Army Form C. 2118.

# WAR DIARY
## or
## INTELLIGENCE SUMMARY.
(Erase heading not required.)

Instructions regarding War Diaries and Intelligence Summaries are contained in F. S. Regs., Part II. and the Staff Manual respectively. Title pages will be prepared in manuscript.

| Place | Date April 1918. | Hour | Summary of Events and Information | Remarks and references to Appendices |
|---|---|---|---|---|
| F.7.a.5.2. (Sheet 56B.) | 9th | | Casualties passing through Unit...... Sick nil. Wounded 231. Horse Transport of the unit moves to FOUQUIERES-LEZ-BETHUNE (H.6. Sheet HAZEBROUCK 5ª) to be parked there. | A.D.S. |
| | 10th | | Casualties passing through Unit...... Sick 1. Wounded 36. Capt. A.C. Collin, R.A.M.C. temporarily attached to this unit, and 242410 Pte J. Hayes, R.A.M.C. proceeded to take over temporary medical charge of Brigade Details, 1st Division. Corps Rein[forcement] Camp. | A.D.S. |
| | 11th | | 20 other Ranks, R.A.M.C. proceeded to No. 18 C.C.S for temporary duty. Sick 2. Wounded nil. Casualties passing through Unit. One Tent Division of Unit moves by march route to Labour Coy. Camp at D.30.d.1.1. Sheet 36 B. N.E. from F.7.a.5.2. Horse Transport rejoins the Unit at D.30.a.1.1. Sheet 36 B. N.E. from FOUQUIERES, H.6, Sheet HAZEBROUCK 5ª. One Bearer Division under charge of Major C.C. Forsyth, R.A.M.C. remains at F.7.a.5.2. Sheet 36 B. N.E., and operates under orders of G.O.C. 3rd Brigade. | A.D.S. |
| D.30.a.1.1. Sheet 36 B. N.E. | 12th | | Casualties passing through Unit. Sick 4. Wounded 22. Bearer Division with 1 Forage Cart, 1 G.S. Wagon, 1 Water Cart, and 3 Motor Ambulance Cars joins this Unit from No. 2 Field Ambulance for temporary duty. Capt. A.C. Collin, R.A.M.C. proceeded from Brigade Details to report to No. 2 Field Ambulance for temporary duty. M2/022059 Pte G.P. Kesler, A.S.C. M.T. attached this Unit, was admitted to the Hospital of this unit suffering from lacerated wounds, face, the result of a motor cycle accident. | A.D.S. |

Army Form C. 2118.

# WAR DIARY
## or
## INTELLIGENCE SUMMARY.
(Erase heading not required.)

Instructions regarding War Diaries and Intelligence Summaries are contained in F. S. Regs., Part II. and the Staff Manual respectively. Title pages will be prepared in manuscript.

| Place | Date April 1918 | Hour | Summary of Events and Information | Remarks and references to Appendices |
|---|---|---|---|---|
| D.30.d.1.1. Sheet 36B N.E. | 13th | | Casualties passing through Unit...... Sick 1. Wounded 1. The 20 Other Ranks attached to No. 18 C.C.S. rejoined this unit for duty. | A.D.P. |
| | 14th | | Casualties passing through Unit...... Sick 1. Wounded nil. | A.D.P. |
| | 15th | | Casualties passing through Unit...... Sick 24. Wounded 10. Test Division of Unit and Horse Transport moves by march route from Labour Corps Camp at D.30.d.1.1. Sheet 36B. to FOUQUIERES and takes over Hospital buildings at E.15.d.1.3. Sheet 36B. and operates as Divisional Main Dressing Station. Major G.C. Forsyth, R.A.M.C. and party of Bearers rejoin rearguard. | A.D.P. |
| E.15.d.1.3. (Sheet 36B) FOUQUIERES | 16th | | Casualties passing through Unit ...... Sick 26. Wounded 35. Capt. L.J. Fane, R.A.M.C. proceeded from Unit to assume temporary medical charge of 1st Bn. Gloucestershire Regt. vice Lieut. A.J. Bailey, M.R.C., U.S.A., "sick," who on relief, rejoined this unit. | A.D.P. |
| | 17th | | Casualties passing through Unit ...... Sick 22. Wounded 24. 38824 Cpl. A. Knapton, R.A.M.C. rejoined the unit for duty from Cyclists Base Depot | A.D.P. |
| | 18th | | Casualties passing through Unit...... Sick 23. Wounded 43. Lieut. A.J. Bailey, M.R.C., U.S.A., proceeded for temporary duty with 2nd Welsh Regt. | A.D.P. |
| | 19th | | Casualties passing through Unit...... Sick 41. Wounded 15. | A.D.P. |
| | 20th | | Casualties passing through Unit...... Sick 26. Wounded 10. 8967 Pte. Y.A. Dowling, R.A.M.C. was admitted to Hospital of this unit, sick, and evacuated to L. of C. | A.D.P. |

Army Form C. 2118.

# WAR DIARY
## or
## INTELLIGENCE SUMMARY.
*(Erase heading not required.)*

Instructions regarding War Diaries and Intelligence Summaries are contained in F.S. Regs., Part II. and the Staff Manual respectively. Title pages will be prepared in manuscript.

| Place | Date April 1918 | Hour | Summary of Events and Information | Remarks and references to Appendices |
|---|---|---|---|---|
| E.15.a.1.5. (Sheet 36B.) FOUQUIERES. | 21st | | Casualties passing through Unit...... Sick. 54. Wounded. 69. Unit vacates Hospital Buildings at E.15.a.1.3. (Sheet 36B) and moves by march route to Labour Corps Camp, HESDIGNEUL, D.30.d.7.1. (sheet 36B.) and opens as Divisional Main Dressing Station. | L.I.P. |
| D.30.d.1.1. (Sheet 36B) | 22nd | | Casualties passing through Unit...... Sick. 29 Wounded. 49. Lieut. H.J. Bailey, M.O.R.C. U.S.A., rejoined unit for duty, from temporary medical duty with the 2nd Bn Welch Regt. 58840. Pte. G. Wood, R.A.M.C., was admitted to Hospital of this unit, sick, and transferred to 1 Corps Skin Depot. Under authority delegated by the Field Marshal Commanding in Chief, the 1 Corps Commander has awarded the Military Medal to the undermentioned men for gallantry and devotion to duty in action :— <br>    M.2/082059 Pte. J.L. Wilson, A.S.C. m.t. attached No.141 Field Ambulance. <br>    M.2/021534 Pte. A.J. Kerr. A.S.C. m.t. attached No.141 Field Ambulance. | L.I.P. |
| | 23rd | | Casualties passing through Unit..... Sick 143 Wounded. 93. Capt. L.J. Favie, R.A.M.C, rejoined unit from temporary medical duty with 1st Gloucesters. | L.I.P. |
| | 24th | | Casualties passing through unit..... Sick. 44 Wounded. 85. 3696 Pte. D. Wild, R.A.M.C., was admitted to Hospital, sick, and transferred to 1 Corps Skin Depot. Unit leaves Labour Corps Camp, HESDIGNEUL, (D.30.d.7.1.) and moves by march route to RUITZ K.20.a.5.5. (Sheet 36B) and opens on arrival as Divisional Main Dressing Station. | L.I.P. |

Army Form C. 2118.

# WAR DIARY
## or
## INTELLIGENCE SUMMARY.
(Erase heading not required.)

Instructions regarding War Diaries and Intelligence Summaries are contained in F. S. Regs., Part II. and the Staff Manual respectively. Title pages will be prepared in manuscript.

| Place | Date April 1918 | Hour | Summary of Events and Information | Remarks and references to Appendices |
|---|---|---|---|---|
| K.20.a.5.5. (Sheet 36 B) RUITZ. | 25th | | Casualties passing through Unit...... Sick. 25. Wounded. 21. Lieut. J.S. Adams, R.A.M.C. and Lieut. M.J. O'Flynn, R.A.M.C. joined this Unit for duty from No 2 Field Ambulance. Lieut. A.J. Bailey, M.O.R.C. U.S.A. proceeded from this unit to report to 5th Army Brigade, R.F.A. for permanent medical duty. | A.D.P. |
| | 26th | | Casualties passing through Unit...... Sick. 42. Wounded 27. The Field Marshal Commanding-in-Chief awards "The Distinguished Service Order" to Capt. (a/Lt. Col.) L.J. Poole, M.C., R.A.M.C., of this Unit. (Authority M.S. No 4/840 dated 23/4/18) | A.D.P. |
| | 27th | | Casualties passing through Unit...... Sick. 28. Wounded. 28. The Field Marshal Commanding-in-Chief awards "The Military Cross" to Capt.(A/Major) C.C. Joseph, R.A.M.C. | A.D.P. |
| | 28th | | Casualties passing through Unit...... Sick. 32. Wounded. 35. 3882H Corpl. A. Knapton, R.A.M.C. was admitted to Hospital of the unit, sick, and evacuated to L. of C. | A.D.P. |
| | 29th | | Casualties passing through Unit...... Sick. 29. Wounded. 34. 12/1429 Pte. R.C. Nixon, A.I.C.H.T. rejoined the Unit for duty from Course of Instruction at Farriery School, ABBEVILLE. 74223 Pte. S.A. Gransden, R.A.M.C. rejoined the Unit for duty from Labour Reinforcement Camp, ABANCOURT. | A.D.P. |

Army Form C. 2118.

# WAR DIARY
## or
## INTELLIGENCE SUMMARY.

(Erase heading not required.)

| Place | Date | Hour | Summary of Events and Information | Remarks and references to Appendices |
|---|---|---|---|---|
| K.20.a.5.5. (Sheet 36B.) RUITZ | April 1918 30th | | Casualties passing through Unit. Sick 26 Wounded 4. Lt. J.S. Adams, R.A.M.C. proceeded to take over temporary medical charge of 1st Bn. South Wales Borderers, vice Capt. L.L. Hadley, M.C., R.A.M.C. 1,390,834. Pte. J. Turner, A.S.C. M.T. joined the unit for duty from 1st Division Train. | L.2.9. |

L.L. Cook Lt Col
R.A.M.C.
O.C. 141st Field Ambulance.

Vol 24
14/2983

Confidential.

War Diary
of
No. 141 Field Ambulance.

From 1st May 1918 to 31st May 1918.
(Volume No. 23.)

Army Form C. 2118.

# WAR DIARY
# INTELLIGENCE SUMMARY.

(Erase heading not required.)

Instructions regarding War Diaries and Intelligence Summaries are contained in F.S. Regs., Part II. and the Staff Manual respectively. Title pages will be prepared in manuscript.

| Place | Date May 1918 | Hour | Summary of Events and Information | Remarks and references to Appendices |
|---|---|---|---|---|
| K.20.a.5.5. (Sheet 36B.) | 1st | | Casualties admitted to Unit. Sick 26. Wounded 4. No. 58890 Pte. G. WOOD, R.A.M.C. and No. 3696 Pte. P. WILD, R.A.M.C. were discharged to duty from Corps Skin Depot. No. T4/240650 Pte. T.T. EDWARDS, A.S.C. H.T. proceeded to report to Headquarters, 1st Infantry Brigade and is accordingly taken off the strength of this Unit. "Candidate for Commission undergoing training". No. 53665 Pte. A. HOUSER, R.A.M.C. was admitted to Hospital of this Unit, sick. | 28. 28. |
| | 2nd | | Casualties admitted to Unit. Sick 21. Wounded 10. | 28. |
| | 3rd | | Casualties admitted to Unit. Sick 33. Wounded 6. One Tent Sub-division, less Officers, proceeded from this Unit to report to No. 22 Casualty Clearing Station, for temporary duty. | 28. |
| | 4th | | Casualties admitted to Unit. Sick 24. Wounded 6. | 28. |
| | 5th | | Casualties admitted to Unit. Sick 30. Wounded 3. No. 28474 Cpl. W. SLATOR, R.A.M.C. joined this Unit for duty from No. 1 Field Ambulance. No. 61111 Pte. J.C. MADDEN, R.A.M.C. joined this Unit for duty from Cyclists' Base Depot. | 28. |
| | 6th | | Casualties admitted to Unit. Sick 31. Wounded 15. | 28. |
| | 7th | | Casualties admitted to Unit. Sick 35. Wounded 4. No. 51436. Pte. E.J. GROGAN, R.A.M.C. rejoined this Unit for duty from 23rd Field Amb, R.C. | 28. |
| | 8th | | Casualties admitted to Unit. Sick 35. Wounded 13. Capt. G.J. FARIE, R.A.M.C. proceeded to assume temporary medical charge of the 1st Bn. Northants Regt. No. 93383. Pte. A. STAFF, R.A.M.C. was admitted to No. 22 Casualty Clearing Station, sick, and evacuated to Base. No. 9502. Pte. J.W. DYKES, R.A.M.C. rejoined unit on this day for duty, from 26 L Field Coy. R.E. | 28. |

# WAR DIARY or INTELLIGENCE SUMMARY

Army Form C. 2118.

| Place | Date May 1918 | Hour | Summary of Events and Information | Remarks and references to Appendices |
|---|---|---|---|---|
| R.20.a.5.5. (Sheet 36B) | 9th | | Casualties admitted to Unit. Sick. 33. Wounded. 2. No. M2/048544 Pte. R.G. Masters. A.S.C. M.T, attached to this Unit, awarded the "VICTORIA CROSS." (Authority:- A.M.S. First Army. No. 21/1859/A.M.S. of 12-5-18.) No. 53665 Pte. A. HOUSIER, R.A.M.C. was evacuated from the unit to L. of C. sick. | App. App. |
| | 10th | | Casualties admitted to Unit. Sick 42. Wounded 6. No. 3/3051 Pte. R. CAMPBELL, R.A.M.C. (T) rejoined this unit on this day for duty from H.Q 9 (Scot.) Field Coy. R.E. | App. |
| | 11th | | Casualties admitted to Unit. Sick. 23. Wounded. 3. | App. |
| | 12th | | Casualties admitted to Unit. Sick. 24. Wounded. 5. | App. |
| | 13th | | Casualties admitted to unit. Sick. 28. Wounded. 3. | App. |
| | 14th | | Casualties admitted to unit. Sick. 39. Wounded. 19. | App. |
| | 15th | | Casualties admitted to unit. Sick. 24. Wounded. 9. | App. |
| | 16th | | Casualties admitted to unit. Sick. 34. Wounded. 5. No. 139085 Dr. F. TURNER, A.S.C. M.T was admitted to Hospital of this Unit. sick. and evacuated to L. of C. | App. |
| | 17th | | Casualties admitted to unit. Sick. 36. Wounded. 2. No. 90409 Pte. O.A. HINDE, R.A.M.C. was admitted to Hospital of this Unit, sick. and evacuated to L. of C. | App. |
| | 18th | | Casualties admitted to unit. Sick. 39. Wounded. 4. Lieut. F.S. ADAMS, R.A.M.C. on this day posted to medical charge of 1st Bn. South Wales Borderers. | App. |
| | 19th | | Casualties admitted to unit. Sick. 22. Wounded. 2. | App. |

Army Form C. 2118.

# WAR DIARY
# INTELLIGENCE SUMMARY.
(Erase heading not required.)

Instructions regarding War Diaries and Intelligence Summaries are contained in F. S. Regs., Part II and the Staff Manual respectively. Title pages will be prepared in manuscript.

| Place | Date May 1918 | Hour | Summary of Events and Information | Remarks and references to Appendices |
|---|---|---|---|---|
| K20.a.5.5. (Sheet 36B) | 20th | | Casualties admitted to Unit. Sick 37. Wounded 14. | A.28. |
| | 21st | | Casualties admitted to Unit. Sick 14. Wounded 13. Lieut. G.E. BIRKETT, R.A.M.C. (S.R.) joined the Unit for duty. | A.28. |
| | 22nd | | Casualties admitted to Unit. Sick 29. Wounded 5. | A.28. |
| | 23rd | | Casualties admitted to Unit. Sick 21. Wounded 4. | A.28. |
| | 24th | | Casualties admitted to Unit. Sick 27. Wounded 28. | A.28. |
| | 25th | | Casualties admitted to Unit. Sick 22. Wounded 22. No. 2852 Private P. BEDFORD, R.A.M.C. joined the Unit for duty from Cyclists Base Depot. | A.28. |
| | 26th | | Casualties admitted to Unit. Sick 23. Wounded 5. No. 736+573 Pte P. WALSH, A.S.C. M.T. joined the Unit for duty from 1st Divisional Train. | A.28. |
| | 27th | | Casualties admitted to Unit. Sick 23. Wounded 9. | A.28. |
| | 28th | | Casualties admitted to Unit. Sick 20. Wounded 63. Lieut. G.E. BIRKETT, R.A.M.C. (S.R.) proceeded from this Unit to assume temporary medical charge of 1st Bn. Royal Highlanders. | A.28. |
| | 29th | | Casualties admitted to Unit. Sick 26. Wounded 13. | A.28. |
| | 30th | | Casualties admitted to Unit. Sick 24. Wounded 19. | A.28. |
| | 31st | | Casualties admitted to Unit. Sick 21. Wounded 11. No. 85698 Private J.H. GILLMAN, R.A.M.C. joined the Unit for duty from Cyclists Base Depot. | A.28. |

J.J. Poole
Lt. Col. R.A.M.C.
O.C., 141st FIELD AMBULANCE.

June 1918

Confidential.

War Diary
of
No. 141 Field Ambulance.
From 1st June 1918 to 30th June 1918.
(Volume No. 24.)

141 2nd Aust
Vol 25
140/30/6

Army Form C. 2118.

# WAR DIARY
## or
## INTELLIGENCE SUMMARY.
(Erase heading not required.)

Instructions regarding War Diaries and Intelligence Summaries are contained in F. S. Regs., Part II. and the Staff Manual respectively. Title pages will be prepared in manuscript.

| Place | Date | Hour | Summary of Events and Information | Remarks and references to Appendices |
|---|---|---|---|---|
| K.20.a.5.5. Sheet 44. B. | June 1918. 1st | | Casualties admitted to Unit. Sick 25. Wounded 9. | L.S.R. |
| | 2nd | | 85698 Pte. J.H. GILLMAN, R.A.M.C. joined the Unit for duty. | L.R. |
| | 3rd | | Casualties admitted to Unit. Sick 25. Wounded 17. | L.S.R. |
| | 4th | | Casualties admitted to Unit. Sick 22. Wounded 11. | L.S.R. |
| | 5th | | Casualties admitted to Unit. Sick 23. Wounded 19. | L.S.R. |
| | | | Casualties admitted to Unit. Sick 66. Wounded 12. | 2.0.P. |
| | | | Interpreter F. GIRAULT, French Mission, attached to this Unit awarded the MILITARY MEDAL. (Authority:- I Corps 7E. A 24/17.) | |
| | 6th | | Casualties admitted to Unit. Sick 22. Wounded 12. | 2.0.P. |
| | 7th | | Casualties admitted to Unit. Sick 24. Wounded 13. | 2.0.P. |
| | 8th | | Casualties admitted to Unit. Sick 28. Wounded 13. | 2.0.P. |
| | 9th | | Casualties admitted to Unit. Sick 17. Wounded 5. | 2.0.P. |
| | 10th | | Casualties admitted to Unit. Sick 10. Wounded 5. | 2.0.P. |
| | 11th | | Casualties admitted to Unit. Sick 28. Wounded 4. | 2.0.P. |
| | 12th | | Casualties admitted to Unit. Sick 114. Wounded 8. | 2.0.P. |
| | 13th | | Casualties admitted to Unit. Sick 68. Wounded 4. | 2.0.P. |
| | | | Lieut and Qr.Mr. J.E. PARTRIDGE, R.A.M.C. proceeded to report to First Army R.A.M.C. School of Instruction for temporary duty. | |
| | | | 40 Other Ranks, R.A.M.C. of this Unit proceeded to No.2 Field Ambulance for temporary duty. | |
| | 14th | | Casualties admitted to Unit. Sick 48. Wounded 4. | 2.0.P. |
| | 15th | | Casualties admitted to Unit. Sick 33. Wounded 6. | 2.0.P. |
| | 16th | | Casualties admitted to Unit. Sick 24. Wounded 8. | |
| | | | The 1st Lab. Division attached to No.22 Casualty Clearing Station rejoined this Unit for duty. | |

Army Form C. 2118.

# WAR DIARY
## or
## INTELLIGENCE SUMMARY.
(Erase heading not required.)

Instructions regarding War Diaries and Intelligence Summaries are contained in F.S. Regs., Part II. and the Staff Manual respectively. Title pages will be prepared in manuscript.

| Place | Date | Hour | Summary of Events and Information | Remarks and references to Appendices |
|---|---|---|---|---|
| K.20.a.5.5. Sheet 44B | June 1918 17th | | Casualties admitted to Unit. Sick. 63. Wounded. 3. No. 15/21 Sgt. Major A.E. ODELL, R.A.M.C. awarded the Meritorious Service Medal. (authority: Supplement to the London Gazette dated 17/6/18.) | 128. |
| | 18th | | Casualties admitted to Unit. Sick. 88. Wounded. 20. Lt. and Q.M. J.E. PARTRIDGE, R.A.M.C. rejoined this Unit for duty from First Army R.A.M.C. School of Instruction. | 128. |
| | 19th | | Casualties admitted to Unit. Sick. 90. Wounded. 20. | 128. |
| | 20th | | Casualties admitted to Unit. Sick. 66. Wounded. 7. Lieut. J.H. WILSON, M.O.R.C. U.S.A. joined this Unit for duty. No. 742/240650 Pte. T.T. EDWARDS, A.S.C. M.T. joined the Unit for duty. | 128. |
| | 21st | | Casualties passing through Unit. Sick 74. Wounded. 4. | 128. |
| | 22nd | | Casualties admitted to Unit. Sick. 61. Wounded. 2. T/10967 Cpl. S. SALTER, A.S.C. M.T. proceeded from this Unit to report to Base Depot (H.T. 45) HAVRE. No. 95880 Pte. J.H. VICKERS, R.A.M.C. and No. 5393 Pte. J.T. ALLCOCK, R.A.M.C. joined this Unit from Cyclists Base Depot. Lieut. M.J. O'FLYNN, R.A.M.C. proceeded from this Unit to assume temporary medical charge of 1st Bn. South Wales Borderers. | 128. |
| | 23rd | | Casualties admitted to Unit. Sick. 53. Wounded. 1. | 128. |
| | 24th | | Casualties admitted to Unit. Sick. 69. Wounded. 4. | 128. |
| | 25th | | Casualties admitted to Unit. Sick. 111. Wounded. 6. The undermentioned men were admitted to the Hospital of this Unit, sick :- 105354 Pte. J.A. BESWICK, 10132 Pte. A. BEAN, 58869 Pte. F. SANDHAM. T/80043 Pte. H. MUNDAY, T/259382 Pte. J.E. MUZZELL. of A.S.C. M.T. DM2/236148 Pte. Y.O. LEE. A.S.C. M.T. | 128. |

# WAR DIARY
## or
## INTELLIGENCE SUMMARY.

(Erase heading not required.)

Army Form C. 2118.

| Place | Date | Hour | Summary of Events and Information | Remarks and references to Appendices |
|---|---|---|---|---|
| K20.a.5.5. Sheet H4B | June 1918 26th | | Casualties admitted to Unit. Sick. 106 Wounded. 6. The undermentioned men were admitted to Hospital of this Unit, sick :- 58128 Pte. R. Duncan, R.A.M.C. and M2/052643 Pte. A. Anderson, M.M., A.S.C.M.T. | 28. |
| | 27th | | Casualties admitted to Unit. Sick. 134 Wounded. 11. T3/12929 Pte. R.H. Mason, A.S.C.H.T. was admitted to Hospital of this Unit, sick. The undermentioned men were discharged to duty from Hospital :- T4/262082 Pte. E. Plant, and T4/108043 Pte. H. Munday, A.S.C.H.T. 58668 Pte. F. Sandham, R.A.M.C. | 28. |
| | | | No. 2 054939 Cpl. H.G. Wheatland, A.S.C.M.T. proceeded to 1st Bn. Headquarters for temporary duty. 315051 Pte. R. Campbell, R.A.M.C. (T) proceeded to Headquarters, First Army, for temporary duty. | 28. |
| | 28th | | Casualties admitted to Unit. Sick. 98 Wounded. 1 57990 Dr. Mn. Sgt. T.C. Hill, R.A.M.C. admitted to Hospital of this unit, sick. The undermentioned men were discharged to duty from this Unit's Hospital :- 105339 Pte. J.A. Beswick, R.A.M.C., DM2/231648 Pte. Y.O. Lee, A.S.C.M.T. and M2/032643 Pte. A. Anderson, M.M., A.S.C.M.T. 34652 Pte. F. Hidons, R.A.M.C. proceeded to 350th and M Coy. R.E. for temporary duty. | 28. |
| | 29th | | Casualties admitted to Unit. Sick. 56 Wounded. 1. 993 Pte. H.W. Round, R.A.M.C. admitted to the Hospital of this Unit sick, and evacuated to C.C.S. The undermentioned men were discharged to duty from Hospital. 58128 Pte. R. Duncan, R.A.M.C., 10132 Pte. A. Bean, R.A.M.C. and T4/069582 Dr. J.F. Muzzell, A.S.C.H.T. | 28. |
| | 30th | | Casualties admitted to Unit. Sick. 41 Wounded. 1. Lieut. G.E. Birkett, R.A.M.C. (S.R.) of this Unit is posted to medical charge of 1st Bn. Gloucestershire Regt. from this date. Capt. H.E. Collier, R.A.M.C. is posted to this unit for duty from 1st Bn. Gloucestershire Regt. Lieut. M.J. O'Flyn, R.A.M.C. of this Unit is posted to 1st Bn. Northamptonshire Regt. from this date. | 28. |

L.J. Nott
LT. COL. R.A.M.C.
O.C. 141st FIELD AMBULANCE.

# CONFIDENTIAL

WAR DIARY

OF

NO. 141 FIELD AMBULANCE

FROM - 1st JULY, 1918
TO   - 31st JULY, 1918.

( VOLUME   NO. 25. )

Army Form C. 2118.

# WAR DIARY
## or
## INTELLIGENCE SUMMARY.
*(Erase heading not required.)*

Instructions regarding War Diaries and Intelligence Summaries are contained in F. S. Regs., Part II. and the Staff Manual respectively. Title pages will be prepared in manuscript.

| Place | Date JULY 1918 | Summary of Events and Information | Remarks and references to Appendices |
|---|---|---|---|
| K.20.a.5.5. Sheet 44 b. | 1st | Casualties admitted to Unit. Sick 44. Wounded 6. No.T.334809 Driver C.Brotherton., ASC"HT" joined the Unit for duty. No.M2/054957 Cpl H.G.Wheatland., ASC"MT" rejoined the Unit from temporary duty at 1st Div. Hd Qrs. Captain H.E.Collier., RAMC. proceeded to Hd Qrs 1st Division for temporary duty. | 47P |
| | 2nd | Casualties admitted to Unit. Sick 6. Wounded 5. No.T2/12929 Driver R.H.Mason., ASC"HT" was discharged to duty from Hospital of this unit. | 42P |
| | 3rd | Casualties admitted to Unit. Sick 37. Wounded 6. Lieut & Qr Mr J.E.Partridge., RAMC. proceeded to report to A.D.M.S., Calais for duty at No.2 Base Depot of Medical Stores. No.57996 Qr Mr Sgt T.C.Hill., RAMC. was discharged to duty from Hospital of this Unit. | 47P |
| | 4th | Casualties admitted to Unit. Sick 30. Wounded Nil. No.34656 Pte F.Hibbins., RAMC. rejoined the Unit from temporary duty at 350th E.&.M.Coy., R.Es. | 47P |
| | 5th | Casualties admitted to Unit. Sick 52. Wounded 4. No.315051 Pte R.Campbell., RAMC. rejoined the unit from temporary duty at Hd Qrs First Army | 36P |
| | 6th | Casualties admitted to Unit. Sick 34. Wounded 8. | 42P |
| | 7th | Casualties admitted to Unit. Sick 33. Wounded 25. | 42P |
| | 8th | Casualties admitted to Unit. Sick 37. Wounded Nil. | 42P |
| | 9th | Casualties admitted to Unit. Sick 23. Wounded 1. | 42P |
| | 10th | Casualties admitted to Unit. Sick 29. Wounded 3. | 42P |
| | 11th | Casualties admitted to Unit. Sick 20. Wounded 5. | 42P |
| | 12th | Casualties admitted to Unit. Sick 18. Wounded 4. | 47P |

Army Form C. 2118.

# WAR DIARY
## or
## INTELLIGENCE SUMMARY.
*(Erase heading not required.)*

Instructions regarding War Diaries and Intelligence Summaries are contained in F. S. Regs., Part II. and the Staff Manual respectively. Title pages will be prepared in manuscript.

| Place | Date July 1918 | Hour | Summary of Events and Information | Remarks and references to Appendices |
|---|---|---|---|---|
| K 20.a.5.5. Sheet 44b. | 13th. | | Casualties admitted to Unit. Sick. 30. Wounded 2. No.CMT 2298 Sgt.H.A.PAGE, A.S.C. MT. joined this Unit for duty from No.1 Divisional M.T.Coy. No.77223 Pte.S.A.GRANSDEN, R.A.M.C. was admitted to the Hospital of this Unit, sick. | A28. |
| | 14th. | | Casualties admitted to Unit. Sick 18 Wounded 2 No M.S.816 Sgt.C.CAMERON, A.S.C. MT. proceeded from this Unit to report to No.1 Divisional M.T Coy for duty. No.85698 Pte.J.H.GILLMAN, R.A.M.C. was admitted to Hospital of this Unit, sick. | A28. |
| | 15th. | | Casualties admitted to Unit. Sick 20 Wounded 4 No T 20178 Staff Sgt.Major R.W.RIDOUT, A.S.C. HT. was admitted to No 11 Stationary Hospital, sick. | A28. |
| | 16th. | | Casualties admitted to Unit. Sick 29 Wounded 1 No T2/59792 Dr.A.J.GRAY, A.S.C. HT. was admitted to Hospital of this Unit, sick, and evacuated to L.of C. No 32989 Sgt.H.V.TURTON, R.A.M.C. was discharged to duty from this Unit's Hospital. No T1/3253 Dr. E.OWEN, A.S.C. HT. was admitted to this Unit's Hospital, sick. | A28. |
| | 17th. | | Casualties admitted to Unit. Sick 28 Wounded Nil. | A28. |
| | 18th. | | Casualties admitted to Unit. Sick 28 Wounded 5 Capt.G.J.FARIE, R.A.M.C. rejoined the Unit from temporary duty with 1st.Bn.Northamptons. | A28. |
| | 19th. | | Casualties admitted to Unit. Sick 34 Wounded 7 No.77223 Pte.S.A.GRANSDEN, R.A.M.C. was evacuated from Hospital of this Unit to L.of C., sick. | A28. |
| | 20th. | | Casualties admitted to Unit. Sick. 26 Wounded 17 No.T 20178 Staff Sgt.Major R.W.RIDOUT, A.S.C. HT. rejoined Unit for duty on discharge from No.11 Stationary Hospital. | A28. |

Army Form C. 2118.

# WAR DIARY
## or
## INTELLIGENCE SUMMARY.
*(Erase heading not required.)*

Instructions regarding War Diaries and Intelligence Summaries are contained in F.S. Regs., Part II. and the Staff Manual respectively. Title pages will be prepared in manuscript.

| Place | Date July 1918. | Hour. | Summary of Events and Information | Remarks and references to Appendices |
|---|---|---|---|---|
| K.20 a.5.5. Sheet 44 B | 21st | | Casualties admitted to Unit.... Sick 26. Wounded.... 7. Captain G.J.Farie., R.A.M.C. and 14 O.Ranks proceeded from Head Qrs and took over from No.2 Field Ambulance the Dressing Station at LABOURSE(Map Refce L.2.d.8.2. Sheet 44 b), relief being completed by 12 noon. Captain T. Clapperton., R.A.M.C. and 39 O.Ranks R.A.M.C. proceeded from Head Qrs and took over from No.2 Field Ambulance the MADELEINE A.Dressing Station (Map Refce G.1.d.4.4. Sheet 44 a) and Relay Posts; relief being completed by 4 p.m. The party working on the new MADELEINE A.D.S. came under the administration of this Unit from 6 p.m. | ADS. |
| | 22nd | | Casualties passing through Advanced Dressing Stations.... Sick 2. Wounded 12. Major O. L. Chalk., M.C., RAMC. and 39 O.Ranks proceeded from Head Qrs and took over from No.2 Field Ambulance the CAMBRIN A.Dressing Station (Map Refce A.26 a.1.8. Sheet 44 a) and Relay Posts; relief being completed by 4 p.m. Captain J. T. Kirkland., M.C., RAMC. and 27 O.Ranks proceeded from No.2 Field Ambulance; relief the A.D.Stn at ANNEQUIN (Map Refce F.29 c.2.3. Sheet 44 b) from No.2 Field Ambulance; relief being completed by 12 noon. Hand over the 1st Div. Main Dressing Station to No.2 Field Ambulance at 10 a.m. and the personnel remaining with Head Qrs move into the Billets vacated by No.2 Field Ambulance at K.20 a.5.5. (Sheet 44 b) No.58233 Private S. T. George RAMC. joined this Unit for duty from the 1st Div.Reception Camp. No.T.390490 Driver W.Hindle., A.S.C. "HT" joined this Unit for duty from 1st Div.Train. | ADS. |
| | 23rd | | Casualties passing through Advanced Dressing Stations.... Sick 2. Wounded 11. Lieut J. H. Wilson., M.O.R.C.,U.S.A. proceeded from Head Quarters to report to CAMBRIN A. D. Station for duty. | ADS. |
| | 24th | | Casualties passing through Advanced Dressing Stations.... Sick 2. Wounded 8. | ADS. |
| | 25th | | Casualties passing through Advanced Dressing Stations.... Sick 6. Wounded 1. | ADS. |
| | 26th | | Casualties passing through Advanced Dressing Stations.... Sick 8. Wounded Nil. No.85698 Pte J.H.Gillman., RAMC. was discharged from Hospital of NO:2 Field Ambce and rejoined this Unit for duty. | ADS. |

Army Form C. 2118.

# WAR DIARY
## or
## INTELLIGENCE SUMMARY.
*(Erase heading not required.)*

Instructions regarding War Diaries and Intelligence Summaries are contained in F. S. Regs., Part II. and the Staff Manual respectively. Title pages will be prepared in manuscript.

| Place | Date | Hour | Summary of Events and Information | Remarks and references to Appendices |
|---|---|---|---|---|
| K.20 a.5.5. Sheet 44 b. | July 1918. | | | |
| | 27th | | Casualties passing through Advanced Dressing Stations... Sick 9. Wounded 2. | A.D.S. |
| | 28th | | Casualties passing through Advanced Dressing Stations... Sick 8. Wounded 2. | A.D.S. |
| | 29th | | Casualties passing through Advanced Dressing Stations... Sick 12. Wounded 3. No.58054 Pte E.M.Davies., M.M., RAMC and No.T2/10568 Driver R.Symonds., ASC"HT" were admitted to Hospital of No.2 Field Ambulance "Sick". | A.D.S. |
| | 30th | | Casualties passing through Advanced Dressing Stations... Sick 8. Wounded 5. Captain G. J. Farie., RAMC. hands over the Dressing Station at LABOURSE to Lieut J.H.Wilson., M.O.R.C., U.S.A. and rejoins Head Quarters for duty. | A.D.S. |
| | 31st | | Casualties passing through Advanced Dressing Stations... Sick 10. Wounded 2. | A.D.S. |

A.D. Part

Lieut-Col R.A.M.C.
O. Commanding 141st Field Ambulance.

CONFIDENTIAL.

WAR DIARY

of

No.141 FIELD AMBULANCE.

From 1st AUGUST 1918 to 31st AUGUST 1918.

( Volume No.26. )

Army Form C. 2118.

# WAR DIARY
## or
## INTELLIGENCE SUMMARY.
*(Erase heading not required.)*

Instructions regarding War Diaries and Intelligence Summaries are contained in F.S. Regs., Part II. and the Staff Manual respectively. Title pages will be prepared in manuscript.

| Place | Date | Hour | Summary of Events and Information | Remarks and references to Appendices |
|---|---|---|---|---|
| K.20.a.5.5. Sheet 44 b. | AUGUST 1918. | | | |
| | 1st | | Casualties passing through Advanced Dressing Stations... Sick 8. Wounded 8. | A.D.S. |
| | 2nd | | Casualties passing through Advanced Dressing Stations... Sick 4. Wounded 2. | A.D.S. |
| | 3rd | | Casualties passing through Advanced Dressing Stations... Sick 5. Wounded 3. Captain H.E.COLLIER., R.A.M.C. rejoined the 1st Div.Head Qrs from a Course at the First Army R.A.M.C. School of Instruction. | A.D.S. |
| | 4th | | Casualties passing through Advanced Dressing Stations... Sick 8. Wounded 3. No.58054 Private E.M.DAVIES., M.M., R.A.M.C. rejoined the Unit for duty on discharge from Hospital of No.2 Field Ambulance. Captain F.E.L.PHILLIPS., R.A.M.C. joined the Unit for duty. Captain H.E.COLLIER., R.A.M.C. was posted to No.1 Field Ambulance for duty. | A.D.S. |
| | 5th | | Casualties passing through Advanced Dressing Stations... Sick 10. Wounded Nil. No.T2/10568 Driver R.SYMONDS., A.S.C. "HT" rejoined the Unit for duty on discharge from Hospital of No.2 Field Ambulance. | A.D.S. |
| | 6th | | Casualties passing through Advanced Dressing Stations... Sick 7. Wounded 4. Captain F.E.L.PHILLIPS., R.A.M.C. proceeded from Head Qrs to relieve Major C.L.CHALK., M.C., R.A.M.C. at the Advanced Dressing Station, CAMBRIN. Major CHALK. on being relieved rejoined Head Quarters for duty. | A.D.S. |
| | 7th | | Casualties passing through Advanced Dressing Stations... Sick 13. Wounded 1. Lieut & Qr Mr S.M.GAWTHORNE., R.A.M.C. joined the Unit for duty. No.21712 Private W&G.HOLBROOK., R.A.M.C. was admitted to Hospital of No.2 Field Ambulance "Sick" | A.D.S. |
| | 8th | | Casualties passing through Advanced Dressing Stations... Sick 11. Wounded 7. | A.D.S. |
| | 9th | | Casualties passing through Advanced Dressing Stations... Sick 14. Wounded Nil. No.58192 Pte C.L.ANNEAR., R.A.M.C. was admitted to Hospital of No.2 Field Ambce "Sick" | A.D.S. |

Army Form C. 2118.

# WAR DIARY
## or
## INTELLIGENCE SUMMARY.
(Erase heading not required.)

Instructions regarding War Diaries and Intelligence Summaries are contained in F.S. Regs, Part II. and the Staff Manual respectively. Title pages will be prepared in manuscript.

| Place | Date | Hour | Summary of Events and Information | Remarks and references to Appendices |
|---|---|---|---|---|
| K.20 a.5.5. Sheet 44 b. | AUGUST 1918. 10th | | Casualties passing through Advanced Dressing Stations... Sick 12. Wounded Nil. Major C.L.CHALK., M.O., R.A.M.C. proceeded from Head Qrs to relieve Capt F.E.L.PHILLIPS., R.A.M.C. at the Advanced Dressing Station, CAMBRIN. Captain PHILLIPS. on being relieved proceeded to report to the First Army R.A.M.C. School of Instruction for temporary duty as Assistant Instructor. Captain D.MacINTYRE., M.C., R.A.M.C. joined the Unit for temporary duty from No.2 Field Ambulance. | A.D.P. |
| | 11th | | Casualties passing through Advanced Dressing Stations...Sick 8. Wounded 6. No.21712 Private W.G.HOLBROOK., R.A.M.C. was discharged to duty from Hospital of No.2 Field Ambulance. Captain G.J.FARIE., R.A.M.C., Lieut J.H.WILSON., M.O.R.C., U.S.A., and No.10255 Private W.D.QUERIPEL., R.A.M.C. proceeded to the First Army R.A.M.C. School of Instruction for the purpose of attending a Course. Major U.C.FORSYTH., M.C., R.A.M.C. relieved Lieut J.H.WILSON., M.O.R.C., U.S.A. at the Dressing Station, LABOURSE. | A.D.P. |
| | 12th | | Casualties passing through Advanced Dressing Stations... Sick 13. Wounded 2. No.5323 Private R.BAILEY., R.A.M.C. was wounded slightly and remained at duty. G.S.W.(Shell) Scalp. | A.D.P. |
| | 13th | | Casualties passing through Advanced Dressing Stations... Sick 8. Wounded 1. No.52262 Lce Cpl N.FRANKS., R.A.M.C. proceeded to report to the 54th Battery R.F.A. for attachment. Candidate for a Commission undergoing training. No.57210 Private D.C.S.SLAUGHTER., R.A.M.C. was admitted to Hospital of No.2 Field Ambulance "Sick". | A.D.P. |
| | 14th | | Casualties passing through Advanced Dressing Stations... Sick 7. Wounded 6. No.56706 Private C.S.GILLINGHAM., R.A.M.C. was admitted to hospital of No.2 Field Ambulance "Sick". | A.D.P. |

Army Form C. 2118.

# WAR DIARY
## or
## INTELLIGENCE SUMMARY.
*(Erase heading not required.)*

Instructions regarding War Diaries and Intelligence Summaries are contained in F. S. Regs., Part II. and the Staff Manual respectively. Title pages will be prepared in manuscript.

| Place | Date | Hour | Summary of Events and Information | Remarks and references to Appendices |
|---|---|---|---|---|
| K.20 a.5.5. Sheet 44 b. | AUGUST 1918. 15th | | Casualties passing through Advanced Dressing Stations... Sick 1. Wounded 5. | A.D.S. |
| | 16th | | Casualties passing through Advanced Dressing Stations... Sick 3. Wounded 6. Draw one Heavy Draught Horse to replace casualty. | A.D.S. |
| | 17th | | Casualties passing through Advanced Dressing Stations... Sick 8. Wounded 3. | A.D.S. |
| | 18th | | Casualties passing through Advanced Dressing Stations... Sick 18. Wounded 1. No.56706 Pte C.S.GILLINGHAM., R.A.M.C. and No.58192 Pte C.L.ANNEAR., R.A.M.C. were discharged from Hospital of No.2 Field Ambulance to duty. No.52304 Pte A.GIBSON., R.A.M.C. rejoined the Unit for duty from temporary duty at the 1st Div. Head Qrs. | A.D.S. |
| | 19th | | Casualties passing through Advanced Dressing Stations... Sick 7. Wounded 4. No.T1/3253 Driver E.OWEN., A.S.C. "HT" rejoined the Unit for duty on discharge from 1st Corps Rest Station. | A.D.S. |
| | 20th | | Casualties passing through Advanced Dressing Stations... Sick Nil. Wounded 2. No.57210 Private D.C.S.SLAUGHTER., R.A.M.C. rejoined the Unit for duty on discharge from Hospital of No.2 Field Ambulance. | A.D.S. |
| | 21st | | Casualties passing through Advanced Dressing Stations... Sick 1. Wounded Nil. No.57927 Staff Sergt A.J.TAIT., M.M., R.A.M.C. was wounded on the evening of the 20th inst. G.S.W. Shell. Rt Forearm (slight) and was admitted to No.22 Casualty Clearing Station on the 21st inst. Hand over Advanced Dressing Stations at CAMBRIN, ANNEQUIN, MADELEINE, the Walking Wounded Collecting Post at LABOURSE, and Head Qrs Billets at RUITZ to the 143th Field Ambulance; relief being completed by 12 noon. The Horsed transport under charge of Major O.C.FORSYTH., M.C., R.A.M.C. moved by march route with Horsed Transport of the 3rd Infantry Brigade Group to new area. Personnel of unit embussed at 6 p.m. under orders of 3rd Infantry Brigade and moved to new area. The Unit on arrival in new area occupied Billets in SAINS-les-PERNES (Map Reference H.13 c. Sheet 44 b) | A.D.S. |

Army Form C.2118.

# WAR DIARY
## or
## INTELLIGENCE SUMMARY.
*(Erase heading not required.)*

Instructions regarding War Diaries and Intelligence Summaries are contained in F. S. Regs., Part II. and the Staff Manual respectively. Title pages will be prepared in manuscript.

| Place | Date AUGUST 1918. | Hour | Summary of Events and Information | Remarks and references to Appendices |
|---|---|---|---|---|
| H.13 c. Sheet 44 b. | 21st (cont'd) | | Captain D. MacINTYRE., M.C., R.A.M.C. proceeded to report to No.2 Field Ambulance for duty. | A.3.P. |
| | 22nd | | Casualties admitted to unit. Sick Nil. Collect and treat sick of the 3rd Infantry Brigade Group. | A.3.P. |
| | 23rd | | Casualties admitted to Unit. Sick 2. Captain J.T.KIRKLAND., M.C., R.A.M.C. and No.69945 Private H.ARCHER., R.A.M.C. proceeded to the 1st Divisional Reception Camp for temporary duty. | A.3.P. |
| | 24th | | Casualties admitted to unit. Sick 3. Capt G.J.FARIE., R.A.M.C., Capt F.E.L.PHILLIPS., R.A.M.C., Lieut J.H.WILSON, M.O.R.C., U.S.A., and No.10255 Private W.D.QUERIPEL, R.A.M.C. rejoined the Unit from a Course at the First Army R.A.M.C. School of Instruction. | A.3.P. |
| | 25th | | Casualties admitted to Unit. Sick 1. No.57927 Staff Sergt A.J.TAIT., M.M., R.A.M.C. rejoined the unit for duty on discharge from Hospital of No.22 Casualty Clearing Station. 40 Other Ranks R.A.M.C. proceeded to report to No.1 Casualty Clearing Station for temporary duty. No.T.20178 Staff Sergt Major R.W.RIDOUT., A.S.C. "HT" was admitted to No.22 Casualty Clearing Station suffering from Accidental injuries. | A.3.P. |
| | 26th | | Casualties admitted to Unit. Sick 4. | A.3.P. |
| | 27th | | Casualties admitted to Unit. Sick 3. Lieut J.H.WILSON., M.O.R.C., U.S.A. proceeded from this unit with instructions to report to the A.D.M.S., 4th Division for duty. | A.3.P. |
| | 28th | | Casualties admitted to unit. Sick 4. | A.3.P. |
| | 29th | | Casualties admitted to Unit. Sick 2. | A.3.P. |

Army Form C. 2118

# WAR DIARY
## or
## INTELLIGENCE SUMMARY.
(Erase heading not required.)

Instructions regarding War Diaries and Intelligence Summaries are contained in F. S. Regs., Part II. and the Staff Manual respectively. Title pages will be prepared in manuscript.

| Place | Date | Hour | Summary of Events and Information | Remarks and references to Appendices |
|---|---|---|---|---|
| | AUGUST 1918. | | | |
| H.13 c. Sheet 44 b. | 30th | | Casualties admitted to Unit. Sick 3. | A.D.S. |
| | 31st | | Casualties admitted to Unit. Sick 8. 40 O.Ranks rejoined the unit for duty from No.1 Casualty Clearing Station. No.69206 Private G.E.YEO., R.A.M.C. was admitted to Hospital "Sick" and evacuated to "L of C" Horsed Transport of Unit, under charge of Major C.C.FORSYTH., M.C., R.A.M.C. left Unit's Head Qrs at 1-15 p.m. and moved with the 3rd Infantry Group Transport by road into the ARRAS Area; staging for the night 31st/1st Sept. at ACE in the FRENIN-CAPELLE Area. | A.D.S. |

J. J. Post
Lieut-Col R.A.M.C.
O.Commanding 141st Field Ambulance.

CONFIDENTIAL.

WAR DIARY

of

No. 141 FIELD AMBULANCE.

From 1st SEPTEMBER 1918 to 30th SEPTEMBER 1918.

(Volume No.27.)

Army Form C. 2118.

# WAR DIARY
## or
## INTELLIGENCE SUMMARY.
*(Erase heading not required.)*

Instructions regarding War Diaries and Intelligence Summaries are contained in F. S. Regs., Part II. and the Staff Manual respectively. Title pages will be prepared in manuscript.

| Place | Date September 1918. | Hour | Summary of Events and Information | Remarks and references to Appendices |
|---|---|---|---|---|
| | 1st | | Dismounted personnel of unit leave PERNES with 3rd Brigade Group by tactical train, detraining at ARRAS. On arrival at ARRAS, unit marches to Billets in Rue de Justice, ARRAS. Transport of Unit moves by march route from AOQ to ACHICOURT. "C" Section Bearer Sub-division under charge of Captain PHILLIPS., R.A.M.C. left Head Qrs at 9 p.m. and moves with 3rd Brigade Group to an assembly area East of WANCOURT. | 128 |
| ARRAS. | 2nd | | "A" Section Bearer Sub-division under charge of Captain CLAPPERTON., R.A.M.C. left Head Qrs at 4 a.m. by march route route and joined "C" Section Bearer Sub-division at 7 a.m. These Bearer Sub-divisions came under the administration of No.1 Field Ambulance. 4 Ambulance Cars and 1 Motor Cycle proceeded to report to No.1 Field Ambulance for duty. No.58868 Pte F.SANDHAM., R.A.M.C. was wounded in action (G.S.W. Shell. Lt Clavicular region) and evacuated to C.C.Station. | 128 |
| | 3rd | | Casualties passing through Unit.  Sick 5.  Wounded 102. Unit moves from Billets and rue de Justice, ARRAS and takes over the Corps Main Dressing Station, Hospice St Jean, ARRAS from No.10 Field Ambulance. "A" Section Bearer Sub-division rejoin Head Qrs for duty. | 128 |
| | 4th | | Casualties passing through Unit.  Sick 3.  Wounded 143. Capt J.S.LLOYD., R.A.M.C. attached 1st Divisional Engineers joined the unit for temporary duty. | 128 |
| | 5th | | Casualties passing through Unit.  Sick 9.  Wounded 75. | 128 |
| | 6th | | Casualties passing through Unit.  Sick 3.  Wounded 66. No.57839 Pte W.G.WOODS., R.A.M.C. was admitted to hospital and evacuated to "L of C" sick. "C" Section Bearer sub-division rejoined Head Qrs for duty. | 128 |
| | 7th | | Casualties passing through unit.  Sick 11. Wounded 113. 4 Motor Ambulances and 1 motor cycle rejoined the Unit from No.1 Field Ambulance for duty. Capt J.S.LLOYD., R.A.M.C. proceeded from Unit to rejoin the 1st D.Engineers for duty. | 128 |

Army Form C. 2118.

# WAR DIARY
## or
## INTELLIGENCE SUMMARY.
*(Erase heading not required.)*

Instructions regarding War Diaries and Intelligence Summaries are contained in F.S. Regs., Part II. and the Staff Manual respectively. Title pages will be prepared in manuscript.

| Place | Date | Hour | Summary of Events and Information | Remarks and references to Appendices |
|---|---|---|---|---|
| | Septr 1918. | | | |
| ARRAS. | 8th | | Casualties passing through Unit. Sick 2. Wounded 10. Hand over Hospital Buildings and Billets to the 2/1st London Field Ambulance, and Unit moves by march route to AVESNES-le-COMTE and are billeted in the old C.C.S. Site on the NOYELLE-VION Road. | A.D.S |
| AVESNES-le-COMTE. | 9th | | Casualties passing through Unit. Sick 15. No.38490 Pte (act Sergt) G.T.WILSON., R.A.M.C., joined the Unit for duty from the ~~Syo~~ R.A.M.C. Base Depot. | A.D.S |
| | 10th | | Casualties passing through Unit. Sick 6. No.10255 Pte W.D.Queripel., R.A.M.C. and No.1910 Pte H.McCabe., R.A.M.C. were admitted to this Unit's Hospital, sick, and evacuated to "L of C". Unit leaves Billets at 5 p.m. and moves by march route to AUBIGNY, and move from there by tactical train to new area. | A.D.S |
| VILLERS BRETONNEUX | 11th | | Casualties passing through Unit. Sick 4. Unit detrains at VILLERS BRETONNEUX at 2 p.m. and march to Billets in the Rue de Cachy. | A.D.S |
| | 12th | | Casualties passing through Unit. NIL. Dismounted personnel embus at 8 a.m. and move to O.33.a.8.2. Sheet 62 C. Transport by march route. Bue Major O.C.Forsyth., M.C., R.A.M.C. with Captains Farie and Kirkland. and "B" Bearer Sub-division left Head Qrs at 7-45 p.m. and established an A.D.Stn at R.26.d.4.2. Sheet 62 C and Bearer Posts in the vicinity of Regimental Aid Posts. | A.D.S |
| O.33.a.8.2. Sheet 62 C | 13th | | Casualties passing through Unit. Sick Nil. Wounded 24. Personnel at Head Qrs move by road to ESTREES-en-CHAUSSEE (P.29.d.6.5.) and establish a Divisional Main Dressing Station. | A.D.S |
| | 14th | | Casualties passing through Unit. Sick 23 Wounded 21 Establish a Walking Wounded Collecting Post at Q.29.d.3.9. Sheet 62 C. | A.D.S |

C O N F I D E N T I A L.

WAR DIARY

of

No.141 Field Ambulance.

From 1st October 1918    to    31st October 1918.

(Volume No.28.)

Army Form C. 2118.

# WAR DIARY
## or
## INTELLIGENCE SUMMARY.
*(Erase heading not required.)*

Instructions regarding War Diaries and Intelligence Summaries are contained in F. S. Regs., Part II. and the Staff Manual respectively. Title pages will be prepared in manuscript.

| Place | Date | Hour | Summary of Events and Information | Remarks and references to Appendices |
|---|---|---|---|---|
| ESTREES en CHAUSSEE | Sept 1918. 15th | | Casualties passing through Unit. Sick 46 Wounded.180 1 Tent Sub division from No.1 Field Ambulance and 1 Tent Sub division from No.2 Field Ambce joined the Unit for temporary duty. The following casualties in personnel occurred on this date:- | |
| | | | No.68562 Pte A.H.Gould., R.A.M.C. G.S.W. Rt Thigh and Left Foot. Died in No.41 C.C.S. | A.D.S. |
| | | | No.55478 Pte A.Bonell., R.A.M.C. G.S.W.Back(perforating) Evacuated to C.C.S. | |
| | | | No.90138 Pte J.Gunn., R.A.M.C. G.S.W. Lt Thigh. Evacuated to C.C.S. | |
| | | | No.35791 Cpl A.F.Davies., M.M.,R.A.M.C. G.S.W. Hands. Evacuated to C.C.S. | |
| | | | No.1062200 Pte S.R.Ashton., R.A.M.C. G.S.W. Face. Remained at duty. | |
| | | | No.43684 Pte W.Milne., R.A.M.C. joined the Unit for duty from 8th Railway Coy. | A.D.S. |
| | | | No.T4/071857 Farr Cpl B.Bennett., A.S.C."H.T" joined the Unit for duty from 1st Divisional Train. | |
| | 16th | | Casualties passing through Unit. Sick 38 Wounded 27 | A.D.S. |
| | 17th | | Casualties passing through Unit. Sick 40 Wounded 115 Hand over A.D.Station at VERMAND and Relay Posts to No.1 and 2 Field Ambulances. Captain J.T.KIRKLAND., M.C., R.A.M.C. proceeded to assume temporary medical charge of the 1st Glosters. | A.D.S. |
| | 18th | | Casualties passing through Unit. Sick 35 Wounded 79 No.46236 Pte A.CARSON., R.A.M.C. joined the Unit for duty from Office of D.D.M.S., IX Corps. Captain J.T.KIRKLAND., M.C., R.A.M.C. tempy attached to 1st Glosters was killed in action. | A.D.S. |
| | 19th | | Casualties passing through Unit. Sick 39 Wounded 1041 | A.D.S. |
| | 20th | | Casualties passing through Unit. Sick 40 Wounded 340 Divisional Main Dressing Station is formed into a Corps Main Dressing Station. 2 Officers and 46 Other Ranks join the Unit for temporary duty from No.17 Field Ambulance. 2 Officers and 46 Other Ranks join the Unit for temporary duty from 1/1 N.Mid.Field Ambce. 1 Officer and 30 O.Ranks join the Unit for temporary duty from No.90 Field Ambulance. Central Bureau for the recording the casualties of the IX Corps is formed at this Unit. | A.D.S. |

Army Form C. 2118.

# WAR DIARY
## or
## INTELLIGENCE SUMMARY.
*(Erase heading not required.)*

Instructions regarding War Diaries and Intelligence Summaries are contained in F.S. Regs., Part II. and the Staff Manual respectively. Title pages will be prepared in manuscript.

| Place | Date Septr 1918 | Hour | Summary of Events and Information | Remarks and references to Appendices |
|---|---|---|---|---|
| ESTREES en CHAUSSEE | 21st | | Casualties recorded by the Central Bureau..... Sick 111. Wounded 161. | 1.D.P. |
| | 22nd | | Casualties recorded by the Central Bureau. Sick 57. Wounded 95. Major C.C.Forsyth., M.C. R.A.M.C. in charge of Bearer Division proceeded to report to 3rd Brigade for duty. | 1.D.P. |
| | 23rd | | Casualties recorded by the Central Bureau. Sick 162. Wounded 230. | 1.D.P. |
| | 24th | | Close down the Main Dressing Station at ESTREES en CHAUSSEE at 4 a.m. and open at the same hour at POEUILLY (Map Refce Q.28.d.8.2. Sheet 62 C). Captain F.E.L.Phillips., R.A.M.C. proceeded from Unit to assume temporary medical charge of the 1st Northants Regt. The following casualties in personnel of Unit occurred on this date:- No.463038 Cpl B.J.Teague., R.A.M.C. GSW (Shell) Lt Arm. Evacuated to C.C.Stn. 57716 Pte F.Bastier., R.A.M.C. Killed in action. 58751 Cpl J.McTurk., M.M., R.A.M.C. GSW(Shell) Head, Neck, Back & Legs. Evac to C.C.Stn. Casualties recorded by the Central Bureau. Sick 123. Wounded 1225. | 1.D.P. |
| POEUILLY. | 25th | | Casualties recorded by the Central Bureau. Sick 134. Wounded 257. | 1.D.P. |
| | 26th | | Casualties recorded by the Central Bureau. Sick 133. Wounded 143. | 1.D.P. |
| | 27th. | | Casualties recorded by the Central Bureau. Sick 126. Wounded 127. | 1.D.P. |
| | 28th | | Casualties recorded by the Central Bureau. Sick 161. Wounded 240. Capt A.G.T.Fisher., M.C., R.A.M.C. joined the Unit for duty. Capt F.E.L.Phillips., R.A.M.C. was posted to medical charge of the 1st Northants Regt. | 1.D.P. |
| | 29th | | Casualties recorded by the Central Bureau. Sick 128. Wounded 1398. | 1.D.P. |
| | 30th | | Casualties recorded by the Central Bureau. Sick 93 Wounded 610 Capt.R.Power., A.A.M.C. and Capt F.G.Power. A.A.M.C. joined the Unit for duty. | 1.D.P. |

L.D.Parr Lieut-Col R.A.M.C.
O.Commanding 141st Field Ambulance.

## 141st FIELD AMBULANCE.

Numbers by Regiments of wounded German Prisoners of War recorded by the Central Bureau during September 1918.

| Regiment. | Number of Prisoners. | Regiment. | Number of Prisoners. |
|---|---|---|---|
| 228. R.I.R. | 1 | 62 Infantry | 1 |
| 71. Infantry. | 1 | 262 do | 31 |
| 270 do | 3 | 263 do | 34 |
| 51 R.I.R. | 25 | 236 do | 1 |
| 40 R.I.R. | 1 | 261 do | 53 |
| 404 Infantry | 1 | 46 R.I.R. | 30 |
| 24 do | 1 | 50 do | 1 |
| 168 R.I.R. | 1 | 58 do | 4 |
| 10 Grenadiers. | 15 | 83 do | 3 |
| 4 do | 28 | 64 Infantry | 2 |
| 456 Infantry | 3 | 168 do | 2 |
| 33 do | 49 | 226 R.I.R. | 2 |
| 12 do | 1 | 13 do | 12 |
| 7 Jaeger | 2 | 27 do | 2 |
| 2 Guard Reserve | 10 | 273 Infantry | 23 |
| 91 Infantry | 1 | 31 Minenwerfer Coy. | 1 |
| 28 do | 10 | 682 Battery Fd Arty. | 1 |
| 14 Jaeger | 1 | 237 Regt Fd Arty. | 1 |
| 25 do | 3 | 20 Regt Active Arty. | 2 |
| 86 Infantry | 1 | Field Arty R.17. | 1 |
| 35 do | 1 | lllrd Abteelung Arty | 1 |
| 252 R.I.R. | 1 | 63 Res. Arty | 1 |
| 249 do | 3 | 279 Minenwerfer Coy. | 1 |
| 373 Infantry | 5 | Res. Pion.Regt. | 81 |
| 1 Grenadiers | 1 | 1 Pioneer Btn | 1 |
| 43 Infantry | 1 | 24 do Regt | 1 |
| 44 Jaeger | 27 | Artillery 4th Btty. | 1 |
| 363 Infantry | 1 | do 1st Regt. | 2 |
| 118 do | 4 | do 90th Btty | 2 |
| 77 Res Inf Regt | 1 | 12 Ers.Btn Fuss.Arty. | 1 |
| 1 Guards Reserve | 1 | 42 Field Artillery. | 1 |
|  |  | Unknown. | 9 |

*L. J. Poot*
Lieut-Col R.A.M.C.
O. Commanding 141st Field Ambulance.

Army Form C. 2118.

# WAR DIARY
## or
## INTELLIGENCE SUMMARY.
*(Erase heading not required.)*

Instructions regarding War Diaries and Intelligence Summaries are contained in F.S. Regs., Part II. and the Staff Manual respectively. Title pages will be prepared in manuscript.

| Place | Date OCTOBER 1918. | Hour | Summary of Events and Information | Remarks and references to Appendices |
|---|---|---|---|---|
| POEUILLY | 1st | | Casualties recorded by the Central Bureau. Sick 129. Wounded 426. | 19P |
| | 2nd | | Casualties recorded by the Central Bureau. Sick 165. Wounded 540. Capt T.CLAPPERTON., R.A.M.C. took over the duties of O.C. Bearers from Major C.C.FORSYTH., M.C. R.A.M.C. who proceeded to the U.K. on leave. Capt A.FISHER., M.C., R.A.M.C. took over the duties of Bearer Officer from Capt CLAPPERTON. Close down the Corps Main Dressing Station at POEUILLY at 0900 and open out at VADENCOURT (Map Refce. R.11.c.1.5. Sheet 62 c) at the same hour. | 19P |
| VADENCOURT. | 3rd | | IX Corps attack on MONTBREHAIN and SEQUEHART. Casualties recorded by the Central Bureau. Sick 194. Wounded 1463. | 19P |
| | 4th | | Casualties recorded by the Central Bureau. Sick 132. Wounded 399. Capt R.POWER., A.A.M.C. took over the duties of Bearer Officer from Capt A.FISHER., M.C., R.A.M.C. who on relief proceeded to report to No.2 Field Ambulance for duty. | 19P |
| | 5th | | Casualties recorded by the Central Bureau. Sick 117. Wounded 148. No.76515 Pte F.M.Young., R.A.M.C. and No. 66959 Pte J.E.Johnson., R.A.M.C. joined the Unit for duty. | 19P |
| | 6th | | Casualties recorded by the Central Bureau. Sick 83. Wounded 156 Capt F. POWER., A.A.M.C. took over the duties of Bearer Officer from Capt R.POWER., A.A.M.C. who on relief proceeded to report to 1st S.W.Borderers for temporary medical duty. | 19P |
| | 7th | | Casualties recorded by the Central Bureau. Sick 109. Wounded 115. | 19P |
| | 8th | | Casualties recorded by the Central Bureau. Sick 129. Wounded 873. | 19P |
| | 9th | | Casualties recorded by the Central Bureau. Sick 110. Wounded 102. | 19P |
| | 10th | | Close down the Corps M.D.Stn at VADENCOURT at 0800 and open out at the same hour at MAGNY la FOSSE (Map Refce H.19 c.9.0. Sheet 62 B) Casualties recorded by the Central Bureau. Sick 75 Wounded 92. No.46938 Pte S.MASON., R.A.M.C. joined the Unit for duty. | 19P |

2353 Wt. W2544/1454 700,000 5/15 D.D. & L. A.D.S.S./Forms/C. 2118.

Army Form C. 2118.

# WAR DIARY
## or
## INTELLIGENCE SUMMARY.
(Erase heading not required.)

Instructions regarding War Diaries and Intelligence Summaries are contained in F.S. Regs., Part II. and the Staff Manual respectively. Title pages will be prepared in manuscript.

| Place | Date October 1918. | Hour | Summary of Events and Information | Remarks and references to Appendices |
|---|---|---|---|---|
| MAGNY la FOSSE | 11th | | Casualties recorded by the Central Bureau. Sick 85. Wounded 165. | 126 |
| | 12th | | Casualties recorded by the Central Bureau. Sick 126. Wounded 135. | 127 |
| | 13th | | Casualties recorded by the Central Bureau. Sick 122. Wounded 21. No.52577 Cpl J.W.Crane., and No.510036 Cpl D.J.Hutchinson., R.A.M.C. joined the Unit for duty. The undermentioned men of this Unit were awarded the MILITARY MEDAL. No.57664 Pte M.W.Bell., R.A.M.C. 57950 Pte R.Elliott. do 5591 Pte B.Price. do 1876 Pte F.M.Elliott. do | 128 |
| | 14th | | Casualties recorded by the Central Bureau. Sick 128. Wounded 25. No.52262 L&c Cpl N.FRANKS., R.A.M.C. rejoined the Unit from temporary duty with the 54th Battery R.F.A. | 129 |
| | 15th | | Casualties recorded by the Central Bureau. Sick 152. Wounded 89. | 128 |
| | 16th | | Casualties recorded by the Central Bureau. Sick 133 Wounded 82 | 129 |
| | 17th | | Casualties recorded by the Central Bureau. Sick 97. Wounded 1138. | 130 |
| | 18th | | Casualties recorded by the Central Bureau. Sick 127. Wounded 270. Close down the Corps M.D.Station at MAGNY-la-FOSSE at 1400 hours and open up at the Civil Hospital, BOHAIN (D.22.a.6.1. Sheet 62 B) at the same hour. No.65923 Private W.PAGE., R.A.M.C. was wounded by Shell Fire. (G.S.W. Left Foot) | 109 |
| BOHAIN | 19th | | Casualties recorded by the Central Bureau. Sick 107. Wounded 89. | 108 |
| | 20th | | Casualties recorded by the Central Bureau. Sick 237. Wounded 173. No.59043 Private S.J.Ashton., R.A.M.C. was wounded by Shell Fire. (G.S.W. Rt Arm) | 129 |

#353 Wt W2544/1454 700,000 5/15 D.D.& L. A.D.S.S./Forms/C. 2118.

Army Form C. 2118.

# WAR DIARY
## or
## INTELLIGENCE SUMMARY.
*(Erase heading not required.)*

Instructions regarding War Diaries and Intelligence Summaries are contained in F. S. Regs., Part II. and the Staff Manual respectively. Title pages will be prepared in manuscript.

| Place | Date October 1918. | Hour | Summary of Events and Information | Remarks and references to Appendices |
|---|---|---|---|---|
| BOHAIB. | 21st | | Casualties recorded by the Central Bureau. Sick 262. Wounded 199. No.76115 Pte F.M.YOUNG., R.A.M.C. was wounded by Shell Fire (G.S.W. Lt Thigh). | K2P |
| | 22nd | | Casualties recorded by the Central Bureau. Sick 262. Wounded 317. | K32 |
| | 23rd | | Casualties recorded by the Central Bureau. Sick 244. Wounded 621. Major C.C.FORSYTH., M.C. re-assumed command of the Bearers on his return from the U.K. off leave. | K2P |
| | | | | K2P |
| | 24th | | Casualties recorded by the Central Bureau. Sick 228. Wounded 131. | K2P |
| | 25th | | Casualties recorded by the Central Bureau. Sick 274. Wounded 120. | K2P |
| | 26th | | Casualties recorded by the Central Bureau. Sick 534. Wounded 80. | K2P |
| | 27th | | Casualties recorded by the Central Bureau. Sick 307. Wounded 87. | K2P |
| | 28th | | Casualties recorded by the Central Bureau. Sick 322. Wounded 63. | K2P |
| | 29th | | Casualties recorded by the Central Bureau. Sick 337. Wounded 97. | K2P |
| | 30th | | Casualties recorded by the Central Bureau. Sick 294. Wounded 106. | K2P |
| | 31st | | Casualties recorded by the Central Bureau. Sick 256 Wounded 46 No.58870 Pte G.Wood., R.A.M.C. was wounded by Shell Fire(G.S.W. Leg & Foot Rt) No.T.1.S.R./396 Coy Sgt Major T.W.TYTLER., A.S.C."HT" joined the Unit for duty. | K2P |

L.O. Post. Lieut-Colonel.
Officer Commanding 141st Field Ambulance.

C O N F I D E N T I A L.

WAR DIARY

of

141st. Field Ambulance.

From 1st. November 1918 to 30th. November 1918.

(Volume No. 29)

Army Form C. 2118.

# WAR DIARY
## or
## INTELLIGENCE SUMMARY.
(Erase heading not required.)

Instructions regarding War Diaries and Intelligence Summaries are contained in F. S. Regs., Part II. and the Staff Manual respectively. Title pages will be prepared in manuscript.

| Place | Date | Hour | Summary of Events and Information | Remarks and references to Appendices |
|---|---|---|---|---|
| BOHAIN | NOVEMBER 1918. 1st | | Casualties recorded by the Central Bureau. Sick 258. Wounded 46. No.2852 Private P.BEDFORD., R.A.M.C. was wounded by shell fire. G.S.W. Forehead (slight) and remained at duty. Captain T.CLAPPERTON., R.A.M.C. was awarded the MILITARY CROSS. | A.R.O. |
| | 2nd | | Casualties recorded by the Central Bureau. Sick 324. Wounded 65. | A.R.O. |
| | 3rd | | Casualties recorded by the Central Bureau. Sick 276. Wounded 134. | A.R.O. |
| | 4th | | Casualties recorded by the Central Bureau. Sick 257. Wounded 801. No.90332 Private H.G.MUNRO., R.A.M.C. was wounded by shell fire G.S.W. Thigh Lt (slight) and remained at duty. | A.R.O. |
| | 5th | | Casualties recorded by the Central Bureau. Sick 396. Wounded 166. Close down the Corps Main Dressing Station at BOHAIN at 1000 hours and open out at the same hour at Q.35. d. Sheet 57 B. Captains R.POWER and F.G.POWER, A.A.M.C. proceeded from Unit to report to the Administrative Head Qrs, Australian Imperial Force, LONDON. | A.R.O. |
| | 6th | Q.35 d. | Casualties recorded by the Central Bureau. Sick 219. Wounded 91. | A.R.O. |
| | 7th | | Casualties recorded by the Central Bureau. Sick 230. Wounded 87. | A.R.O. |
| | 8th | | Casualties recorded by the Central Bureau. Sick 145. Wounded 56. | A.R.O. |
| | 9th | | Casualties recorded by the Central Bureau. Sick 137. Wounded 26. The Corps Resuscitation Team with the necessary equipment moves to CARTIGNIES and is established there in the Girls School at O.11 b.1.3. Sheet 57 A. The Central Bureau moves to the Corps Walking Wounded Station at CATILLON (Map Refce R.23 b.1.8. Sheet 57 B) | A.R.O. |
| | 10th. | | Casualties recorded by the Central Bureau. Sick.141 Wounded.9 | A.R.O. |

Army Form C. 2118.

# WAR DIARY
## or
## INTELLIGENCE SUMMARY.
*(Erase heading not required.)*

Instructions regarding War Diaries and Intelligence Summaries are contained in F.S. Regs., Part II. and the Staff Manual respectively. Title pages will be prepared in manuscript.

| Place | Date Nov.1918. | Hour | Summary of Events and Information | Remarks and references to Appendices |
|---|---|---|---|---|
| Q 35.d. Sheet 57b. | 11th. | | Casualties recorded by the Central Bureau. Sick 215 Wounded.4 44736 Pte.T.M.SMITHSON, RAMC evacuated sick to C.C.S. | AO |
| | 12th. | | Casualties recorded by the Central Bureau. Sick 207 Wounded.7 T31755 Cpl./a/Sgt.T.H.RAWLINSON, A.S.C. joins Unit for duty from 1st.Div.Train. | AO |
| | 13th. | | Casualties recorded by the Central Bureau. Sick 225 Wounded.Nil. Lt.Col.L.T.POOLE, D.S.O., M.C., R.A.M.C. proceeds to the United Kingdom on Leave granted from 15/11/18 to 15/12/18., and the Command of the Ambulance devolves on Major C.L.CHALK, M.C, R.A.M.C. The Stores at the Corps Main Dressing Station are handed over to O.C. 44 M.A.C. at LA GROISE M 22 a.2.6. Sheet 57 b. | AO |
| BAZUEL. R.8.b. Sheet 57b. | 14th. | | Casualties recorded by the Central Bureau. Sick 312 Wounded.Nil. Unit moves from Q 35.d. to BAZUEL, by march route, to rejoin the 3rd.Infantry Brigade Group. Horse Transport accompanies the Unit. The following personnel, who were attached to this Unit, are left at the C.M.D.S.Site Q 35 d. preparatory to rejoining their units :- 1 Officer & 11 Other Ranks 1/1 N.Mid.Field Ambce. 1 Officer & 11 Other Ranks 1/2 N.Mid.Field Ambce. 1 Officer & 10 Other Ranks 1/3 N.Mid.Field Ambce. 6 N.C.Os. and 52 Men 17th.Field Ambulance. 1 N.C.O. and 6 Men. 16th.Field Ambulance. 14 Other Ranks, No.2 Field Ambulance proceed to rejoin their Unit from temporary duty with this Unit. 5393 Pte.J.T.ALLCOCK, RAMC evacuated sick to C.C.S. The undermentioned has been awarded the Medal for Long Service and Good Conduct under A.O.305 of 1918.:- Lt. and Qr.S.M.GAWTHORNE, R.A.M.C. T/4270 Sgt.E.J.WATTS, A.S.C. HT. is appointed a/C.S.M. (W.O.Cl.2) 2.11.18 to complete establishment of No.1 Field Ambulance. Assumed duties with pay 10.11.18.CSM WATTS joined No.1 Field Ambulance on 11/11/18. | AO |

Army Form C. 2118.

# WAR DIARY
## or
## INTELLIGENCE SUMMARY.

*(Erase heading not required.)*

Instructions regarding War Diaries and Intelligence Summaries are contained in F. S. Regs., Part II and the Staff Manual respectively. Title pages will be prepared in manuscript.

| Place | Date | Hour | Summary of Events and Information | Remarks and references to Appendices |
|---|---|---|---|---|
| | November 18 | | | |
| | 15th. | | Casualties recorded by the Central Bureau. Sick Nil. Wounded. Nil. Ambulance moves by march route to MARBAIX, I 16.d.8.8. Sheet 57 a. Horse Transport accompanying. Central Bureau at the SUCRERIE, CATILLON, closes down at 1200. | |
| MARBAIX I 16.d.8.8. Sheet 57a.. | 16th. | | Casualties admitted by Unit. NIL. Ambulance moves by march route to SARS POTERIES, F 19.d.8.2. Sheet 57 a., transport accompanying. The undermentioned reinforcements joined the Unit for duty from R.A.M.C. Base Depot :- <br> 82059 Pte.G.H.Riley, RAMC    100432 Pte.P.H.Warren, RAMC <br> 143433 Pte.T.Wilkinson, RAMC    155447 Pte.Heggerty, G.,RAMC <br> 136525 Pte.S.Smith, RAMC <br> 15 Other Ranks, No.1 Field Ambulance proceed to rejoin that Unit from temporary duty with this Unit. | |
| SARS POTERIES F 19.d.8.2. Sheet 57a.. | 17th. | | Casualties admitted by Unit. NIL. | |
| | 18th. | | Casualties admitted by Unit. NIL. Unit moves by march route to BEAUMONT, C 4.80.80. Sheet NAMUR 1/100,000. Horse Transport accompanying. The undermentioned Officers are posted to this Unit for duty : <br> Capt.J.F.C.HASLAM, M.C., R.A.M.C.    Capt.L.G.FERGUSON, R.A.M.C. | |
| BEAUMONT. C 4.80.80. NAMUR 1:100000 | 19th. | | Casualties admitted by Unit. NIL. Unit moves by march route to WALCOURT, F.4. NAMUR 1:100000, Transport accompanying. T 259792 Dr.A.J.GRAY, A.S.C. HT. evacuated sick, to C.C.S. Under authority delegated by His Majesty the King, the Corps Commander has awarded the Military Medal to :- <br> M2/022059 Pte.G.R.LESTER, A.S.C. MT. attached 141st.Field Ambulance. <br> (Authority: IX Corps No.H.R./704 dated 15:11:18.) | |
| WALCOURT. F.4. NAMUR 1:100000 | 20th. | | Casualties admitted by the Unit. NIL. 1 N.C.O. and 18 Men R.A.M.C. proceed to No.1 Field Ambulance for temporary duty. The undermentioned men are evacuated sick, to C.C.S. <br> 143433 Pte.T.WILKINSON, R.A.M.C.    53898 Pte.J.H.BIRKETT, R.A.M.C. | |

Army Form C. 2118.

# WAR DIARY
## or
## INTELLIGENCE SUMMARY.
*(Erase heading not required.)*

Instructions regarding War Diaries and Intelligence Summaries are contained in F.S. Regs., Part II. and the Staff Manual respectively. Title pages will be prepared in manuscript.

| Place | Date November 1918. | Hour | Summary of Events and Information | Remarks and references to Appendices |
|---|---|---|---|---|
| WALCOURT. F 4. Namur 1/100000 | 21st. | | Casualties admitted by Unit. Sick. Nil. Wounded Nil. 519036 Cpl.D.J.HUTCHINSON, R.A.M.C. evacuated sick, to C.C.S. Captain T.CLAPPERTON, M.C., R.A.M.C. having been ordered to report to the W.O. for early release, is struck off the strength of this Unit. | |
| | 22nd. | | Casualties admitted by Unit. Sick Nil. Wounded Nil. | |
| | 23rd. | | Casualties admitted by Unit. Sick Nil. Wounded Nil. Unit moves by march route to FLORENNES, 3 H, 2504 Sheet NAMUR 8, 1/100000, Horse transport accompanying. | |
| FLORENNES. 3 H 25.04. | 24th. | | Casualties admitted by Unit. Sick. Nil. Wounded Nil. | |
| | 25th. | | Casualties admitted by Unit. Sick Nil. Wounded Nil. | |
| | 26th. | | Casualties admitted by Unit. Sick Nil. Wounded Nil. | |
| | 27th. | | Casualties admitted by Unit. Sick. Nil. Wounded Nil. | |
| | 28th. | | Casualties admitted by Unit. Sick Nil. Wounded Nil. | |
| | 29th. | | Casualties admitted by Unit. Sick Nil. Wounded Nil. | |
| | 30th. | | Casualties admitted by Unit. Sick Nil. Wounded Nil. No.9502 Pte.J.W.Dykes, M.M., R.A.M.C. evacuated, sick, to C.C.S. | |

Major
a/O.C. 141st FIELD AMBULANCE R.A.M.C.

CONFIDENTIAL.

WAR DIARY

of

141st FIELD AMBULANCE.

From 1st December 1918 to 31st DECEMBER 1918.

( Volume No. 30 )

Army Form C. 2118.

# WAR DIARY
## or
## INTELLIGENCE SUMMARY.
*(Erase heading not required.)*

Instructions regarding War Diaries and Intelligence Summaries are contained in F. S. Regs., Part II. and the Staff Manual respectively. Title pages will be prepared in manuscript.

| Place | Date Decr 1918 | Hour | Summary of Events and Information | Remarks and references to Appendices |
|---|---|---|---|---|
| | 1st | | Casualties admitted to Unit............ N I L Unit moves by march route to CORENNES. Map Refce 3 I. 18.03. Sheet Namur 1/100000. Horse Transport accompanying. | A.P. |
| CORENNES | 2nd | | Casualties admitted to Unit............ N I L. Unit moves by march route to WEILLEN. Map Refce 3 J. 95.12. Sheet Namur 1/100000. Horse Transport accompanying. No.463009 L.Sgt (Act Sgt) P.L.Brown., R.A.M.C. was evacuated sick to Cas. Clearing Stn. | A.P. |
| WEILLEN | 3rd | | Casualties admitted to Unit............ N I L. Unit moves by march route to BOISEILLES. Map Refce 4 L.90.86. Sheet Namur 1/100000. Horse Transport accompanying. | A.P. |
| BOISEILLES | 4th | | Casualties admitted to Unit............ N I L. | A.P. |
| | 5th | | Casualties admitted to Unit............ N I L. | A.P. |
| | 6th | | Casualties admitted to unit............ N I L. | A.P. |
| | 7th | | Casualties admitted to Unit............ N I L. | A.P. |
| | 8th | | Casualties admitted to Unit............ N I L. No.5591 Private B.H.Price., R.A.M.C. proceeded to Transportation Troops Base Depot for duty and is accordingly taken off the strength of this unit. | A.P. |
| | 9th | | Casualties admitted to Unit............ N I L. Unit moves by march route to CHEVETOGNE ABBEY 4 D.59.65. Sheet Marche 9. 1/100,000. Horse Transport accompanying. | A.P. |
| CHEVETOGNE ABBEY. | 10th | | Casualties admitted to Unit............ N I L. Unit moves by march route to BAILLONVILLE, 3 E. 05.42. Marche 9. | A.P. |
| BAILLONVILLE | 11th | | Casualties admitted to unit............ N I L. Unit moves by march route to DEULIN. Map Refce 5 E.30.29. Sheet Marche 9. Horse Transport accompanying. | A.P. |

A 583+ Wt.W4973/M687 750,000 8/16 D.D.&L.Ltd. Forms/C.2118/13.

Army Form C. 2118.

# WAR DIARY
## or
## INTELLIGENCE SUMMARY.
(Erase heading not required.)

Instructions regarding War Diaries and Intelligence Summaries are contained in F. S. Regs., Part II. and the Staff Manual respectively. Title pages will be prepared in manuscript.

| Place | Date December 1918. | Hour | Summary of Events and Information | Remarks and references to Appendices |
|---|---|---|---|---|
| DEULIN. | 12th | | Casualties admitted to Unit......... N I L. | A.28. |
| | 13th | | Casualties admitted to Unit......... N I L. No.59801 Pte C.E.Greenwood., R.A.M.C. was evacuated sick to C.C.Stn. | A.28. |
| | 14th | | Casualties admitted to Unit......... N I L. Unit moves by march route to SADZOT. Map Refce 2 H.15.41. Sheet Marche 9. Horse Transport accompanying. | A.28. |
| SADZOT. | 15th | | Casualties admitted to Unit......... N I L. Unit moves by march route to VAUX CHAVANNE. 3 I.37.64. Sheet Marche 9. Horse Transport accompanying. | A.28. |
| VAUX CHAVANNE | 16th | | Casualties admitted to Unit......... N I L. Unit moves by march route to BIHAIN Map Refce 4 J.70.81. Sheet Marche 9. Horse Transport accompanying. | A.28. |
| BIHAIN. | 17th | | Casualties admitted to Unit......... N I L. Unit moves by march route to HONVELEZ 7 B.24.42.Sheet Germany 1 M. Horse Transport accompanying. | A.28. |
| HONVELEZ | 18th | | Casualties admitted to Unit......... N I L. Unit moves by march route to MALDINGEN. 7 D.04.39. Sheet Germany 1 M. Horse Transport accompanying. No.47810 Sergt H.G.Scorer., M.M. R.A.M.C. was evacuated sick to C.C.Stn. Captain J.F.C.Haslam., M.C., R.A.M.C. proceeded to report to the D.D.M.S. ROUEN for duty. | A.28. |
| MALDINGEN. | 19th | | Casualties admitted to Unit......... N I L. Unit moves by march route to SCHONBERG. Map Refce 5 G.40.04. Sheet Germany 1 M. Horse Transport accompanying. | A.28. |
| SCHONBERG. | 20th | | Casualties admitted to Unit......... N I L. | A.28. |

Army Form C. 2118.

# WAR DIARY
## or
## INTELLIGENCE SUMMARY.
*(Erase heading not required.)*

Instructions regarding War Diaries and Intelligence Summaries are contained in F. S. Regs., Part II. and the Staff Manual respectively. Title pages will be prepared in manuscript.

| Place | Date Decr 1918 | Hour | Summary of Events and Information | Remarks and references to Appendices |
|---|---|---|---|---|
| SCHONBERG. | 21st | | Casualties admitted to Unit........ N I L.<br>Unit moves by march route to BAASEM. Map Refce 3 J.70.02. Sheet Germany 1 M. Horse Transport accompanying. | L2P |
| BAASEM. | 22nd | | Casualties admitted to Unit........ N I L.<br>Unit moves to SCHMIDTHEIM. 2 K.69.09. Sheet Germany 1 M. Horse Transport accompanying. | L2P |
| SCHMIDTHEIM. | 23rd. | | Casualties admitted to Unit........ N I L.<br>Unit moves to EICHERSCHEID. Map Refce 11 H.78.14. Sheet Germany 1 L. Horse Transport accompanying. | L2P |
| EICHERSCHEID. | 24th | | Casualties admitted to Unit........ N I L.<br>Unit moves to ODENDORF. Map Refce 9 A.62.47. Sheet Germany 2 L. Horse Transport accompanying. | L2P |
| ODENDORF. | 25th | | Casualties admitted to Unit........ Sick 5. | L2P |
| | 26th | | Casualties admitted to Unit........ Sick 5. | L2P |
| | 27th | | Casualties admitted to Unit........ Sick 8. | L2P |
| | 28th | | Casualties admitted to Unit........ Sick 15. | L2P |
| | 29th | | Casualties admitted to Unit........ Sick 5.<br>1st Lieut T.A.PITTS., M.O.R.C. is posted to this Unit for duty. | L2P |
| | 30th | | Casualties admitted to Unit........ Sick 21.<br>Lieut T.A.PITTS., M.O.R.C. proceeded to report to Office of D.D.M.S., IX Corps for temporary duty.<br>No.68875 Cpl H. Storry., R.A.M.C. joined the unit for duty. | L2P |
| | 31st | | Casualties admitted to Unit........ Sick 5. | L2P |

L.J.Job.
Lieut-Colonel.
Commanding 141st Field Ambulance.

BEF
1 DIV TROOPS

141 FLD AMB

1919 JAN TO 1919 JUNE

Box 926

CONFIDENTIAL,

WAR DIARY

of

141st FIELD AMBULANCE.

From 1st January 1919 To 31st January 1919.

(Volume No.31.)

Army Form C. 2118.

# WAR DIARY
## or
## INTELLIGENCE SUMMARY.
(Erase heading not required.)

Instructions regarding War Diaries and Intelligence Summaries are contained in F.S. Regs., Part II and the Staff Manual respectively. Title pages will be prepared in manuscript.

| Place | Date | Hour | Summary of Events and Information | Remarks and references to Appendices |
|---|---|---|---|---|
| | January 1919. | | | |
| ODENDORF. | 1st | | Casualties admitted to Unit...... Sick 14 | |
| | 2nd | | Casualties admitted to Unit...... Sick 8 Unit moves to RHEINBACH by march route and opens up as the Divisional Sick Station at the Convent, sufficient personnel being left behind to staff the Hospital at ODENDORF which remains open for the reception of slight cases from the 3rd Brigade Group, 1st Divisional Artillery and 1st Divisional Engineers. | |
| RHEINBACH. | 3rd | | Casualties admitted to Unit...... Sick 10 | |
| | 4th | | Casualties admitted to Unit...... Sick 6 | |
| | 5th | | Casualties admitted to Unit...... Sick 12 | |
| | 6th | | Casualties admitted to Unit...... Sick 11 | |
| | 7th | | Casualties admitted to Unit...... Sick 19 | |
| | 8th | | Casualties admitted to Unit...... Sick 22 No.T-21508 Act Staff Sgt Major H.W.Flackfield., A.S.C. "HT" joined the Unit for duty. | |
| | 9th | | Casualties admitted to Unit...... Sick 29 No.T1.S.R/596 Coy Sergt Major T.W.Tytler., A.S.C. "HT" proceeded from the Unit to report to 35th Divisional Train for duty. | |
| | 10th | | Casualties admitted to unit...... Sick 2 | |
| | 11th | | Casualties admitted to Unit...... Sick 27 | |
| | 12th | | Casualties admitted to Unit...... Sick 3 A dispersal draft consisting of 16 Other Ranks R.A.M.C. proceeded from this Unit to report to the Second Army Concentration Camp. | |

Army Form C. 2118.

# WAR DIARY
## or
## INTELLIGENCE SUMMARY.
*(Erase heading not required.)*

Instructions regarding War Diaries and Intelligence Summaries are contained in F.S. Regs., Part II and the Staff Manual respectively. Title pages will be prepared in manuscript.

| Place | Date January 1919 | Hour | Summary of Events and Information | Remarks and references to Appendices |
|---|---|---|---|---|
| RHEINBACH | 13th | | Casualties admitted to Unit.... Sick 23. No.463009 Sergt P.L.Brown, R.A.M.C. joined the Unit from R.A.M.C. Base Depot. | |
| | 14th | | Casualties admitted to Unit.... Sick 32. Major C.C.FORSYTH., R.A.M.C. proceeded to report to No.83 General Hospital for transfer to the Michelham Home, CAP MARTIN. | |
| | 15th | | Casualties admitted to Unit.... Sick 24. A dispersal draft consisting of 1 Other Rank R.A.M.C. proceeded from Unit to report to the Second Arey Concentration Camp. | |
| | 16th | | Casualties admitted to Unit.... Sick 8. No.7347 Private A.J.Friend, R.A.M.C. joined the Unit for duty from D.D.M.S., IX Corps. | |
| | 17th | | Casualties admitted to Unit.... Sick 23. | |
| | 18th | | Casualties admitted to Unit.... Sick 7. | |
| | 19th | | Casualties admitted to Unit.... Sick 6. | |
| | 20th | | Casualties admitted to Unit.... Sick 27. | |
| | 21st | | Casualties admitted to Unit.... Sick 3. | |
| | 22nd | | Casualties admitted to Unit.... Sick 9. Captain C.K.CARROLL, M.C. R.A.M.C. is attached to this Unit for duty from this date. | |
| | 23rd | | Casualties admitted to unit.... Sick 23. | |
| | 24th | | Casualties admitted to Unit.... Sick 5. | |

Army Form C. 2118.

# WAR DIARY
## or
## INTELLIGENCE SUMMARY.
*(Erase heading not required.)*

Instructions regarding War Diaries and Intelligence Summaries are contained in F. S. Regs., Part II. and the Staff Manual respectively. Title pages will be prepared in manuscript.

| Place | Date | Hour | Summary of Events and Information | Remarks and references to Appendices |
|---|---|---|---|---|
| | JANUARY. 1919. | | | |
| RHEINBACH | 25th | | Casualties admitted to Unit.... Sick 10. | |
| | 26th | | Casualties admitted to Unit.... Sick 6. Captain J.P.DUNCAN., R.A.M.C. joined the Unit for duty. | |
| | 27th | | Casualties admitted to Unit.... Sick 24. Lt-Col L.T.Poole, D.S.O., M.C., R.A.M.C. proceeded to the Office of A.D.M.S., 1st Div. for temporary duty and during his absence the command of the Field Ambulance devolves on Captain L.C.Ferguson., R.A.M.C. | |
| | 28th | | Casualties admitted to Unit.... Sick 6. | |
| | 29th | | Casualties admitted to Unit.... Sick 11. Captain C.K.Carroll., M.C., R.A.M.C. proceeded to assume temporary medical charge of the 1st D.A.C. | |
| | 30th | | Casualties admitted to Unit.... Sick 12. | |
| | 31st | | Casualties admitted to Unit.... Sick 10. | |

Lionel Curfman Captain R.A.M.C.
a/O.C., 141st Field Ambulance.

Vol 33
140/5524

No. 141st. Field Ambulance.
*********************************

WAR DIARY

for the period 1st. to 28th.

FEBRUARY 1919.

Volume No. 32.

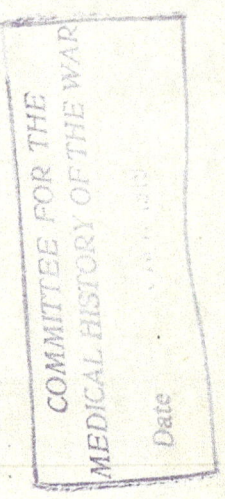

Feb. 1919

Army Form C. 2118.

# WAR DIARY
## or
## INTELLIGENCE SUMMARY.
*(Erase heading not required.)*

Instructions regarding War Diaries and Intelligence Summaries are contained in F. S. Regs., Part II. and the Staff Manual respectively. Title pages will be prepared in manuscript.

| Place | Date 1919. | Hour | Summary of Events and Information | Remarks and references to Appendices |
|---|---|---|---|---|
| RHEINBACH. Germany 2L 9 B. | FEBRUARY 1st. | | Casualties admitted to the Unit. Sick. 8 58080 Pte.J.R.Davies, R.A.M.C. was admitted to Hospital sick, and evacuated to C.C.S. | 128 |
| | 2nd. | | Casualties admitted to the Unit. Sick. 6 The u/m N.C.Os. and Men reported at Dispersal Stations whilst on leave to the U.K. on the dates shown below, and are accordingly struck off the strength of this Unit :- <br>On 11/1/19..... No.52577 Cpl.J.W.Crane, R.A.M.C. <br>On 16/1/19..... No.52262 L/C N.Franks, R.A.M.C. <br>                No.33090 Pte.G.H.Macnaughton, R.A.M.C. <br>On 18/1/19..... No.57947 Pte.J.Wilson, R.A.M.C. <br>                No.29294 Pte.J.Beswick, R.A.M.C. <br>On 21/1/19..... No.57948 Pte.D.D.P.Douglas, R.A.M.C. <br>                No.104349 Pte.J.Cheesman, R.A.M.C. | 128 |
| | 3rd. | | Casualties admitted to the Unit. Sick. 6 | 128 |
| | 4th. | | Casualties admitted to the Unit. Sick. 10 90009 Cpl.E.Grice, R.A.M.C. to be Lance Sergeant with pay from this date. | 128 |
| | 5th. | | Casualties admitted to the Unit. Sick. 9 57996 Qr.Mr.Sgt.T.C.Hill, R.A.M.C. proceeded to Concentration Camp - a draft for demobilization - and is struck off the strength accordingly. Major C.C.FORSYTH, M.C., R.A.M.C. was evacuated, sick, to England on 21/1/19 and is taken off the strength of this Unit. | 128 |
| | 6th. | | Casualties admitted to the Unit. Sick. 24 | 128 |
| | 7th. | | Casualties admitted to the Unit. Sick. 9 | 128 |
| | 8th. | | Casualties admitted to the Unit. Sick. 8 | 128 |
| | 9th. | | Casualties admitted to the Unit. Sick. 17 T1/4346 Dr.T.Grainger, R.A.S.C. HT admitted to Hospital, sick, and evacuated to C.C.S. | 128 |

Army Form C. 2118.

# WAR DIARY
## or
## INTELLIGENCE SUMMARY.
(Erase heading not required.)

Instructions regarding War Diaries and Intelligence Summaries are contained in F. S. Regs., Part II. and the Staff Manual respectively. Title pages will be prepared in manuscript.

| Place | Date 1919. | Hour | Summary of Events and Information | Remarks and references to Appendices |
|---|---|---|---|---|
| RHEINBACH. | 10th. | | Casualties admitted to the Unit. Sick. 27 | |
| | 11th. | | Casualties admitted to the Unit. Sick. 17 | |
| | 12th. | | Captain C.K.CARROLL, M.C., R.A.M.C. rejoined the Unit from temporary duty with 1st.D.A.C. | |
| | | | Casualties admitted to the Unit. Sick. 10 | |
| | | | Major G.L.CHALK, M.C., R.A.M.C. rejoined the Unit off leave to the U.K. and took over temporary command of the Unit. | |
| | | | Captain C.K.CARROLL, M.C., R.A.M.C. proceeded to take over temporary medical charge of the 1st. Bn.Cameron Highlanders. | |
| | | | T 24408 Dr.A.Millar, R.A.S.C. HT was demobilised whilst on leave to the U.K. and is struck off the strength from 12/1/19. | |
| | 13th. | | Casualties passing through Unit. Sick 23 | |
| | 14th. | | Casualties admitted to the Unit. Sick 22 | |
| | | | The undermentioned men were demobilised whilst on leave to the U.K. and are struck off the strength from the dates shown : | |
| | | | 58103 Pte.W.L.McClenaghan, R.A.M.C.   31/1/19. | |
| | | | 58136 Pte.H.C.Butler, R.A.M.C.   3/2/19. | |
| | 15th. | | Casualties admitted to the Unit. Sick 9 | |
| | | | 17421 T/Q.M.S. P.Plume, R.A.M.C. appointed Act.Sergt.Major with effect from 18/1/19. | |
| | | | 58097 Sergt. A.J.Tait, M.M., R.A.M.C. appointed Act.Staff Sergt. with effect from 18/1/19. | |
| | 16th. | | Casualties admitted to the Unit. Sick 6 | |
| | | | Lt-Col.L.T.Poole, D.S.O., M.C., R.A.M.C. rejoined the Unit from temporary duty at 1st.Div.H.Q. and re-assumed command. | |
| | 17th. | | Casualties admitted to the Unit. Sick 10 | |
| | 18th. | | Casualties admitted to the Unit. Sick 22 | |

Army Form C. 2118.

# WAR DIARY
## or
## INTELLIGENCE SUMMARY.
(Erase heading not required.)

Instructions regarding War Diaries and Intelligence Summaries are contained in F. S. Regs., Part II and the Staff Manual respectively. Title pages will be prepared in manuscript.

| Place | Date 1919. | Hour | Summary of Events and Information | Remarks and references to Appendices |
|---|---|---|---|---|
| RHEINBACH GERMANY. | FEBRUARY 19th. | | Casualties admitted to the Unit. Sick 20 | |
| | 20th. | | Casualties admitted to the Unit. Sick 7 58121 L/Cpl.J.J.JONES, R.A.M.C. passed through Dispersal Station in England on 8/2/19 and is accordingly struck off the strength of this unit. The undermentioned sisters reported to the Unit for temporary duty :- Sister E.P.WRIGHT.  A.A.N.S.) From No.3 Aust.C.C.S. Sister J.C.GILES,   A.A.N.S.) Sister C.I.G.Southwell, Q.A.R.) From Sister's Hostel, COLOGNE. Sister P.M.Gill,          Q.A.R.) | |
| | 21st. | | Casualties admitted to the Unit. Sick 6 | |
| | 22nd. | | Casualties admitted to the Unit. Sick 27 | |
| | 23rd. | | Casualties admitted to the Unit. Sick 4 | |
| | 24th. | | Casualties admitted to the Unit. Sick 20 56706 Pte.C.S.GILLINGHAM, R.A.M.C. passed through Dispersal Station in England on 9/1/19 and is accordingly struck off the strength of this Unit. | |
| | 25th. | | Casualties admitted to the Unit. Sick 9 | |
| | 26th. | | Casualties admitted to the Unit. Sick 11 81718 Pte.D.CROSS, R.A.M.C. proceeded to No.5 G.H.Q. School of Chemistry for a Course in Pharmacy. | |
| | 27th. | | Casualties admitted to the Unit. Sick 22 1st.Lieut.L.B.FARRIOR, M.O.R.C., U.S.A., M.C. joined the Unit for duty. Sister E.P.WRIGHT, A.A.N.S. and Sister J.C.GILES, A.A.N.S. proceeded to No.3 Aust.C.C.S. for tempy.duty with this Unit. Staff Nurse J.GALBRAITH, Q.A.R. and Staff Nurse K.CARR, Q.A.R. joined the Unit for tempy.duty. | |

Army Form C. 2118.

# WAR DIARY
## or
## INTELLIGENCE SUMMARY.

*(Erase heading not required.)*

Instructions regarding War Diaries and Intelligence Summaries are contained in F. S. Regs., Part II. and the Staff Manual respectively. Title pages will be prepared in manuscript.

| Place | Date 1919. | Hour | Summary of Events and Information | Remarks and references to Appendices |
|---|---|---|---|---|
| RHEINBACH GERMANY. | FEBRUARY 28th. | | Casualties admitted to the Unit. Sick 5. 51617 Pte.J.J.MULDOON, R.A.M.C. was admitted to Hospital and evacuated to C.C.S. | |

Lieut.Colonel R.A.M.C.
Commanding 141st.Field Ambulance.

141st. Field Ambulance.

War Diary

1st. March 1919 to 31st. March 1919.

Volume No. 33.

17 JUL 1919

Army Form C.2118.

# WAR DIARY
## or
## INTELLIGENCE SUMMARY.
*(Erase heading not required.)*

Instructions regarding War Diaries and Intelligence Summaries are contained in F.S. Regs., Part II. and the Staff Manual respectively. Title pages will be prepared in manuscript.

| Place | Date MARCH 1919. | Hour | Summary of Events and Information | Remarks and references to Appendices |
|---|---|---|---|---|
| RHEINBACH GERMANY. | 1st. | | Casualties admitted to the Unit.  Sick 9. 88135 Pte.(a/L/Cpl) J.P.ROBERTSON, R.A.M.C. appointed Act.Sergt.with pay from 18/1/19. | 28. |
| | 2nd. | | Casualties admitted to the Unit.  Sick 6. Capt.E.FORBES, M.C., R.A.M.C. Medical Officer i/c 1st.Bn.Cameron Highlanders is posted to this Unit for duty from 28/2/19. | 28. |
| | 3rd. | | Casualties admitted to the Unit.  Sick 10. 57544 Pte.J.R.BUTLER, R.A.M.C. appointed Act.L/Cpl.with pay from today's date. | 28. |
| | 4th. | | Casualties admitted to the Unit.  Sick 9. T 260082 Dr.F.J.FITCH, R.A.S.C. HT. admitted to Hospital sick, and evacuated to C.C.S. | 28. |
| | 5th. | | Casualties admitted to the Unit.  Sick 25. 57944 S/Sgt.W.MARLEY, M.M., R.A.M.C. appointed Act.Q.M.S. with pay with effect from 10/2/19. | 28. |
| | 6th. | | Casualties admitted to the Unit.  Sick 6. 57999 Pte.W.G.JACKSON, R.A.M.C. appointed Act.L/Cpl.with pay. 57935 Pte.B.STEVENSON, R.A.M.C. appointed Act.L(Cpl.with pay. | 28. |
| | 7th. | | Casualties admitted to the Unit.  Sick 28. The undermentioned N.C.Os passed through Dispersal Stations whilst on leave to the U.K. and are struck off the strength from the dates shown :  58431 Cpl.(Act L/Sgt) F.Tovey, R.A.M.C.  13/1/19. 58024 Pte.(Act L/Cpl) T.G.Howard, R.A.M.C.  11/1/19. 58195 Pte.(Act.L/Cpl) C.Newman, R.A.M.C.  19/1/19. CMT 2298 Sgt.H.A.PAGE, R.A.S.C. MT proceeded to report to 1st.Div.M.T.Coy. for Demobilization. Lieut T.A.PITTS, M.O.R.C., U.S.A. proceeded to take over Medical Charge of 1st.Bn.Gloucesters. Capt.E.FORBES, M.C., R.A.M.C. proceeded to take over Medical Charge of 1st.Bn.S.Wales Bords. | 28. |

Army Form C. 2118.

# WAR DIARY
## or
## INTELLIGENCE SUMMARY.
*(Erase heading not required.)*

Instructions regarding War Diaries and Intelligence Summaries are contained in F.S. Regs., Part II. and the Staff Manual respectively. Title pages will be prepared in manuscript.

| Place | Date 1919. | Hour | Summary of Events and Information | Remarks and references to Appendices |
|---|---|---|---|---|
| RHEINBACH. GERMANY. | MARCH 8th. | | Casualties admitted the Unit. Sick.7 | A.D.S. |
| | 9th. | | Casualties admitted to the Unit. Sick 5. | A.D.S. |
| | 10th. | | Casualties admitted to the Unit. Sick 8. | A.D.S. |
| | 11th. | | Casualties admitted to the Unit. Sick 16. | A.D.S. |
| | 12th. | | Casualties admitted to the Unit. Sick 11<br>The undermentioned ladies proceeded to the Sisters Hostel, COLOGNE, from temporary duty with this Unit :<br>    Staff Nurse J.GALBRAITH, Q.A.R.<br>    Staff Nurse K.CARR, Q.A.R. | A.D.S. |
| | 13th. | | Casualties admitted to the Unit. Sick 8<br>The undermentioned men were demobilized whilst on leave to the U.K. and are struck off the strength accordingly.<br>54309 Pte.A.Walton.    57724 Pte.A.Adlington.    56990 Pte.E.T.Jardine.<br>105357 Pte.J.A.Beswick.    106220 Pte.S.R.Ashton.    56499 Pte.E.A.Hicks.<br>58116 Pte.E.Williams.    1138 Pte.F.J.Murray.    82059 Pte.G.H.Riley.<br>65291 Pte.A.Ballam.    74277 Pte.A.Bamfield.    58751 Pte.J.Kirkby.<br>90539 Pte.W.Macpherson. | A.D.S. |
| | 14th. | | Casualties admitted to the Unit. Sick 7 | A.D.S. |
| | 15th. | | Casualties admitted to the Unit. Sick 8<br>Capt.L.O.FERGUSON, R.A.M.C. proceeded for demobilization to Concentration Camp, Duren. | A.D.S. |
| | 16th. | | Casualties admitted to the Unit. Sick 8 | A.D.S. |
| | 17th. | | Casualties admitted to the Unit. Sick 4<br>Capt.G.J.FARIE, R.A.M.C. proceeded for demobilization, independently, via Boulogne. | A.D.S. |

Army Form C. 2118.

# WAR DIARY
## or
## INTELLIGENCE SUMMARY.

*(Erase heading not required.)*

Instructions regarding War Diaries and Intelligence Summaries are contained in F.S. Regs., Part II. and the Staff Manual respectively. Title pages will be prepared in manuscript.

| Place | Date 1919. | Hour | Summary of Events and Information | Remarks and references to Appendices |
|---|---|---|---|---|
| RHEINBACH GERMANY. | 18th. | | Casualties admitted to the Unit. Sick 10 | |
| | 19th. | | Casualties admitted to the Unit. Sick 5 Capt.A.WILSON, R.A.M.C. joined the Unit for duty. | |
| | 20th. | | Casualties admitted to the Unit. Sick 10 | |
| | 21st. | | Casualties admitted to the Unit. Sick 8 The undermentioned N.C.O. and men joined the Unit for duty : 1548 Cpl.(T/Sgt) R.J.Paskell. 84786 Pte.F.Hills. 84635 Pte.F.Holmes. 98471 Pte.R.Lord. 79813 Pte.J.N.Moorcock. | |
| | | | The undermentioned officers joined the Unit for duty : Capt.T.L.CRAWHALL, R.A.M.C. (S.R.) Capt.F.CAMERON, R.A.M.C. (S.R.) | |
| | 22nd. | | Casualties admitted to the Unit. Sick 9 | |
| | 23rd. | | Casualties admitted to the Unit. Sick 6 Capt.A.WILSON, R.A.M.C. proceeded to take over medical charge of 25th.Bde.R.F.A. | |
| | 24th. | | Casualties admitted to the Unit. Sick 7 1st.Lieut.L.B.FARRIOR, M.C., M.O.R.C. is struck off the strength of this Unit from 19th.inst. on transfer to the Home Establishment. | |
| | 25th. | | Casualties admitted to the Unit. Sick 4 Major C.L.CHALK, M.C., R.A.M.C. proceeded independently to the U.K. for dispersal. Capt.J.S.LLOYD, R.A.M.C. joined the Unit for duty and proceeded to the Office of the A.D.M.S. Western Division for temporary duty. | |
| | 26th. | | Casualties admitted to the Unit. Sick 4 81111 Pte.J.C.Madden, R.A.M.C. proceeded to Concentration Camp for dispersal. | |

Army Form C. 2118.

# WAR DIARY
## or
## INTELLIGENCE SUMMARY.

*(Erase heading not required.)*

Instructions regarding War Diaries and Intelligence Summaries are contained in F.S. Regs., Part II. and the Staff Manual respectively. Title pages will be prepared in manuscript.

| Place | Date 1919 | Hour | Summary of Events and Information | Remarks and references to Appendices |
|---|---|---|---|---|
| RHEINBACH, GERMANY. | MARCH 27th. | | Casualties admitted to the Unit. Sick 5. 15212 Sgt.G.Gillespie, R.A.M.C. appointed Act.Staff Sergt. with pay from 10/2/19. | ADS. |
| | 28th. | | Casualties admitted to the Unit. Sick 3 | ADS |
| | 29th. | | Casualties admitted to the Unit. Sick 10 Capt.F.CAMERON, M.C., R.A.M.C. and 12 Other Ranks proceeded to MUNSTEREIFEL to relieve a detachment of No. 1 Field Ambulance, and take over the Hospital there. | ADS. |
| | 30th. | | Casualties admitted to the Unit. Sick 5 | ADS |
| | 31st. | | Casualties admitted to the Unit. Sick 19 Capt.E.FORBES, M.C., R.A.M.C. joined the Unit for duty. | ADS |

Lieut Colonel.
Officer Commanding 141st. Field Ambulance.

141st. Field Ambulance.
************************

WAR        DIARY

for the period

1st. April 1919.   to   30th. April 1919.

Volume No. 34.

*Confidential.*

*April 1919.*

Army Form C. 2118.

# WAR DIARY
## or
## INTELLIGENCE SUMMARY.

*(Erase heading not required.)*

Instructions regarding War Diaries and Intelligence Summaries are contained in F. S. Regs., Part II. and the Staff Manual respectively. Title pages will be prepared in manuscript.

| Place | Date | Hour | Summary of Events and Information | Remarks and references to Appendices |
|---|---|---|---|---|
| RHEINBACH, GERMANY. | 1st. | | Casualties admitted to the Unit. Sick 10 | ADP. |
| | 2nd. | | Casualties admitted to the Unit. Sick 19 | ADP. |
| | 3rd. | | Casualties admitted to the Unit. Sick 27. 66948 Pte. E. SMITH, R.A.M.C. evacuated sick, to C.C.S. Sister J. GILL, Q.A.R., and Sister C.I.G. SOUTHWELL, Q.A.R. proceeded to the Sisters' Hostel, COLOGNE, from temporary duty with this Unit. | ADP. |
| | 4th. | | Casualties admitted to the Unit. Sick 11 31713 Pte. D. CROSS, R.A.M.C. rejoined the Unit from a Course at No.5 G.H.Q., Chemistry School. The following men proceeded to Concentration Camp, DUREN for dispersal :- 35223 Pte. U. DEMPSEY, R.A.M.C. ET 48150 Dvr. W. JONES, R.A.S.C. HT. | ADP. |
| | 5th. | | Casualties admitted to the Unit. Sick 13 The undermentioned men are struck off the strength from the dates shown :- 57028 Pte. H. P. JONES, R.A.M.C. Demobilised in the U.K. on 15/2/19. 78910 Pte. A. K. CROWE, R.A.M.C. Discharged from the Service, medically unfit, on 15/1/19. | ADP. ADP. ADP. |
| | 6th. | | Casualties admitted to the Unit. Sick 7 | ADP. |
| | 7th. | | Casualties admitted to the Unit. Sick 16 | ADP. |
| | 8th. | | Casualties admitted to the Unit. Sick 18 | ADP. |
| | 9th. | | Casualties admitted to the unit. Sick 12 | ADP. |
| | 10th. | | Casualties admitted to the Unit. Sick 16 | ADP. |

Army Form C. 2118.

# WAR DIARY
## or
## INTELLIGENCE SUMMARY.
*(Erase heading not required.)*

Instructions regarding War Diaries and Intelligence Summaries are contained in F.S. Regs., Part II. and the Staff Manual respectively. Title pages will be prepared in manuscript.

| Place | Date 1919. | Hour | Summary of Events and Information | Remarks and references to Appendices |
|---|---|---|---|---|
| RHEINBACH, Germany. | 11th. | | Casualties admitted to the Unit. Sick 4. Capt.D.C.PARMENTER, R.A.M.C. is posted to this Unit for duty from the 9th.inst. Capt.J.P.DUNCAN, R.A.M.C. is taken on the strength of this Unit from this date. | A.D. |
| | 12th. | | Casualties admitted to the Unit. Sick 19. Capt.T.A.PITTS, M.O.R.C., U.S.A. is taken on the strength of the Unit from this date. | A.D. |
| | 13th. | | Casualties admitted to the Unit. Sick 5. 57274 Sgt.W.A.LEE, R.A.M.C. proceeded to Concentration Camp for dispersal. | A.D. |
| | 14th. | | Casualties admitted tot the Unit. Sick 11. Capt.D.C.PARMENTER, R.A.M.C. is posted to No.2 Field Ambulance and is attached to this Unit. | A.D. |
| | 15th. | | Casualties admitted to the Unit. Sick 12. | A.D. |
| | 16th. | | Casualties admitted to the Unit. Sick 16. | A.D. |
| | 17th. | | Casualties admitted to the Unit. Sick 13. | A.D. |
| | 18th. | | Casualties admitted to the Unit. Sick 3. The undermentioned men joined the Unit for duty from West.Div.M.T.Coy :- M 303192 Pte.F.MASSAM, M 351635 Pte.A.DALES. M 266204 Pte.R.H.METCALFE, M 182828 Pte.W.G.BRADLEY. | A.D. |
| | 19th. | | Casualties admitted to the Unit. Sick 10. The undermentioned N.C.O. and man proceeded to Concentration Camp for dispersal :- T4 /071857 Farr.Dr.B.BENNETT, RASC H.T. T 31055 Dr.E.W.JONES, RASC H.T. The undermentioned men proceeded to report to West.D.M.T.Coy. for demobilization :- M2 /022059 Pte.G.R.LESTER, MM, RASC M.T. M2 /031658 Pte.L.WIDDOWS, RASC M.T. M2 /021524 Pte.A.Y.KERR, MM, RASC M.T. M2 /048544 Pte.R.G.MASTERS, VC, RASC M.T. | A.D. |

Army Form C. 2118.

# WAR DIARY
## or
## INTELLIGENCE SUMMARY.
*(Erase heading not required.)*

Instructions regarding War Diaries and Intelligence Summaries are contained in F. S. Regs, Part II. and the Staff Manual respectively. Title pages will be prepared in manuscript.

| Place | Date APRIL 1919. | Hour | Summary of Events and Information | Remarks and references to Appendices |
|---|---|---|---|---|
| RHEINBACH, Germany. | 20th. | | Casualties admitted to the Unit. Sick. 5. The undermentioned men proceeded to Concentration Camp for dispersal :— 42754 a Cpl.T.H.UNCLES, RAMC. 63161 L/Cpl.C.THOMSON, RAMC. 79675 Pte.W.O'NEILL, RAMC. | AP. |
| | | | The undermentioned men joined this Unit for duty from 130th.Field Ambulance :— 96810 Pte.A.H.CODD, RAMC. 357534 Pte.H.SHIERS, RAMC. 126587 Pte.G.R.HARYOTT, RAMC. | AP. |
| | | | M2/052643 Pte.A.ANDERSON, MM, RASC.M.T. proceeded to report to West.Div.M.T.Coy. for demob'n. | AP. |
| | 21st. | | Casualties admitted to the Unit. Sick 9. 78898 Pte.R.COLLIER, RAMC. appointed A/t.L/Cpl.with pay from today's date. | AP. |
| | 22nd. | | Casualties admitted to the Unit. Sick 28. | AP. |
| | 23rd. | | Casualties admitted to the Unit. Sick 17. The undermentioned men joined this Unit for duty from No.1 Coy. West.Div.Train :— T 306544 Dr.R.CAMPBELL, RASC H.T. T 30571 Dr.A.DANIELS, RASC H.T. | AP. |
| | 24th. | | Casualties admitted to the Unit. Sick 9. | AP. |
| | 25th. | | Casualties admitted to the Unit. Sick 13. | AP. |
| | 26th. | | Casualties admitted to the Unit. Sick 20. The undermentioned men proceeded to report to West.Div.M.T.Coy. for demobilization. M2/054957 Cpl.H.G.Wheatland, RASC MT. M2/045486 Pte.S.Rayner, RASC MT. M2/153780 Pte.A.R.Full, RASC MT. | AP. |
| | | | Capt.A.WILSON, M.C., R.A.M.C. joined the Unit for duty. | |
| | 27th. | | Casualties admitted to the Unit. Sick 7. T 364573 Dr.P.WALSH, R.A.S.C. HT. admitted to hospital, sick, and evacuated to L.of C. | AP. |

Army Form C. 2118.

# WAR DIARY
## or
## INTELLIGENCE SUMMARY.

(*Erase heading not required.*)

| Place | Date 1919. | Hour | Summary of Events and Information | Remarks and references to Appendices |
|---|---|---|---|---|
| RHEINBACH, Germany. | 28th. | | Casualties admitted to the Unit. Sick 9. | |
| | 29th. | | Casualties admitted to the Unit. Sick 11. | |
| | 30th. | | Casualties admitted to the Unit. Sick 6. | |

LT. COL. R.A.M.C.
O.C. 141st FIELD AMBULANCE.

May 1919

May 1919

War Diary

No 1441 Field Ambulance

Army Form C. 2118.

# WAR DIARY
## or
## INTELLIGENCE SUMMARY.

(Erase heading not required.)

Instructions regarding War Diaries and Intelligence Summaries are contained in F.S. Regs., Part II. and the Staff Manual respectively. Title pages will be prepared in manuscript.

| Place | Date 1919 | Hour | Summary of Events and Information | Remarks and references to Appendices |
|---|---|---|---|---|
| RHEINBACH. Germany. | MAY 1st. | | Casualties admitted to the Unit. Sick 4. | Q |
| | 2nd. | | Casualties admitted to the Unit. Sick 4. 82363 Pte. A. RHODES, R.A.M.C. joined the Unit for duty from Camp Commandant IX Corps. | Q |
| | 3rd. | | Casualties admitted to the Unit. Sick 8. | Q |
| | 4th. | | Casualties admitted to the Unit. Sick 2. T2/1404 Dr. A.S. MOLSON, R.A.S.C. HT. appointed Act. L/Cpl. with pay and transferred to No. 1 Coy. Western Division Train for duty. The under-mentioned men proceeded to Concentration Camp for dispersal :- 2424 Pte. H. WINSTANLEY, RAMC. 5323 Pte. R. BAILEY, RAMC. 3696 Pte. P. WILD, RAMC. | Q |
| | 5th. | | Casualties admitted to the Unit. Sick 18. Lt. Col. L.T. POOLE, D.S.O., M.C., R.A.M.C. proceeded to the United Kingdom on leave granted from 5th. to 19th. May 1919, and the command of the Ambulance during his absence devolves on Capt. E. FORBES, M.C., R.A.M.C. | Q |
| | 6th. | | Casualties admitted to the Unit. Sick 10. Lt. & Qr. Mr. S.M. GAWTHORNE, R.A.M.C. proceeded to Concentration Camp for dispersal. | Q |
| | 7th. | | Casualties admitted to the Unit. Sick 10. The under-mentioned men proceeded to Concentration Camp for dispersal :- 1742 Pte. P. McBRIDE, RAMC. 5346 Pte. E.J. GROGAN, RAMC. 7347 Pte. A.J. FRIEND, RAMC. | Q |
| | 8th. | | Casualties admitted to the Unit. Sick 11. T 30571 Dr. A. DANIELS, R.A.S.C. HT. was admitted to Hospital, sick, and evacuated to C.C.S. The result of an accident. Capt. J.S. LLOYD, R.A.M.C. appointed D.A.D.M.S. Western Division with effect from 7.4.19. and is struck off the strength accordingly. | Q |
| | 9th. | | Casualties admitted to the Unit. Sick 5. | Q |

Army Form C. 2118.

# WAR DIARY
## or
## INTELLIGENCE SUMMARY.
*(Erase heading not required.)*

Instructions regarding War Diaries and Intelligence Summaries are contained in F. S. Regs., Part II. and the Staff Manual respectively. Title pages will be prepared in manuscript.

| Place | Date MAY 1919 | Hour | Summary of Events and Information | Remarks and references to Appendices |
|---|---|---|---|---|
| RHEINBACH. Germany. | 15th.(contd) | | 33 Men joined the Unit for temporary duty from 9th.Bn.Cheshire Regt. for training in R.M.C. duties. Capt.R.H.ALEXANDER, M.C., R.A.M.C. joined the Unit for duty from 84th.Bde.R.G.A. and proceeded to take over the temporary medical charge of 52nd.South Wales Borderers during the absence on leave of the Medical Officer of that Battalion. | |
| | 16th. | | Casualties admitted to the Unit.  Sick 5. The undermentioned men proceeded to Concentration Camp for dispersal and are struck off the strength of the Unit from this date :- 26900 Pte.J.F.GATEHOUSE, RAMC.   38233 Pte.S.T.GEORGE, RAMC. | |
| | 17th. | | Casualties admitted to the Unit.  Sick 6. | |
| | 18th. | | Casualties admitted to unit.  Sick 6. | |
| | 19th. | | Casualties admitted to the Unit.  Sick. 4. The undermentioned men proceeded to Concentration Camp for dispersal and are struck off the strength of the unit from this date:- 43684 Pte W.Milne, RAMC. 40599 Pte J.P.Howland, RAMC. 38740 Pte T.F.Webb, RAMC. 58092 Pte G.Nuttall, RAMC.   42931 Pte J. Dewhurst, RAMC. | |
| | 20th | | Casualties admitted to the unit.  Sick. 8. 20 Men joined unit for temporary duty and instruction in R.A.S.C. work from 52nd Bn. Cheshire Regt. | |
| | 21st | | Casualties admitted to the unit.  Sick 8. No. 54463 Pte T.Clifford, RAMC. rejoined unit this date from temporary duty with Western Div. M.T. Coy. The undermentioned N.C.O. and men proceeded to Concentration Camp for Dispersal and are struck off the strength of the unit from this date. 88135 Sgt. J.P.Robertson, RAMC. 28474 Cpl. R.W.Slator, RAMC. 19477 Pte A.Cook, RAMC. 155477 Pte J.Hegarty, RAMC. 45275 Pte T.E.Phillips, RAMC. | |

Army Form C. 2118.

# WAR DIARY
## or
## INTELLIGENCE SUMMARY.
*(Erase heading not required.)*

Instructions regarding War Diaries and Intelligence Summaries are contained in F.S. Regs, Part II. and the Staff Manual respectively. Title pages will be prepared in manuscript.

| Place | Date MAY 19 19. | Hour | Summary of Events and Information | Remarks and references to Appendices |
|---|---|---|---|---|
| RHEINBACH. Germany. | 9th.(contd) | | The undermentioned N.C.O. and men proceeded to Concentration Camp for dispersal and are struck off the strength accordingly :- <br><br> 52989 Sgt.H.V.TURTON, RAMC. 1876 Pte.F.M.ELLIOTT, MM, RAMC. 26512 Pte.F.BOOTHBY, RAMC. | A |
| | 10th. | | Casualties admitted to the Unit. Sick 5. | A |
| | 11th. | | Casualties admitted to the Unit. Sick 4. <br> The undermentioned men proceeded to Concentration Camp for dispersal and are struck off the strength from this date :- <br><br> 344186 Pte.B.G.HODDER, RAMC T. 51347 Pte.B.RIDING, RAMC. 34656 Pte.F.HIBBINS, RAMC. | A |
| | 12th. | | Casualties admitted to the Unit. Sick 12. | A |
| | 13th. | | Casualties admitted to the Unit. Sick 5. <br> The undermentioned man joined the Unit for duty from West.Div.M.T.Coy.:- <br><br> M/42009 Pte.T.J.SWINDEN, R.A.S.C. MT. | A |
| | 14th. | | Casualties admitted to the Unit. Sick 5. <br> The undermentioned N.C.Os. and Man proceeded to Concentration Camp for dispersal and are struck off the strength from this date :- <br><br> 90009 Cpl(a. Sgt) E.GRICE, R.A.M.C. 40838 Cpl.F.W.MALIN, RAMC. 10132 Pte.A.BEAN, RAMC. <br><br> The undermentioned N.C.O. joined the Unit for duty from West.Div.M.T.Coy.:- <br><br> M2/167805 a Cpl.J.LUCK, R.A.S.C. MT. | |
| | 15th. | | Casualties admitted to the Unit. Sick 9. <br> Capt.A.WILSON, M.C., R.A.M.C. proceeded on 14th.inst. to 84th.Bde.R.G.A. for duty and is struck off the strength from that date. | A |

Army Form C. 2118.

# WAR DIARY
## or
## INTELLIGENCE SUMMARY.

(Erase heading not required.)

Instructions regarding War Diaries and Intelligence Summaries are contained in F. S. Regs., Part II. and the Staff Manual respectively. Title pages will be prepared in manuscript.

| Place | Date MAY 1919 | Hour 19 | Summary of Events and Information | Remarks and references to Appendices |
|---|---|---|---|---|
| RHEINBACH GERMANY. | 22nd | | Casualties admitted to the Unit. Sick 9 Lt.Col.L.T.POOLE, D.S.O. M.C. R.A.M.C. rejoined Ambulance and resumed command. | 2 |
| | 23rd | | Casualties admitted to the Unit. Sick 3 | 2 |
| | 24th | | Casualties admitted to the Unit. Sick 7 The undermentioned men proceeded to Concentration Camp for dispersal and are struck off the strength of the Unit from this Date.:- 1113 Pte R.HOLLIDAY. R.A.M.C. 52776 Pte A.MEDDINGS. R.A.M.C. 54518 Pte D.CLARK. R.A.M.C. 50515 Pte W.H.GARDNER. R.A.M.C. 54463 Pte T.CLIFFORD. R.A.M.C. | 2 |
| | 25th | | Casualties admitted to the Unit. Sick 21 Capt.T.A.PITTS. M.O.R.C. proceeded to report to Commanding General, 1st Replacement Camp, St AIGNAN, FRANCE. for demobilisation and was struck of the strength of the Unit on the 24.5.19 | 2 |
| | 26th | | Casualties admitted to the Unit. Sick 6 The undermentioned N.C.Os and men proceeded to Concentration Camp for dispersal and are struck off the strength of the Unit from this date:- 90134 Sgt A.M.Wilson, R.A.M.C. 55415 Pte J.MILLARD. R.A.M.C. 57999 L/Cpl W.G.JACKSON.RAMC. 10843 Pte A.H.HEFFORD. R.A.M.C. 56252 Pte T.BAILEY. R.A.M.C. | 2 |
| | 27th | | Casualties admitted to the Unit. Sick 7 | 2 |
| | 28th | | Casualties admitted to the Unit. Sick 5 | 2 |
| | 27th | | 26 R.A.M.C. N.C.Os and men joined this Unit from No 1 Field Ambulance on the 27th and are taken on the strength of this Unit from that date. 17 men of the 9th Cheshire Regt joined this Unit for temporary duty and instruction in R.A.M.C. work | 2 |
| | 28th | | 5622 Pte W.H.FISHER, (MM) R.A.M.C. was admitted to hospital, sick, and evacuated to 47 C.C.S. | 2 |
| | 29th | | Casualties admitted to the Unit. Sick 4 | 2 |
| | 30th | | Casualties admitted to the Unit. Sick 5 | 2 |
| | 31st | | Casualties admitted to the Unit. Sick 5 | 2 |

L.D. Poole
Lt. Col. R.A.M.C.
O.C. 146 Field Ambulance.

No. 141st Field Ambulance.

WAR   DIARY

for the period 1st to 30th

JUNE   1919.

Volume No. 36.

# WAR DIARY
## or
## INTELLIGENCE SUMMARY.

*(Erase heading not required.)*

Army Form C. 2118.

| Place | Date 1919. | Hour | Summary of Events and Information | Remarks and references to Appendices |
|---|---|---|---|---|
| RHEINBACH, Germany. | June 1st | | Casualties admitted to the unit. Sick. 6. 57979 Pte R. Eliott, R.A.M.C. rejoined unit from temp. duty with West Div. R.E. | 12A |
| | 2nd | | Casualties admitted to the unit. Sick. 8. The u/m N.C.Os. and men proceeded to No. 1 Concentration Camp, Cologne, for dispersal and were accordingly struck off the strength. 30369 S/Sgt. R.Henderson, RAMC. 57344 L/Cpl J.R.Butler, RAMC. 79535 Pte E.G.Greenwood, RAMC. 57941 Pte G. Holt, RAMC. 56256 Pte F.R.Long, RAMC. 56738 Pte T.Atkinson, RAMC. 57278 Pte F. Bennison, RAMC. 56528 Pte G.Blurton, RAMC. 57279 Pte A.Gardiner A. RAMC. 56279 Pte D. Robertson D. 55881 Pte W. Hutchison, RAMC. rejoined unit from temp.duty with West.Div. Hostel, COLOGNE. | 12B |
| | 3rd. | | Casualties admitted to the unit. Sick. 2. | 12C |
| | 4th. | | Casualties admitted to the unit. Sick. 4. The u/m N.C.O. and men proceeded to No. 1 Concentration Camp, COLOGNE, for dispersal, and were accordingly struck off the strength. 2346 Cpl. P.Noonan, RAMC. 752 Pte H.White, RAMC. 6280 Pte A.E.Gurr. RAMC. 57382 Pte C. McHenry, RAMC. 57809 Pte Tanner, RAMC. 56-132 Pte G. Higgins.RAMC. 37288 Cpl. L.G.Wilson, R.A.MC. 127192 Pte J.E. Bailey, RAMC. 57219 Pte D.C.S.Blaughter.RAMC. 57664 Pte M.Bell, RAMC. 57970 Pte Eliott, R. RAMC. 56355 Pte T.Hope, RAMC. | 12D |
| | 5th | | Casualties admitted to the unit. Sick. 7. | 12E |
| | 6th | | Casualties admitted to the unit. Sick. 16. | 12F |
| | 7th | | Casualties admitted to the unit. Sick. 4. The u/m men proceeded to report to No. 1 Concentration Camp, COLOGNE. for dispersal, and were accordingly struck off the strength. 24249 Pte J. Hayes, RAMC. 56221 Pte W.H. Fisher, RAMC. 57935 L/C B.Stevenson, RAMC. T2/17305 Dr. J.Ruane, RASC.HT. T1/2233 Dr. W.H.Langmead, R.A.S.C. HT. T2/9575 Dr. D.G. Perrett, R.A.S.C. | 12G |
| | 8th | | Casualties admitted to the unit. Sick. 3. | 12H |

Army Form C. 2118.

# WAR DIARY
## or
## INTELLIGENCE SUMMARY.

*(Erase heading not required.)*

Instructions regarding War Diaries and Intelligence Summaries are contained in F.S. Regs., Part II. and the Staff Manual respectively. Title pages will be prepared in manuscript.

| Place | Date 1919 | Hour | Summary of Events and Information | Remarks and references to Appendices |
|---|---|---|---|---|
| RHEINBACH. Germany. | June 9th | | Casualties admitted to the unit. Nil. 58161 Cpl. T.Scanlan, RAMC. awarded the Meritorious Service Medal (London Gazette 4/6/19) | 12A. |
| | 10th | | Casualties admitted to the unit. Sick. 2. | 12A. |
| | 11th | | Casualties admitted to the unit. Sick. 12. | 12A. |
| | 12th | | Casualties admitted to the unit. Sick. 9. | 12A. |
| | 13th | | Casualties admitted to the unit. Sick. 7. | 12A. |
| | 14th | | Casualties admitted to the unit. Sick. 3. The u/m men proceeded to No. 1 Concentration Camp, COLOGNE, for Dispersal, and were accordingly struck off the strength. T4/058947 Dr. G.Hoy, R.A.S.C. T2/11084 Dr. F.Lauder, R.A.S.C. T1/2210 Dr.J.Robertson, RASC. T2/14087 Dr. W.Cross, RASC. T2/9426 Dr. W.K.Damerall, RASC. T4/240650 Dr. T.T.Edwards, RASC. 54/108045 Dr. H.Munday, RASC. T4/262082 Dr. E.Plant, RASC. T1/5072 Dr. C.Munday, RASC. T2/017250 Dr. T.Purcell, RASC. T2/12929 Dr. R.H.Mason, RASC. | 12A. |
| | 15th | | Casualties admitted to the unit. Sick. 1. M2/032059 Pte J.L.Wilson, RASC.MT. proceeded to report to O.C. West.Div.M.T.Coy. and was accordingly struck off the strength. The u/m N.C.O. and men proceeded to report to No. 1 Concentration Camp, COLOGNE, for Dispersal, and were accordingly struck off the strength. 58097 S/Sgt. A.J.Tait, RAMC. 30358 Pte T.J.Wensley, RAMC. 41880 Pte J.Spedding, RAMC. 56337 Pte A.Young, RAMC. 58120 Pte F.Graham, RAMC. 58040 Pte F.J.Hailston, RAMC. 66959 Pte J.F.Johnson, RAMC. 58066 Pte G.Smith, RAMC. 58112 Pte G.F.Hooper, RAMC. 58128 Pte R.Duncan, RAMC. | 12A. |
| | 16th | | Casualties admitted to the unit. Sick. Nil. T21508 S.S.M.Flackfield, R.A.S.C.HT. proceeded to report for duty to O.C. No. 3 Coy. Western Div. Train and was accordingly struck off the strength. T20683 S.S.M.Bland, D.C.M. joined the unit for duty from O.C. No. 3 Coy. West Div. Train. | 12A. |

# WAR DIARY or INTELLIGENCE SUMMARY

Army Form C. 2118.

Instructions regarding War Diaries and Intelligence Summaries are contained in F. S. Regs., Part II. and the Staff Manual respectively. Title pages will be prepared in manuscript.

(Erase heading not required.)

| Place | Date | Hour | Summary of Events and Information | Remarks and references to Appendices |
|---|---|---|---|---|
| Rheinbach. Germany. | 17th | | Casualties admitted to the unit. Sick. 5. | 19L. |
| | 18th | | Casualties admitted to the unit. Sick. 3. | 19L. |
| | 19th | | Casualties admitted to the unit. Sick. 7. | 19L. |
| Lengsdorf. Germany. | 20th | | Unit moved from Rheinbach to Lengsdorf, Germany. Casualties admitted to unit. Sick. 22. | 19L. |
| | 21st | | Casualties admitted to the unit. Sick. 5. The u/m men proceed to No. 1 Concentration Camp, COLOGNE. for dispersal and were accordingly struck off the strength. T2/60092 Dr. T. Harrison, R.A.S.C. H.T. T4/145648 Dr. W. Kaye, R.A.S.C. H.T. | 19L. |
| | 22nd | | Casualties admitted to the unit. Sick. 20. | 19L. |
| | 23rd | | Casualties admitted to the unit. Sick. 4. | 19L. |
| | 24th | | Casualties admitted to the unit. Sick. 3. | 19L. |
| | 25th | | Casualties admitted to the unit. Sick. 3. The u/m men joined this unit from No. 1 Field Ambulance, along with two Auston Cars, one Ford Car and Motor cycle. M2/18843 Pte E.Bamber, R.A.S.C. M2/200237 Pte T. Larkin, R.A.S.C. DM2/189546 Pte J. Bird, R.A.S.C. M2/194116 Pte J. Dawson. | |
| | 26th | | Casualties admitted to the unit. Sick. 1. | 19L. |
| | 27th | | Casualties admitted to the unit. Sick. 3. | 19L. |
| | 28th | | Casualties admitted to the unit. Sick. 3. | 19L. |
| | 29th | | Casualties admitted to the unit. Sick. 3. | 19L. |
| | 30th | | Casualties admitted to the unit. Sick. 3. | 19L. |

L.J. Post.
LT. COL. R.A.M.C.
O.C. 141st FIELD AMBULANCE.

141st Field Ambulance.

WAR    DIARY

JULY

1919.

Army Form C. 2118.

# WAR DIARY
## or
## INTELLIGENCE SUMMARY.
(Erase heading not required.)

Instructions regarding War Diaries and Intelligence Summaries are contained in F. S. Regs., Part II. and the Staff Manual respectively. Title pages will be prepared in manuscript.

| Place | Date | Hour | Summary of Events and Information | Remarks and references to Appendices |
|---|---|---|---|---|
| RHEINBACH. Germany. | July, 1919. 1st. | | Unit moved from LENGSDORF to RHEINBACH. Casualties admitted to the unit. 16. | Rme |
| | 2nd | | Casualties admitted to the Unit. 1 The undermentioned N.C.O. and men proceeded to No.1 Concentration Camp, COLOGNE, for dispersal and were struck off the strength accordingly. 463009 Sgt P.L.BROWN,R.A.M.C. 58104 Pte E.G.ADES,R.A.M.C. 93341 Pte H.W.FLACK,R.A.M.C. 58161 Cpl T.SCANLAN,R.A.M.C. 101208 Pte G.D.GUEST,R.A.M.C. 21210 Pte H.W.HAMILTON,R.A.M.C. 58882 Pte F.MARGINSON,R.A.M.C. 61063 Pte J.MARTIN,R.A.M.C. 58106 Pte C.PAYNE,R.A.M.C. 100223 Pte A.W.TERRY,R.A.M.C. 58189 Pte D.J.REEVE,R.A.M.C. 58192 Pte C.L.ANNEAR,R.A.M.C. 62304 Pte A.GIBSON,R.A.M.C. 21156 Pte J.C.HARROP,R.A.M.C. 58118 Pte W.H.HESKETH,R.A.M.C. 46938 Pte S.MASON,R.A.M.C. 58160 Pte W.PARKER,R.A.M.C. 58462 Pte E.J.QUAYLE,R.A.M.C. 75540 Pte J.GILDEA,R.A.M.C. 58866 Pte F.YATES,R.A.M.C. | Rme |
| | 3rd | | Casualties admitted to the Unit. Nil. | Rme |
| | 4th | | Casualties admitted to the Unit. 10 The undermentioned N.C.O. and men proceeded to No.1 Concentration Camp, COLOGNE, for dispersal and were struck off the strength accordingly. 78898 Sgt R.COLLIER,R.A.M.C. 72304 Pte H.R.ASHTON,R.A.M.C. 69945 Pte H.A.ARCHER,R.A.M.C. 93329 Pte J.BOWMAN,R.A.M.C. 78763 Pte BRADFORD,J.R.A.M.C. 72597 Pte J.J.GREEN,R.A.M.C. 101671 Pte T.GUEST,R.A.M.C. 21712 Pte W.G.HOLBROOK,R.A.M.C. 56462 Pte R.G.HASSALL,R.A.M.C. 67912 Pte C.L.SAY,R.A.M.C. | Rme |
| | 5th | | Casualties admitted to the Unit. 8 85698 Pte J.H.GILLMAN,R.A.M.C,was transferred to 47 C.C.S. | Rme |
| | 6th | | Casualties admitted to the Unit. 4 Capt. & Q.M. REEVE H.J. M.C. R.A.M.C. joined this Unit for duty and was taken on the strength accordingly. | Rme |
| | 7th | | Casualties admitted to the Unit. 4 | Rme |

Army Form C. 2118.

# WAR DIARY
## or
## INTELLIGENCE SUMMARY.

*(Erase heading not required.)*

Instructions regarding War Diaries and Intelligence Summaries are contained in F. S. Regs., Part II. and the Staff Manual respectively. Title pages will be prepared in manuscript.

| Place | Date | Hour | Summary of Events and Information | Remarks and references to Appendices |
|---|---|---|---|---|
| Rheinbach, Germany. | *7th | Cont. | TS/7913 Farr.Dvr B.WILSON,R.A.S.C. proceeded to report to No.4.Coy, West.Div.Train. and was taken off the strength accordingly. | RMO |
| | | | TS/8523 Farr.Dvr T.O'GRADY,R.A.S.C. joined this Unit for duty from No.2 Coy West.Div.Train. and was taken on the strength accordingly. | RMO |
| | 8th | | Casualties admitted to the Unit. 7 | RMO |
| | 9th | | Casualties admitted to the Unit. 6 | RMO |
| | 10th | | Casualties admitted to the Unit. 6 | RMO |
| | 11th | | Casualties admitted to the Unit. 3 | RMO |
| | 12th | | Casualties admitted to the Unit. 10 | RMO |
| | 13th | | Casualties admitted to the Unit. 5 | RMO |
| | | | The undermentioned M.C.O. and men proceeded to No.1 Concentration Camp, COLOGNE, for dispersal and were struck off the strength accordingly. | |
| | | | 75685 Cpl T.D.Gaunt R.A.M.C. 79146 Pte M.SCULLY,R.A.M.C. 88277 Pte J.G.GUTHRIE, R.A.M.C. 74232 Pte C.SIDDONS,R.A.M.C. 69562 Pte S.SMITH,R.A.M.C. 72330 Pte A.C.SAINT,R.A.M.C. 93373 Pte L.V.RENEL, R.A.M.C. | RMO |
| | 14th | | Casualties admitted to the Unit 6 | RMO |
| | 15th | | Casualties admitted to the Unit 6 | RMO |
| | 16th | | Casualties admitted to the Unit 6 | RMO |
| | *7th | | Lieut.Colonel L.T.Poole, D.S.O. M.C. R.A.M.C. proceeded to Paris to represent the in charge of the R.A.M.C.Detachment representing the IX Corps, Rhine Army. in the "Victory March" on 14-7-19. | RMO |
| | | | The undermentioned W.O. and man represented the 141st Field Ambulance. 17421 Sergt Major Plume P. R.A.M.C. 68875 Corpl Storry H. M.M. R.A.M.C. | |
| | 17th | | Casualties admitted to the Unit 7 | RMO |
| | | | The undermentioned Men.proceeded to No.1 Concentration Camp COLOGNE for dispersal and were struck off the strength accordingly. | |
| | | | 70711 Pte Rance J. R.A.M.C. 154862 Pte Thomas T.L. R.A.M.C. 103740 Pte Harrop G.V. R.A.M.C. 81133 Pte Whelan T. R.A.M.C. | |
| | 18th | | Casualties admitted to the Unit. 3 | RMO |
| | 19th | | Casualties admitted to the Unit 8 | RMO |
| | 20th | | Casualties admitted to the Unit 10 | RMO |
| | 21st | | Casualties admitted to the Unit, 8 | RMO |
| | 22nd | | Casualties admitted to the Unit. 5 | RMO |

Army Form C. 2118.

# WAR DIARY
## or
## INTELLIGENCE SUMMARY.
*(Erase heading not required.)*

| Place | Date | Hour | Summary of Events and Information | Remarks and references to Appendices |
|---|---|---|---|---|
| Rheinbach Germany. | 23rd | | Casualties admitted to the Unit.   Sick 2 | |
| | 24th | | Casualties admitted to the Unit.   Sick 4 | |
| | 25th | | Casualties admitted to the Unit.   Sick 4 | |
| | | | 42 Infantry were transferred to R.A.M.C. and were taken on the strength of this Unit. | |
| | 26th | | Casualties admitted to the Unit.   Sick 2 | |
| | 27th | | Casualties admitted to the Unit.   Sick 3 | |
| | 28th | | The undermentioned men with 3 Ambulances proceeded to report to West.Divl M.T.Coy and are struck off the strength of the Unit. | |
| | | | M551635 Pte Dales A. R.A.S.C.(MT) M2/94118 Pte Dawson J. R.A.S.C.(MT) M42009 Pte Swinden T.J. R.A.S.C.(MT) | |
| | 29th | | Casualties admitted to the Unit   Sick 4 | |
| | | | Casualties admitted to the Unit   Sick 3 | |
| | | | The undermentioned N.C.Os. and man proceeded to report to No.1 Concentration Camp COLOGNE for Dispersal and were struck off the strength accordingly. | |
| | | | 68875 Cpl Storry H. R.A.M.C. 58758 L.Cpl Hymans W. R.A.M.C. 82363 Pte Rhodes A. R.A.M.C. | |
| | 30th | | Casualties admitted to the Unit   Sick 5 | |
| | | | The undermentioned men joined this Unit for duty with R.A.S.C.(HT) and were taken on the strength. | |
| | | | T/453176 Dr Keenen E. R.A.S.C.(HT) T/453187 Dr York A. R.A.S.C.(HT) T/453191 Dr Mann E. R.A.S.C.(HT) | |
| | 31st | | Casualties admitted to the Unit   Sick 5 | |
| | | | The undermentioned men joined this Unit for training in R.A.M.C. work and were taken on the strength. | |
| | | | 83821 Pte Evans W. 65773 Pte Malley W. 84376 Pte Kelly J.E. 66261 Pte Watkins E. 69557 Pte Breeze D. 81503 Pte Bingham G. | |

141 Ha Ambee.

Received from
P.R.O. therefore
no Reg. No.

COMMITTEE FOR THE
25 SEP 1919
MEDICAL HISTORY OF THE WAR

No 141. J. A.

August 1919.

Army Form C. 2118.

# WAR DIARY
## or
## INTELLIGENCE SUMMARY.
*(Erase heading not required.)*

Instructions regarding War Diaries and Intelligence Summaries are contained in F. S. Regs., Part II. and the Staff Manual respectively. Title pages will be prepared in manuscript.

| Place | Date | Hour | Summary of Events and Information | Remarks and references to Appendices |
|---|---|---|---|---|
| RHEINBACH GERMANY. | AUGUST | | | |
| | 1st | | Casualties admitted to the Unit. Sick 3 | |
| | | | 16 Infantrymen were approved for transfer to R.A.S.C.(HT) and were taken on the strength of the Unit. | |
| | 2nd | | Casualties admitted to the Unit. Sick 5 | |
| | 3rd | | Casualties admitted to the Unit. Sick 4 | |
| | 4th | | Casualties admitted to the Unit. Sick 3 | |
| | 5th | | Casualties admitted to the Unit. Sick 6 | |
| | | | The undermentioned man was admitted to Hospital sick on the 2nd August and evacuated to C.C.S. on this date. Struck off the strength of the Unit. | |
| | | | 169702 Pte Davies H. R.A.M.C. | |
| | 6th | | Casualties admitted to the Unit. Sick 3 | |
| | 7th | | Casualties admitted to the Unit. Sick 6 | |
| | 8th | | Casualties admitted to the Unit. Sick 6 | |
| | | | The undermentioned man joined this unit for duty from No.2 Field Ambulance and was taken on the strength accordingly. | |
| | | | M/321468 Dvr Jones D. R.A.S.C.(MT) | |
| | 9th | | Casualties admitted to the Unit. Sick 3 | |
| | | | The undermentioned man proceeded to No.1 Concentration Camp, COLOGNE. for dispersal in U.K. and was struck off the strength of the Unit. | |
| | | | 58149 Pte Page A.W. R.A.M.C. | |
| | 10th | | 1 W.O.5 N.C.Os. and 23 men joined the unit for a week's instruction in First Aid. | |
| | | | Casualties admitted to the Unit. Sick 1 | |
| | 11th | | Casualties admitted to the Unit. Sick 2 | |
| | | | The undermentioned man rejoined the Unit from Hospital and was taken on the strength accordingly. | |
| | | | 169702 Pte Davies H. R.A.M.C. | |
| | 12th | | Casualties admitted to the Unit. Sick 4 | |
| | 13th | | Casualties admitted to the Unit. Sick 1 | |
| | | | The undermentioned N.C.O. was appointed act.Sgt with effect from 21.5.19. | |
| | | | 78898 L.Cpl Collier R. R.A.M.C. | |
| | 14th | | Casualties admitted to the Unit. Sick 3 | |
| | | | The undermentioned man was promoted to act.L.Cpl with pay from the 13th inst. | |
| | | | 32001 Pte Bullwinkle J. R.A.M.C. | |

Army Form C. 2118.

# WAR DIARY
## or
## INTELLIGENCE SUMMARY.

(Erase heading not required.)

Instructions regarding War Diaries and Intelligence Summaries are contained in F. S. Regs., Part II. and the Staff Manual respectively. Title pages will be prepared in manuscript.

| Place | Date | Hour | Summary of Events and Information | Remarks and references to Appendices |
|---|---|---|---|---|
| | 14th Cont. | | The undermentioned N.C.O.joined this unit for duty from No.3 Coy Train and was taken on the strength accordingly. | |
| | | | T4/158064 Sgt Novell R. R.A.S.C.(HT) | Rua. |
| | 15th | | Casualties admitted to the Unit. Sick 4 | Rua. |
| | 16th | | Casualties admitted to the Unit. Sick 5 | Rua. |
| | 17th | | Casualties admitted to the Unit. Sick 4 | Rua. |
| | | | The wagons and equipment of the unit proceeded to Bonn in preparation for the transfer of the Division to ENGLAND | |
| | 18th | | Casualties admitted to the Unit Sick 4 | Rua. |
| | | | The undermentioned man proceeded to report to No.1 Concentration Camp, COLOGNE, for dispersal inU.K. 84635 Pte Holmes F. R.A.M.C. | |
| | | | The horses of the Unit were despatched to No.24 Vet. Hospital in preparation for the transfer of the Division to ENGLAND. | |
| | 19th | | Casualtie admitted to the Unit. Sick 3 | Rua. |
| | 20th | | Casualties admitted to the Unit Sick 4 | Rua. |
| | 21st | | Casualties admitted to the Unit Sick 2 | Rua. |
| | 22nd | | Casualties admitted to the Unit Sick 2 | Rua. |
| | | | 169721 Pte Seddon W. R.A.M.C. was admitted to Hospital on this date and evacuated to No.2 C.C.S. the same day. | |
| | 23rd | | Casualties admitted to the Unit. Sick 1 | Rua. |
| | | | The undermentioned N.C.O and man proceeded to the U.K. on advance party for the Unit. | |
| | | | 1548Sgt Paskell R.J. 169731 Pte Matthews F.T. R.A.M.C. | |
| | 24th | | Casualties admitted to the Unit. Sick 2 | Rua. |
| | 25th | | The Unit entrained at ROISDORF for U.K. at 15.00 hours. | Rua. |
| | 26th | | NIL. | Rua. |
| | 27th | | The Unit detrained at Calais; crossed over to Dover and entrained for RHYL. | |
| | 28th | | The Unit detrained at RHYL and proceeded to Kinmel Park Camp. | |
| Kinmel Park Camp. | 29th | | Nil. | Rua. |
| | 30th | | Nil. | Rua. |
| | 31st | | Nil, | Rua. |

O.C. 141st FIELD AMBULANCE.

No. 141 Field Ambulance

COMMITTEE FOR THE
JAN 1920
MEDICAL HISTORY OF THE WAR

HISTORY. 23.

Nursing Service.

Leave and recreation for members of the Nursing Service.

Regulation of leave.

Arrangements to enable Matron-in-Chief to keep in touch with all
members of the Nursing Services.
Appointment of A/Principal Matron to each army.
Training of Nursing sisters to administer anaesthetics.

Army Form C. 2118.

# WAR DIARY
## or
## INTELLIGENCE SUMMARY.

(Erase heading not required.)

Instructions regarding War Diaries and Intelligence Summaries are contained in F. S. Regs., Part II, and the Staff Manual respectively. Title pages will be prepared in manuscript.

| Place | Date | Hour | Summary of Events and Information | Remarks and references to Appendices |
|---|---|---|---|---|
| Kinmel Park. | September 1st | | NIL. | |
| | 2nd | | The undermentioned men proceeded for dispersal on this date and were struck off the strength of the Unit. | Rura. |
| | 3rd | | 79815 L.Cpl Moorcock J.N. R.A.M.C. 557534 Pte Shirrs H. R.A.M.C. 81718 Cpl Cross D. R.A.M.C. | Rura |
| | 4th | | NIL. | Rura |
| | 5th | | Nil. | RMA |
| | | | The R.A.S.C. personnel attached to this unit proceeded to rejoin the No.4 Coy Train. 169699 Pte Crook A. R.A.M.C. rejoined unit for Kinmel Park Military Hospital. | |
| | 6th | | The undermentioned men were transferred to R.A.M.C. for 9th Cheshire Regt and joined this unit for duty. | Rura |
| | | | 83821 Pte Evans W. 94376 Pte Kelley J.E. 66201 Pte Watkins E. | |
| | 7th | | NIL. | Rura |
| | 8th | | 86185 Pte Taylor W.B. 51st Welsh Regt attached to this unit for a course of chiropody proceeded | Rura |
| | 9th | | to rejoin his unit in Ireland. | Rura |
| | 10th | | NIL. | Rura |
| | 11th | | NIL | Rura |
| | 12th | | NIL | Rura |
| | 13th | | NIL | Rura |
| | 14th | | NIL | Rura |
| | 15th | | NIL | Rura |
| | 16th | | NIX The undermentioned men proceeded for dispersal and are struck off the strength of this unit. | Rura |
| | | | 169691 L.Cpl ANDREWS E. R.A.M.C. 169692 Pte ASTELL R. R.A.M.C. 169695 Pte Barrow G. R.A.M.C. 142298 Pte Campion J.E. R.A.M.C. 169728 Pte Derry H. R.A.M.C. 84441 Pte Farnworth A. R.A.M.C. 169712 Ptr McGrail J. R.A.M.C. | |
| | 17th | | The undermentioned N.C.O,s and man proceeded for dispersal and were struck off the strength of the unit. | Rura |
| | | | 186587 Bgt HARYOTT G.R. R.A.M.C. 95880 Cpl VICKERS J.H. R.A.M.C. 96810 Cpl CODD A.H. R.A.M.C. 84786 Pte HILLS F. R.A.M.C. | |
| | 18th. | | nil. | Rura |
| | 19th. | | Nil. | Rura |
| | 20th. | | The under-mentioned men proceeded for dispersal and are struck off the strength of this unit. | Rura |
| | | | 169700 Pte. Chilton E. 90332 Pte. Munro H.G. R.A.M.C. | |

Army Form C. 2118.

# WAR DIARY
## or
## INTELLIGENCE SUMMARY.

*(Erase heading not required.)*

continued.

Instructions regarding War Diaries and Intelligence Summaries are contained in F. S. Regs., Part II. and the Staff Manual respectively. Title pages will be prepared in manuscript.

| Place | Date | Hour | Summary of Events and Information | Remarks and references to Appendices |
|---|---|---|---|---|
| | 21st. | | Instructions received from A.D.M.S. Kinmel Park Camp for disposal of retainable R.A.M.C. of this Unit | Orig. |
| | | |     To Military Hospital Oswestry    40 O.R.s | |
| | | |     "    "          Liverpool      5 " | |
| | | |     " Officers Hospital Llangamarch  2 " | |
| | | |     " Grangethorpe Military Hospital  3 " | |
| | | | The Canteen, Officers, & Sgts. Mess accounts have been audited and reports rendered to Kinmel Park Camp. | |
| | | | The Medical Equipment having been checked by board was handed in to O.C. Military Hospital Kinmel Park Camp pending instructions as to its disposal | |
| | | | Unit Records etc. have been forwarded to Officer I/C Records for safe custody | |
| | | | Army Books etc. have been returned to H.M.Stationery Office Manchester | |

O.T. Alexander
Major, R.A.M.C.,
A.D.C.141st. Field Ambulance.

www.ingramcontent.com/pod-product-compliance
Lightning Source LLC
Chambersburg PA
CBHW080610240426
43664CB00052B/2747